PORTUGUESE STUDIES

Volume 35 Number 2
2019

Transnational Portuguese Women Writers

Guest Editors
Maria Luísa Coelho
Cláudia Pazos-Alonso

Founding Editor
Helder Macedo

Editors
Jane-Marie Collins
Catarina Fouto
Tori Holmes
Paulo de Medeiros
Paul Melo e Castro
Hilary Owen
Claire Williams

Editorial Assistant
Richard Correll

Production Editor
Graham Nelson

MODERN HUMANITIES RESEARCH ASSOCIATION

PORTUGUESE STUDIES

A peer-reviewed biannual multi-disciplinary journal devoted to research on the cultures, literatures, history and societies of the Lusophone world

International Advisory Board

David Brookshaw
João de Pina Cabral
Ivo José de Castro
Thomas F. Earle
John Gledson
Anna Klobucka

Maria Manuel Lisboa
Kenneth Maxwell
Laura de Mello e Souza
Maria Irene Ramalho
Silviano Santiago

Portuguese Studies and other journals published by the MHRA may be ordered from Turpin Distribution (http://ebiz.turpin-distribution.com/).

The **Modern Humanities Research Association** was founded in Cambridge in 1918 and has become an international organization with members in all parts of the world. It is a registered charity number 1064670, and a company limited by guarantee, registered in England number 3446016. Its main object is to encourage advanced study and research in modern and medieval European languages, literatures, and cultures by its publication of journals, book series, and its Style Guide. Further information about the activities of the Association and individual membership may be obtained from the Membership Secretary, email membership@mhra.org.uk, or from the website at: www.mhra.org.uk

Disclaimer: Statements of fact and opinion in the content of *Portuguese Studies* are those of the respective authors and contributors and not of the journal editors or of the Modern Humanities Research Association (MHRA). MHRA makes no representation, express or implied, in respect of the accuracy of the material in this journal and cannot accept any legal responsibility or liability for any errors or omissions that may be made.

Parts of this work may be reproduced as permitted under legal provisions for fair dealing (or fair use) for the purposes of research, private study, criticism, or review, or when a relevant collective licensing agreement is in place. All other reproduction requires the written permission of the copyright holder who may be contacted at rights@mhra.org.uk.

ISSN 0267–5315 (print) ISSN 2222–4270 (online)
ISBN 978-1-78188-889-6

© 2019 The Modern Humanities Research Association
Salisbury House, Station Road, Cambridge CB1 2LA, United Kingdom

Portuguese Studies Vol. 35 No. 2

Transnational Portuguese Women Writers

CONTENTS

Introduction Maria Luísa Coelho and Cláudia Pazos-Alonso	129
Teresa Margarida da Silva Orta (1711–1793): A Minor Transnational of the Brown Atlantic Ana Margarida Martins	136
The Empires Write Back: Tracing Transnational Indias in the Work of Maria Ermelinda dos Stuarts Gomes Hilary Owen	154
Early Twentieth-Century Portuguese Feminist Writers as Transnational Cultural Mediators: Virgínia de Castro e Almeida and Ana de Castro Osório Chatarina Edfeldt	167
'Nem uma coisa nem outra': Nomadic Subjectivity in the *Crónicas* of Ilse Losa Rosa Churcher Clarke	185
O mapa cor de rosa by Maria Velho da Costa: Migration, Dis-location and the Production of Unstable Cartographies Maria Luísa Coelho	199
Éukié: Maria Velho da Costa's Alice and the Absurd Maria Irene Ramalho	216
The Polyhedral Victim and the Patchwork Abuser: A Comparative Study of Names and Naming in Vladimir Nabokov's *Lolita* (1955) and Maria Velho da Costa's *Myra* (2008) Tom Stennett	228
Reviews	244
Abstracts	253

NOTES FOR CONTRIBUTORS

Articles to be considered for publication may be on any subject within the field but must not exceed 7,500 words, and should be submitted in a form ready for publication in English, sent as an email attachment to the Editorial Assistant at portuguese@mhra.org.uk.

Contributions whose standard of English is inadequate will be returned. Any quotations in Portuguese must be accompanied by an English translation. Submissions in Portuguese may be considered, but full peer review and publication will be conditional on provision of a satisfactory translation by or on behalf of the author. The Editorial Assistant may undertake translations on request for a reasonable charge.

Text and references should conform precisely to the conventions of the *MHRA Style Guide*, 3rd edn, 2013 (978-1-78188-009-8), £9.50, $19.00, €12.00, obtainable in print or online version from www.style.mhra.org.uk. All articles are subject to independent, anonymous peer review by experts in the field; authors receive written feedback on the editors' decision and guidance on any revisions required. *Portuguese Studies* regrets it must charge contributors for the cost of corrections in proof deemed excessive.

It is a condition of publication in this journal that authors of articles and reviews assign copyright, including electronic copyright, to the MHRA. Inter alia, this allows the General Editor to deal efficiently and consistently with requests from third parties for permission to reproduce material. The journal has been published simultaneously in printed and electronic form since January 2001. Permission, without fee, for authors to use their own material in other publications, after a reasonable period of time has elapsed, is not normally withheld. Authors may make closed-access deposit of accepted manuscripts in their academic institution's digital repository upon acceptance. Full open access to the accepted manuscript is permitted no sooner than 12 months following publication of the Contribution by the MHRA. Contributions may also be republished on authors' personal websites without seeking further permission from the Association, but no earlier than 12 months after publication by the MHRA.

Books for review should be sent to: Reviews Editor, *Portuguese Studies*, Dr Paul Melo e Castro, School of Modern Languages and Cultures, 221b, Hetherington Building, University of Glasgow, Bute Gardens, Glasgow G12 8RS.

Transnational Portuguese Women Writers

Maria Luísa Coelho and Cláudia Pazos-Alonso

The three most representative names of Portuguese literature are widely acknowledged, both within and outside Portugal, to be Luís de Camões, Eça de Queirós, and Fernando Pessoa. All three can be regarded, in different ways, as transnational writers, firstly in terms of their biographical trajectories and, secondly, of the global circulation of their writings. The fact that none of them is female tellingly reflects the perceived — historically sedimented — limited capacity of women to contribute to the shaping of Portuguese culture or its visibility within world literature.[1] Yet, in the last four decades and a half the most widely translated and internationally circulated Portuguese text, after Camões's *Lusiads* and alongside Pessoa, has been *New Portuguese Letters* by the Three Marias (Maria Velho da Costa, Maria Isabel Barreno and Maria Teresa Horta).[2]

The time is ripe, then, to revisit 'Portuguese' women's experiences of mobility across national borders.[3] In the current volume we embrace this challenge by interrogating through a transcultural perspective the conditions that mediate the development of their creativity and thought, their reception and impact. As Hilary Owen and Claire Williams put it, in their introduction to *Transnational Portuguese Studies*, what a transnational methodology offers us is

> a means of thinking beyond the disciplinary frames of the nation-state, aiming instead to highlight flows of mobility, transcultural points of contact and the dialogues created by the intersectional [...] exploring what is meant by the 'nation' in any given context, and how 'the nation' is always simultaneously in contact with, and shaped by, other transnational and transcultural influences, movements and ideas.[4]

While dislocation and relocation have always been human impulses, the visibility of economic migrant movements and the scale of their political, social and cultural repercussions in the contemporary world have given new impetus and urgency to transnational research, as attested by the numerous journals,

---

[1] This volume came into being in the aftermath of the International Conference on Transnational Portuguese Women Artists held at Wadham College, Oxford, 16–18 March 2017. The conference, jointly organized by Cláudia Pazos-Alonso, Hilary Owen and Maria Luísa Coelho, was generously supported by Wadham College and by the Modern Humanities Research Association, to whom we wish to record our thanks.

[2] See *New Portuguese Letters to the World: International Reception*, ed. by Ana Luísa Amaral, Ana Paula Ferreira and Marinela Freitas (Oxford: Peter Lang, 2015).

[3] The use of 'Portuguese' in quotation marks is intended to draw attention to the multiple belongings of several of the intellectuals discussed in the following articles.

[4] Owen and Williams, eds, 'Introduction', *Transnational Portuguese Studies* (Liverpool University Press, forthcoming 2020).

conferences and networks devoted to this theme. Mimi Sheller and John Urry thus refer to a new mobilities paradigm and emphasize how an understanding of complex and rhyzomatic cultural and social phenomena, through which individuals and communities connect across different times and spaces, has replaced a rigid, geographically stable and nation-based notion of community and culture.[5] Lusophone Studies have not been immune to this re-centring of knowledge, especially given Portuguese imperial and colonial history and its necessary re-assessment through the lens of post-colonial criticism. Nevertheless, the specificities of the geographical movements of women writers and intellectuals across borders, sometimes across continents, remain largely understudied.[6] Exceptions to this omission that seek to address migration explicitly from a gendered perspective are a special issue of the *Interdisciplinary Journal of Portuguese Diaspora Studies* (2015) and the edited volume *Exiliance au Féminin dans le Monde Lusophone (XX–XXI Siècles)* (2017).[7]

The general lack of critical engagement with the mobility of 'Portuguese' women is partially derived from the conditions affecting these migrant subjects, as Ana Margarida Fonseca contends:

> na retaguarda dos poderes instituídos, as mulheres migrantes, sejam elas colonizadoras, e/migrantes, exiladas ou refugiadas, são as últimas a fazerem-se ouvir, pois à marginalidade do deslocado soma-se a secundarização da mulher no espaço público, tanto o de origem como o de chegada.
>
> [at the rear of established powers, migrant women, be they colonizers, migrants, exiles or refugees, are always the last ones to make themselves heard; to the marginality of the displaced one must add the sidelining of women in the public space, both that of origin and of arrival.][8]

Fonseca's comments underscore some of the questions which are central to this volume, namely, the traditional separation between private and public spaces along gendered lines and the way this divide has intersected with the diasporic condition of the female subject. Several essays in the present issue consider this question but they also suggest a more nuanced view of the matter, demonstrating that in parallel to women's marginalization, migration may also contribute to their liberation, independence and agency. Displacement may therefore create the necessary pre-requisites for women to speak and, ultimately, be heard. In other words, by 'writing outside the nation', transnational women may subversively position themselves within the public sphere, making *exiliance* (in the sense the term has been coined by Alexis Nouss, that is, as condition

---

[5] Mimi Sheller and John Urry, 'The New Mobilities Paradigm', *Environment and Planning A*, 38 (2006), 207–26.
[6] There are, however, studies on individual Portuguese writers such as Maria Ondina Braga and Maria Gabriela Llansol, and a vast amount of scholarship on the painter Paula Rego.
[7] *Interdisciplinary Journal of Portuguese Diaspora Studies*, 4.1 (2015); Maria Graciete Besse et al., *Exiliance au Féminin dans le Monde Lusophone (XX–XXI Siècles)* (Paris: Éditions Hispaniques, 2017).
[8] Ana Margarida Fonseca, '"Tudo termina em clichés"? Representações de mulheres migrantes nas narrativas de Lídia Jorge', in *Exiliance au Féminin dans le Monde Lusophone* (2017), pp. 43–53 (p. 43).

and conscience) an ambivalent process which becomes a multi-dimensional experience and increases agency.[9]

When focusing on processes of dis-location in the case of women, we must, as Fonseca does, search for what is common to different circumstances and experiences, in order to address the specificities of gender difference in migration and diaspora studies. However, we also need to take a locational perspective (what Adrienne Rich calls a politics of location) capable of producing situated knowledge, which in turn reflects the intersection of gender and other dimensions of subjective experience.[10] This approach lies at the core of the essays in this volume and is particularly visible in those that discuss race and ethnicity (often in the context of Portuguese imperial past), or that expose the pivotal function of elite education in migrant women's access to public voice and space. Moreover, according to Rich, a politics of location must not begin 'with a continent or a country or a house, but with the geography closest in — the body'.[11] A politics of women's corporeal experience in the terms offered by Rich is very much central to the discussion of a female transnational experience, in which the female body not only lies at the intersection between the personal and the political, the private and the public, but also between past and present, subject and nation, self and other.

The intellectuals discussed in this volume have either lived abroad for extended periods of time or have multiple national roots and alliances, prompting them to problematize (national) identity and cultural difference and to replace these certainties with hybridism and/or fragmentation. They are cultural agents who have written across cultures, often developing productive discussions across national boundaries. For most of them, the written word 'has become the means to re-encounter and re-configure identities scattered through space, time, and circumstances'.[12] But through their written and public work they have also been able to promote translocal relations and an ethical relation to otherness, disrupting fixed notions of subjective and national identity.

Given the predominantly marginal position that women have traditionally occupied by virtue of being the gendered other, or the other within, these transnational women have been particularly well positioned, on the one hand, to function as shuttles between languages and cultures (Braidotti) and, on the other, to provide a self-reflexive interrogation and critical re-vision of their cultural and social roots.[13] Although recent studies dedicated to Lusophone

---

[9] Azade Seyhan, *Writing Outside the Nation* (Princeton, NJ: Princeton University Press, 2001); Alexis Nouss, *La Condition de l'exilé: penser les migrations contemporaines* (Paris: Maison des Sciences de l'Homme, 2015).
[10] Adrienne Rich, 'Notes Toward a Politics of Location', in *Blood, Bread and Poetry: Selected Prose, 1979–1985* (New York: Norton, 1986).
[11] Rich, 'Notes Toward a Politics of Location', p. 212.
[12] Dora Nunes Gago, 'Words in Exile', *Interdisciplinary Journal of Portuguese Diaspora Studies*, 4.1 (2015), 7–10 (p. 10).
[13] Rosi Braidotti, 'L'Usure des langues', *Cahiers du GRIF*, 39 (1988), 73–81; Susan R. Suleiman, *Risking*

women in a migrant context, such as the afore-mentioned *Exiliance au Féminin* and *Interdisciplinary Journal of Portuguese Diaspora Studies*, gathered evidence of this dual process in the context of contemporary mass migration and global circulation, the present volume begins by tracing such movements further back in time, starting with the context of Portugal's imperial past.

The opening two articles therefore examine two women born outside Portugal, in Brazil and Goa respectively: the eighteenth-century Teresa Margarida da Silva e Orta (1711–1793) and Maria Ermelinda dos Stuarts Gomes (1889–1937). Ana Margarida Martins's article proposes a new reading of the São Paulo-born, Portugal-based Teresa Orta as a 'minor transnational' of the Brown Atlantic,[14] as she cogently makes the case for revaluing Orta as an Afro-Brazilian literary precursor, through the recovery of her matrilineal heritage. Furthermore, Martins shows how, under the cover of characters drawn from the Classical world, Orta acts as a pioneer in the way she brings to the fore the question of slavery, as well as the social conditions that impede the development of women's agency in the Age of Reason and Enlightenment.

Over the course of the nineteenth century, women's agency and the transnational circulation of their ideas was boosted in incremental steps through periodical culture. It may not be a coincidence that the activism of three of the most remarkable nineteenth-century journalists, Antónia Gertrudes Pusich, Francisca Martins de Assis Wood and Guiomar Torresão, was underpinned by first-hand experiences of early displacement: Pusich and Torresão spent their childhood in Cape Verde, while Wood lived in Britain from the age of fourteen, staying for several decades.[15] It is this shift, as women became de facto public intellectuals, that paved the way for Ana de Castro Osório and Olga Moraes Sarmento da Silveira's periodical *Sociedade futura* (1902), at the dawn of the twentieth century. Moreover, it is surely not coincidental that their periodical recovered a transnational eighteenth-century foremother, Leonor da Fonseca Pimentel, as a recent article by Bezari cogently shows.[16]

Osório was the author of *Às mulheres portuguesas* (1905), widely regarded as the first Portuguese feminist manifesto. Osório's foundational role for Portuguese feminism is not, however, exempt from what we may regard as a kind of a Lusotropicalist blindspot *avant la lettre*, problematized in the current volume by Hilary Owen's discussion of the more nuanced positioning of the Goan Maria Ermelinda dos Stuarts Gomes. Indeed Owen shows how,

Who One Is: Encounters with Contemporary Art and Literature (Cambridge, MA, and London: Harvard University Press, 1994), p. 176.
[14] Françoise Lionnet and Shu-mei Shih, *Minor Transnationalism* (Durham, NC, and London: Duke University Press, 2005).
[15] For more information on the transnational mindset of Francisca Wood, see Cláudia Pazos Alonso, 'Spreading the Word: The "Woman Question" in the Periodicals *A Voz Feminina* and *O Progresso* (1868–9)', *Angelaki: Journal of the Theoretical Humanities*, 22 (2017), 61–75; reprinted in *Women Writing across Cultures: Past, Present and Future*, ed. by Pelagia Goulimari (New York: Routledge, 2018).
[16] Christina Bezari, 'Transnational Perspectives in Early Twentieth-Century Portugal: The Emergence of the Periodical *Sociedade Futura* (Lisbon, 1902–04)', *Portuguese Studies*, 35 (2019), 39–54.

as an Indo-Portuguese woman writing in the context of burgeoning antiimperial struggles in the neighbouring British Raj, Gomes re-interprets female commonalities as well as political differences in relation to Portuguese Republican and Liberal feminist politics.

Notwithstanding the arguably self-limiting nationalistic ideology of Ana de Castro Osório, her significance as a dynamic transnational cultural mediator deserves recognition, and is examined here by Chatarina Edfeldt. The gendering of transcultural flows has often been neglected, even though women's role as translators has been vital to the circulation of world literature. Edfeldt brings to light the correspondence exchanged in the first two decades of the twentieth century between Ana de Castro Osório and the Swedish Göran Björkman, who was a special advisor on the Romance languages to the Nobel Committee on Literature. She further highlights Virgínia de Castro e Almeida's pioneering 1913 work *A Mulher: história da mulher, a mulher moderna — educação*, for its engagement with and dissemination of transnational feminism, notably the positions of the Swedish feminist Ellen Key.

By the time Castro Osório died, in 1935, the normative curbing of women's intellectual horizons that would soon become associated with the Salazar dictatorship was already underway, evidenced through the subtle and not-sosubtle de-authorizing of non-conforming women such as Irene Lisboa (who studied in Switzerland and Belgium in the 1930s), or the later censorship of vocal activists such as Maria Lamas (who lived in Angola as a young woman and in exile in Paris in the 1960s). Here displacement is tackled from a less frequently discussed angle, by showcasing Ilse Losa, who fled her native Germany as a Jewish refugee in 1934 to settle in Portugal. Rosa Churcher Clarke analyses how Losa's self-understanding and creative imagination was profoundly shaped by her forced dislocation. Her compilation of *crónicas* [chronicles], published in 1997 under the title *À flor do tempo*, which brings cultural figures from German and Portuguese history into contact with one another, is explored through the prism of Braidotti's notion of nomadic subjectivity. At the intersection of journalism and literature, *crónicas*, as a hybrid genre disseminated via the so-called ephemeral press, allow and indeed arguably privilege subjectivity, hybridity, fragmentation. The appeal of the genre for its women practitioners, aside from the pragmatic reason of offering paid work, is worth underlining. For Losa, *crónica*-writing becomes an exercise in creative and intellectual freedom, a reaction against the stifling atmosphere of the Salazar dictatorship.

The last three articles of the volume discuss the vast *oeuvre* of Maria Velho da Costa (1938–), with a special focus on the transnational experiences and transcultural genealogies that inform her thinking and artistic practice. Perhaps still best known in an English-speaking context as one of the authors of *Novas Cartas Portuguesas* (1972), since none of her own novels has been translated into English to date — an absence that disproportionately tends to affect women writers (including those considered in this volume), but is nevertheless particularly conspicuous in her case — Velho da Costa's work had been marked by a spirit of de-centring even before she lived for an extended period of time outside her country of birth. In 1980, she moved to London, where she worked for about six years as Portuguese *leitora* at King's College London, before spending a spell as cultural attaché in Cape Verde in the late 1980s.

It was during her time in England that Velho da Costa wrote and published the compilation *O mapa cor de rosa: cartas de Londres* (1984). The texts were originally published in the Lisbon newspaper *A Capital*, between 1981 and 1982, as a series of *crónicas* about life in London in the early 1980s. As Maria Luísa Coelho discusses, these letters (as they became labelled in *O mapa cor de rosa*) create an unstable geographic and cultural cartography, through which personal, national and linguistic identities are seen as always in transit and in which the specific instances of a diasporic feminine are given literary representation. If it is true that Velho da Costa's writing has always been traversed by transcultural references, Coelho further argues that the writer's migrant experience undoubtedly contributed to the de-territorialization of her writing and the re-writing of the self.

The last two articles in this issue consider those transcultural currents underpinning Velho da Costa's fictional work. Maria Irene Ramalho tackles the broad sweep of Velho da Costa's *oeuvre*, from *Maina Mendes* (1969) to *Myra* (2008), through an examination of the novelist's imaginative re-deployment of Lewis Carroll's *Alice in Wonderland* and *Through the Looking Glass*. Ramalho argues that the use of serious nonsense, paradox and the absurd provides Velho da Costa with poetic tools that display the power of language to speak and unspeak at the same time. Ramalho shows that, by playing on the indefinite proliferation of naming (discussed by Deleuze in *Logic of Sense* precisely in connection with Carroll), Velho da Costa can embrace perplexity as a sophisticated deconstructive move that spotlights at various junctures individual and/or collective contradictions and shortcomings.

Finally, Tom Stennett centres his analysis on Velho da Costa's most recent novel, *Myra* (2008), through a thought-provoking comparison that contrasts the perspectives deployed in *Myra* and its predecessor in time, Nabokov's *Lolita* — the latter (in)famously narrated from the male predator's point of view. The tribulations of Myra, a vulnerable Russian teenage migrant, end in a harrowing suicide. Her *via crucis*, underscored by violent and unequal power relations, problematizes her lack of voice while nevertheless foregrounding her limited agency through her ultimate act of self-annihilation. Nearly 250 years earlier, Orta's protagonist had enjoyed a better outcome, as Ana Margarida Martins reminds us: by disguising herself as a man, Hemirena managed to survive and was ultimately reunited with her family, who resolved to ban slavery on their utopian island.

In a twenty-first-century world, Velho da Costa can no longer partake in the optimism of the Age of Enlightenment. But what she can, and does, do is sensitively bear witness to the plight of an adolescent who poignantly articulates her subaltern subjectivity as follows: 'fui proibida de existir. Fui roubada de poder ser' [I was not allowed to exist. I was cheated out of the possibility of being].[17] This line may be an oblique allusion to Pessoa's interrogation: 'Que jaz no abismo sob o mar que se ergue? | Nós, Portugal, o poder ser' [What lies in the abyss beneath the rising sea? We, Portugal, the possibility of being].[18] If so, it is worth noting that the imagined community envisioned by Pessoa was tellingly verbalized as a unifying collective, 'Nós, Portugal', in a line that sought to transform the darkness of abyssal chaos into cosmos through the power of rhetoric. By contrast, in Velho da Costa's work, exclusions predicated on gender, race and class asymmetries within the twenty-first-century nation are never far from the surface. The ethical repercussions of these exclusions resonate across a novel that privileges de-centring and de-territorialization through the perspective of the nomadic Myra, for whom the 'possibility of being' remains forever deferred, as she stares into the abyss.

In short, this special issue seeks to showcase women and transnational encounters. For the comparatively privileged intellectuals and cultural creators considered here, by and large migration created opportunities for fertile personal transformation, and new perceptions of place and dis-placement — in spite of, or perhaps precisely because of, their first-hand experience of varying degrees of trauma, most obvious in the case of the forced migration of Losa. If there is a common thread running through the seven articles that make up this volume, it is perhaps that the cosmopolitan perspectives of the female cultural agents discussed here lead them to repeatedly interrogate opposite terms, such as 'location' and 'dislocation', 'home' and 'foreign', 'past' and 'present'. As writers infused with transnational sensibilities, Margarida da Silva e Orta, Ana de Castro Osório, Virgínia de Castro e Almeida, Maria Ermelinda dos Stuarts Gomes, Ilse Losa and, last but not least, Maria Velho da Costa become, in a post-imperial context, discursive shuttles, connecting different times, spaces, languages and beings. Ultimately the transcultural space they inhabit, and which their readers are invited to join, is perceived as relational and fluid; what is more, it is one where individual and collective identities are represented as always being in transit.

---

[17] Maria Velho da Costa, *Myra* (Lisbon: Assírio e Alvim, 2008), p. 55.
[18] These lines come from the poem titled 'Tormenta' from *Mensagem* (1934). See <http://arquivopessoa.net/textos/2279>. The title plays on the two meanings of the word, 'torment' and 'tempest', and may also reference Shakespeare's *The Tempest*.

Teresa Margarida da Silva Orta (1711–1793): A Minor Transnational of the Brown Atlantic

ANA MARGARIDA MARTINS

University of Exeter

Introduction

1752 was an interesting year for women writing in Portuguese. This was the year when Rosa Maria Egipcíaca da Vera Cruz (1719–1778), brought from Costa da Mina to Brazil when she was six years old to work as a slave, penned a letter to her ex-slaveowner, Pedro Rodrigues Arvelos, which stands today as the oldest known manuscript authored by a slave woman in Brazil. Egipcíaca, who would spend most of her life writing, also penned *Sagrada teologia do amor de Deus luz brilhante das almas peregrinas*, recognized today as the oldest book ever written by a black woman in Brazil.[1] Also in 1752, the first novel written by a woman in Portuguese was published in Lisbon, under the title *Máximas de virtude e de formosura com que Diófanes, Clymenea e Hemirena, príncipes de Tebas, venceram os mais apertados lances da desgraça*.[2] The original edition of this book survives to this day with only a couple of pages lost. Its cover attributes authorship to Dorothea Engrássia Tavareda Dalmira, a partial anagram of Teresa Margarida da Silva Orta (1711–1793), a São Paulo-born, Lisbon-based woman.[3] The novel was dedicated to a Princess, D. Maria Francisca Isabel Josefa Antónia Gertrudes Rita Joanna, who would become the first Queen of Portugal in 1777. Despite their incredibly significant literary achievements, and although, according to two recent studies, both women were of African descent, the inclusion of Egipcíaca's and Orta's work in canonical postcolonial studies of Afro-Brazilian literature is often controversial.[4] This is,

---

[1] *Sagrada teologia do amor de Deus luz brilhante das almas peregrinas* and its author were deemed heretical by the Inquisition. Today, only a few pages of the book remain. See Luis Mott, *Rosa Egipcíaca: uma santa africana no Brasil* (Rio de Janeiro: Bertrand Brasil, 1993).

[2] Teresa Margarida da Silva Orta, *Máximas de virtude e de formosura com que Climenea e Hemirena, príncipes de Tebas, venceram os mais apertados lances da desgraça* (Lisbon: Oficina de Miguel Manescal da Costa, 1752). Manuscript located in the Biblioteca Nacional de Portugal. I will henceforth refer to this book as *Máximas de virtude e de formosura* in the main text. All quotes from the book are taken from the 1752 edition and all translations are mine.

[3] The acclaimed Portuguese writer Maria Teresa Horta is related to Teresa Margarida da Silva Orta, on her father's side.

[4] Dejair Dionísio, *Ancestralidade Bantu na literatura afro-brasileira: reflexões sobre o romance Ponciá Vicêncio de Conceição Evaristo* (Belo Horizonte: Nandyala, 2013), p. 37. Fábio Mário da Silva,

in large part, due to their transatlantic crossings, which make them harder to pin down to a particular territory.

James Clifford has noted that 'it is now widely understood that the old localizing strategies — by bounded *community*, by organic *culture*, by *region*, by *center* and *periphery* — may obscure as much as they reveal'.[5] What these strategies tend to obscure are the stories of those who inhabit the borders and are the agents of transatlantic crossings. Afro-Brazilian literary criticism often revolves around questions about community and nation, privileging literature produced by black writers born and bred in Brazil, as the title of Eduardo Assis Duarte's ground-breaking study *Literatura e afrodescendência no Brasil* confirms.[6] Although critics of Afro-Brazilian literature have often focused on the need to question the myth of cohesion, harmony and uniformity as regards Brazilian literature, they have done so in an effort to show the diverse ways that forgotten voices have imagined the nation artistically, from within. This strategic framing of Afro-descended writers against the white (and male) centre has been used to justify the exclusion of controversial voices such as the aforementioned women, as noted by Assis Duarte in an essay also titled 'Literatura e afrodescendência':

> A inclusão de ambas as autoras na Literatura Brasileira é polêmica. No caso de Teresa Margarida, pelos motivos exaustivamente debatidos [the writer left Brazil at a young age and wrote about European matters]. Já sobre Rosa Egipcíaca pesa o fato de não ser brasileira, nem ter, até ao momento, seus escritos publicados e divulgados.[7]
>
> [The inclusion of both authors in Brazilian Literature is controversial. In the case of Teresa Margarida, due to reasons that have been thoroughly discussed. As for Rosa Egipcíaca, we must consider the fact that she is not Brazilian, and that her writings have not, so far, been published and disseminated.]

This may partly explain why Maria Firmina dos Reis, born in São Luís do Maranhão in 1825, is recognized today as the black author of the first novel published in Brazil by a woman, titled *Úrsula: romance original brasileiro, por uma Maranhense*, although it only came out in 1859, a hundred and seven years after the publication of *Máximas de virtude e de formosura*.[8] Reis's novel is celebrated also as the first abolitionist novel in Brazilian literature, as attested by Luiza Lobo's chapter included in the first volume of Assis Duarte's seminal

---

'As mulheres em trânsito no contexto luso-brasileiro', *Café com letras: revista de literatura*, 2 (2016), 60–63 (p. 61).
[5] James Clifford, 'Diasporas', *Cultural Anthropology*, 9.3 (1994), 302–38 (p. 303). Author's emphasis.
[6] Eduardo Assis Duarte (ed.), *Literatura e afrodescendência no Brasil: antologia crítica*, 1 (Belo Horizonte: UFMG, 2011).
[7] Assis Duarte, *Literatura e afrodescendência* (2017), <http://www.letras.ufmg.br/literafro2/artigos/artigos-teorico-conceituais/150-eduardo-de-assis-duarte-literatura-e-afrodescendencia> [accessed 2 November 2017].
[8] Maria Firmina dos Reis, *Úrsula: romance original brasileiro por uma Maranhense* (Rio de Janeiro: Gráfica Olímpica Editora LTDA, 1975).

anthology: 'Úrsula [...] é o primeiro romance de autoria feminino brasileiro — bem como o primeiro romance abolicionista e o quinto publicado no Brasil' [Úrsula [...] is the first Brazilian novel written by a woman — as well as the first abolitionist novel, and the fifth published in Brazil].[9] By using the terms 'brasileiro' and 'Brasil' rather than 'Afro-Brazilian' in this quote, Lobo grants status as Brazilian to a black woman who, like most women with a hyphenated identity in that country, has been, for too long, ignored by Brazilian letters as a writer in her own right. In this chapter, Reis is presented alongside key nineteenth-century male authors:

> A escritora aparece ao lado da famosa plêiade de autores maranhenses do século XIX, como Gonçalves Dias (1823–1864), Aluízio de Azevedo (1857–1913), Artur Azevedo (1855–1908), Joaquim de Sousândrade (1832–1902), além do primo materno, o gramático Sotero dos Reis (1800–1871), e o tradutor de Homero, Odorico Mendes (1799–1864).[10]

> [The writer appears alongside the famous pleiad of nineteenth-century authors from Maranhão, such as Gonçalves Dias (1823–1864), Aluízio de Azevedo (1857–1913), Artur Azevedo (1855–1908), Joaquim de Sousândrade (1832–1902), as well as her maternal cousin, the grammarian Sotero dos Reis (1800–1871), and the translator of Homer, Odorico Mendes (1799–1864).]

By placing Reis in relation to male literary discourse rather than other minor, controversially 'Brazilian', Afro-descended, female voices, such as that of Egipcíaca and Orta, Lobo favours the nation-bound, vertical relationship of opposition or assimilation that leads up to the male centre, since the aim is not only to recognize Reis's full status as a Brazilian writer, but also to dismiss any doubts that might still persist about *Úrsula*'s pioneer status as a novel in Brazil:

> Compreende-se o desejo de recuar a gênese do romance brasileiro de autoria feminina até o final do séc. XVIII. No entanto, Teresa Margarida se mudou com a família portuguesa para Portugal quando contava 5 anos de idade, sem mais retornar ao Brasil. Além disso, o tema ilustrado de seu romance epistolar *As Aventuras de Diófanes* (1777), que se inspira em *A Viagem de Telêmaco*, de Fénelon, tem suas raízes no contexto cultural europeu. Desse modo a autora faz parte da literatura portuguesa, fato que já foi suficientemente comprovado.[11]

> [It is understandable that one might desire to root the genesis of the female-authored Brazilian novel in the end of the eighteenth century. However, Teresa Margarida moved with her Portuguese family to Portugal when she was five years old, never to return to Brazil. Besides, the theme of her epistolary novel *As Aventuras de Diófanes* (1777), inspired by *Les Aventures de Télémaque*, by Fénelon, has its roots in the European cultural context.

---

[9] Luiza Lobo, 'Maria Firmina dos Reis', in *Literatura e afrodescendência no Brasil: antologia crítica*, ed. by Eduardo de Assis Duarte, 4 vols (Belo Horizonte: UFMG, 2011), I, 111–26 (p. 113).
[10] Lobo, p. 111.
[11] Lobo, p. 113. In fact, *As Aventuras de Diófanes* is not an epistolary novel.

In this way, the author is part of Portuguese literature, a fact that has been sufficiently proven.]

Whilst Afro-Brazilian studies have moved Orta into closer alignment with Portugal, as this quote suggests, it is important to recognize the writer's Brazilian roots, specifically via her mother, which are still too little acknowledged and researched, and to push back against some of the assumptions that have mischaracterized Orta as belonging to a 'família portuguesa' through an exclusive focus on her Portuguese father.

Orta's father, José Ramos da Silva, was, indeed, Portuguese, having emigrated from Porto to Bahia in 1695, when he was twelve years old, to work as a servant. An intuitive businessman, he soon became one of the richest men in São Paulo, due to his successful dealings with the *Bandeirantes*.[12] In 1704 he married Dona Catarina Dorta, from a wealthy *paulista* family, and they had three children. While there is detailed information available on Orta's Portuguese father, little has been written on her Brazilian mother. Dejair Dionísio describes her as an 'Afro-descendente desterrada' [Afro-descendant in exile].[13] Fábio Mário da Silva corroborates this ethnic description in a study where Dona Catarina Dorta is depicted as 'brasileira de sangue mestiço' [Brazilian of mixed-race blood].[14] Whilst more research is needed in order to test this hypothesis, it seems, at least, that a challenge to views of Orta as only Portuguese (and only white) is in order.

If, on the Afro-Brazilian side, Orta has been rendered more Portuguese and, according to the studies of Dionísio and Silva, whiter than she actually was, on the Portuguese side critics have been quiet about the issue of race. Instead, they have associated her with the Luso-Brazilian group of *estrangeirados* by noting that Orta's articulation, in her novel, of the absence of the motherland and her allegory of autonomy as regards the 'reino dos bárbaros' [kingdom of slaves] confirms her as belonging to the group of Brazilian *desterrados*, to which her brother Matias Aires and her friend Alexandre de Gusmão belonged. Jaime Cortesão considers the novel to be Luso-Brazilian and representative of the rationalist and liberalist philosophical ideas of the time, represented by a group of Brazilians living in Portugal, also known as *ultramarinos*, who influenced the reforms of the Portuguese eighteenth century.[15] Santa-Cruz follows this line of argument in her study, suggesting that the plot resonates with the themes chosen by this group of eighteenth-century Luso-Brazilians who felt torn between their love for the Brazilian homeland and their love for the Portuguese metropolis, and who fought for social and intellectual emancipation from the Church and against political absolutism:

> Dorothea Ingrássia será luso-brasileira — como todos os que, na época, enobreceram a mesma língua portuguesa, estando vinculados ao Brasil

[12] For more on *Bandeirantes* see Boris Fausto, *A Concise History of Brazil*, trans. by Arthur Brakel (Cambridge: Cambridge University Press, 1999), pp. 47–54.
[13] Dionísio, *Ancestralidade Bantu*, p. 37.
[14] Silva, 'As mulheres em trânsito', p. 61.
[15] Jaime Cortesão, *Alexandre de Gusmão e o Tratado de Madrid* (Lisbon: Livros Horizonte, 1984).

pelo menos pelo nascimento e a infância e, quase sempre, pela adolescência, antes de virem para Coimbra.[16]

[Dorothea Ingrássia may be Luso-Brazilian — like all of those who, at the time, ennobled the same Portuguese language, being tied to Brazil through at least their birth and childhood and, almost always, adolescence, before travelling to Coimbra.]

However, Orta's mobility from Brazil to Portugal is, to some extent, distinguishable from that of the typical *estrangeirado*, *desterrado* or *ultramarino*, labels that designate a group of flexible and cosmopolitan individuals, usually male, who, having travelled through Europe in order to study and work, adopt the costumes and ways of life of other kingdoms as they attempt to improve their own. Although she moved amongst this powerful elite group, Orta had not chosen to leave Brazil (she was too young to decide for herself), and she never left Portugal, unlike Matias Aires and Alexandre de Gusmão, who both studied and worked abroad (France, Italy and Spain). Although her family was wealthy, she struggled with financial issues all her life, largely because of her father's decision to leave all of his fortune to his son, whilst sending his daughter to be educated in a convent. Orta was able to leave the convent and marry Pedro Jansen Moller, against her father's wishes, by alleging that she was pregnant. However, Moller, despite having influential friends among the Portuguese Crown, was not wealthy, and they struggled to make ends meet, a situation that led Orta to raise a number of cases in Court against her father and brother in an attempt to secure what was lawfully hers. She was also imprisoned by the Marquis of Pombal between 1770 and 1777 in the Monastery of Ferreira de Aves, for having lied to the King D. José about the secret relationship maintained between her youngest son Agostinho and Teresa José Xavier da Cunha e Melo, a wealthy young Portuguese woman. Orta died in 1793, at the age of eighty, leaving behind a life of noncompliance with patriarchal rules, as well as a novel and other writings documenting social revolution and female emancipation.

What her life experiences demonstrate is not so much, or not only, her membership of the group of *ultramarinos*, but rather her marginality in relation to that particular minor centre of ideas and power. The automatic association of her minority voice with that of the *desterrados* fails to account for the complex ways in which Orta, and also her novel, frame and are reframed by the various sides of her identity, including her ethnic identity (which requires further research), and not just the white male minority based in Portugal, to which she was also attached, albeit marginally. In what follows, I will discuss the work of Orta as a minor transnational whose real and imagined mobility may shed light on minor, or horizontal, forms of interaction with other networks of minoritized cultures, and prevent us from universalizing, from the viewpoint of Brazil, the experience of black female deterritorialization.

[16] Maria de Santa-Cruz, 'Crítica e confluência em *Aventuras de Diófanes*' (unpublished PhD dissertation, Faculdade de Letras da Universidade de Lisboa, 1990), p. 79.

Minor Transnationalism and the Question of Authenticity

Before we can begin to grasp the possibilities opened by the inclusion of controversial literary forerunners such as Orta and Egipcíaca in discussions of transnational mobility in what Miguel Vale de Almeida has called the 'Brown Atlantic', it is necessary, first, to further address the question of authenticity, which lies at the heart of the process that both invites and restricts literary representative roles of women with hyphenated identities in Brazil.[17] In fact, there is more to be said about the silence surrounding these women's work than the references to their birthplaces and countries of residence. I would also argue that the Afro-Brazilian character of their voices is contested because their work is not perceived today as being 'Afro' and 'oppositional' enough. While Egipcíaca turned to the Catholic Church in order to affirm herself as a writer, a visionary and a saint — her visions included breastfeeding baby Jesus, and Jesus combing her hair — Orta wrote about supposedly 'European' matters and set her novel in Ancient Greece.

In this context, the recognition of Reis as *the* forerunner (Afro-)Brazilian woman writer, above Egipcíaca and Orta, can only be understood within the realm of the 'authentic'. According to Emily Lee in 'The Epistemology of the Question of Authenticity', the authentic viewpoint is defined by the hierarchical correspondence between immediate experience and claim to knowledge, and by a focus on the social construction and community validation of both experience and knowledge: 'Knowledge of a culture does not develop solely from visceral experience but must fit with the ongoing web of knowledge and be confirmed by the community'.[18] In celebrating Reis's claim to representation, Lobo confirms perceptions of the writer as the authentic representative of Afro-Brazilian literature as opposed to the supposedly inauthentic outsiders Egipcíaca and Orta. What is celebrated here is the image of a homogeneous and static, though hyphenated, artistic self, authentically Afro-Brazilian because born, bred and based in Brazil.[19]

---

[17] Miguel Vale de Almeida, *An Earth-Colored Sea: 'Race', Culture and the Politics of Identity in the Postcolonial Portuguese-Speaking World* (New York: Berghahn Books, 2004). Almeida's concept expands Paul Gilroy's notion of the Black Atlantic (1993) to include a Lusophone, African-based, Atlantic cultural interconnectedness based on the experience of slavery.

[18] Emily Lee, 'The Epistemology of the Question of Authenticity, in Place of Strategic Essentialism', *Hypathia*, 26.2 (2011), 258–79 (p. 271).

[19] Maria Firmina dos Reis was recently honoured at the First National Encounter *Mulherio das Letras*, which took place on 12–15 October 2017 in the Fundação Casa de José Américo, Cabo Branco, Fernando Pessoa. The event celebrated the 100th anniversary of Reis's death (11 November 1917). On the event's website, the organizers highlight her life-long Brazilian residency: 'Foi na ilha de São Luís do Maranhão, berço de escritores como Gonçalves Dias e Aluízio de Azevedo, que Maria Firmina dos Reis nasceu; mas foi na remota vilazinha maranhense de Guimarães, terra natal de Sousândrade, que passou toda a sua vida e produziu sua pioneira obra literária' [It was on the island of São Luís do Maranhão, cradle of writers such as Gonçalo Dias and Aluízio de Azevedo, that Maria Firmina dos Reis was born; but it was in the small, remote town of Guimarães in Maranhão, birth place of Sousândrade, that she spent all of her life and produced her pioneering literary work] (see <https://www.mulheriodasletras.com/centenariofirmina>) [accessed 5 November 2017].

It is important to note that authenticity is empowering and even, I would argue, necessary here, as a tool to reclaim Reis's suppressed minority discourse. As noted by Lee, authenticity remains epistemologically valid, since it 'holds a kernel of truth', which stems from the connection between who one is and what one knows.[20] Nevertheless, precisely because it is based on the hierarchical correspondence between immediate experience and claim to knowledge, authenticity may also contribute to silencing women who are deemed 'insiders', since they are not expected to produce informed knowledge about contexts other than their own. Furthermore, cultivating the perception of an authentic, Brazil-based, black representative writer may contribute to keeping alive the image of a homogenous, static and essentialist culture, making it harder to clarify misconceptions about Brazil, Brazilian women, feminism and racism.[21] This may lead to forms of cultural essentialism, not to mention the denial of literary citizenship to other, seemingly Afro-descended, women who, like Egipcíaca and Orta, are the product of transmigrations, multiple encounters and spaces of contact, both within and beyond the nation state.[22] As Lee writes: 'one can learn about a culture, and individual visceral experience of culture does not found experience'.[23]

I argue that it is only by paying attention to the intersection of other, more disordered or irreverent forms of participation in the national and the transnational that we may come face to face with complex, unexpected and multiply located 'minor' voices that are, on the one hand, located in relation to the major, whilst also interacting in minor-to-minor networks. In this context, I follow Françoise Lionnet and Shu-mei Shih's concept of minor transnationalism, a term that aims to focus on horizontal communication amongst minorities both within and beyond the nation.[24] In their theoretical considerations of what a minor transnationalism might entail, Lionnet and Shih draw on Edward Glissant's definition of creolization, according to which cultural orientations are always already creolized, hybrid and relational. Instead of being 'transnational' because they transcend the national, minority cultural workers are transnational 'because their cultural orientations are by definition creolized in Glissant's sense'.[25]

An increasingly popular term since the 1990s, when it was used within migrant studies to prioritize the empowerment of migrants as important social agents, transnationalism is today applied to a variety of phenomena, and broadly refers to the durable ties and interactions that link people across

---

[20] Lee, 'The Epistemology of the Question of Authenticity', p. 265.
[21] Ibid.
[22] In much Afro-Brazilian criticism, the expression 'Afro-Brazilian literature and culture' has come to stand for texts that can be seen to exist mostly in relation to a well-defined centre, their value measured in terms of its opposition to a dominant discourse (e.g., white, black male, Brazilian).
[23] Lee, 'The Epistemology of the Question of Authenticity', p. 271.
[24] Françoise Lionnet and Shu-mei Shih, *Minor Transnationalism* (Durham, NC, and London: Duke University Press, 2005), p. 8.
[25] Lionnet and Shih, *Minor Transnationalism*, p. 9.

the borders of nation states. In their introduction to *Minor Transnationalism*, Lionnet and Shih recognize that the transnational is part of the process of globalization and, as such, needs to be questioned as a homogenizing force. Dominant formulations of the transnational arguably reinforce binary models by continuing to adhere to a north/south, dominant/resistant model of culture. The contrast is suggested by means of the distinction between what is often defined as transnationalism from 'above' and 'below'. The former is associated with utopian views of globalization, which celebrate the overcoming of national and other boundaries for the constitution of a liberal global market, the hybridization of cultures, and the expansion of democracies. Transnationalism from below, in contradistinction to the elitist forces of transnationalism from above, generates counter-hegemonic powers among non-elites, creating dystopian views by those who refuse to be assimilated into the interests of the few. Because these non-elites refuse to be assimilated into one given state, transnationalism from below translates into a more or less romanticized politics of the local.

The expression 'minor transnationalism', with its focus on horizontal communication amongst minorities both within and beyond the nation, intervenes in both formulations of transnationalism, by revising their assumptions. The minority and diasporic peoples participate in the moment of transnationalism but their cultural practices and networks of communication exceed the parameters of these theories: 'what is lacking in the binary model of above-and-below, the utopic and the dystopic, and the global and the local is an awareness and recognition of the creative interventions that networks of minoritized cultures produce within and across national boundaries'.[26]

Elleke Boehmer has outlined one of minor transnationalism's blind spots, which is that it may lead us away from a 'critical reflection on nations, minor and major, and their relation to the transnational'.[27] Beyond the larger political and epistemological concern that relates to the marketability of the trans-border perspective, which always risks reproducing the power structures of corporate globalization, Bohemer argues that, despite the contributors' best intentions, the question of location in *Minor Transnationalism* remains problematic: not only are all the articles in the collection produced by academics based in the US, but they also fail to reflect on the nation-state and its relation to the transnational. In this study I will attempt to move beyond this blindspot by asking if there is anything in the binary model of centre/margin in which Orta moved (in between Brazil and Portugal) that encourages transnational minoritized action (or writing) as an oppositional practice. I suggest that the hegemonic identities of the nations she belonged to contributed to shaping her literary identity as a minor transnational (i.e., as someone who identified laterally with other

[26] Lionnet and Shih, *Minor Transnationalism*, p. 7.
[27] Elleke Boehmer, 'Minor Transnationalism (review)', *Journal of Colonialism and Colonial History*, 6.3 (2005). Online at < https://muse.jhu.edu/article/192166#info_wrap> [accessed 11 November 2019].

minority groups rather than vertically in opposition to a dominant discourse). Through her novelistic intervention in debates about slavery, race and gender relations, Orta was able to find common ground with other minor subjects, rather than engaging only with the centre(s) as an end in itself.

Towards a Minor Transnational Understanding of Orta's Work and Mobility

Orta published *Máximas de virtude e de formosura* when she was approximately forty years old. Its first readers, the censors of the *Santo Ofício*, delayed the publication of the novel by two years before they finally allowed it to be published, contrary to what happened to the book authored by her brother Matias Aires, *Reflexões sobre a vaidade dos homens*, which, having been presented to the censors in 1752, was licensed for publication that same year.[28] Orta's novel was so successful that it was published three times in less than fifty years: 1752, 1777 and 1790.[29] *Aventuras de Diófanes* became the preferred abridged title of *Máximas de virtude e de formosura*, following the 1790 edition of the book, which assigned the authorship to Alexandre de Gusmão (1695–1753), an influential diplomat who, like Orta, was born in Brazil but had moved to Portugal. An abridged edition of the novel came out in 1818 under a new title, *História de Diófanes, Climenea e Hemirena, príncipes de Tebas*, its authorship now assigned mysteriously to 'Huma Senhora Portugueza'.[30] As a result of these authorial controversies, much of the available discussion of the novel revolves around the issue of its authorship, which was questioned when the third edition of 1790 was attributed to Gusmão. As noted by Furquim, Gusmão had been dead for 37 years by the time the third edition of the book came out, a detail that significantly problematizes a possible male authorship.[31] In *História da inteligência brasileira* Wilson Martins argues that the publisher's decision to attribute authorship to Gusmão rather than to Orta may have been simply a commercial strategy.[32] Cortesão adds that this could have been orchestrated as a political strategy to protect Orta from being targeted by the authorities, since the Marquis of Pombal had already put her in prison for seven years, as mentioned above.[33] Controversies aside, it is possible to argue that the debate surrounding the book's authorship, initiated with the publication of the third

---

[28] Santa-Cruz, 'Crítica e confluência', p. 58.
[29] Orta, *Máximas de virtude e de formosura* (Lisbon: Oficina de Miguel Manescal da Costa, 1752, 1777); Alexandre de Gusmão, *Aventuras de Diófanes imitando o sapientíssimo Fénelon na sua viagem de Telêmaco* (Lisbon: Régia Oficina Tipográfica, 1790). Both were published under the pseudonym of Dorothea Engrássia Tavareda Dalmira.
[30] Huma Senhora Portugueza [Orta], *História de Diófanes, Climenea e Hemirena, príncipes de Tebas* (Lisbon: Oficina Rolandiana, 1818).
[31] Tânia Magali Ferreira Furquim, 'Aventuras instrutivas: Teresa Margarida da Silva Orta e o romance setecentista' (unpublished master's dissertation, Universidade Estadual de Campinas, 2003), p. 26.
[32] Wilson Martins, *História da inteligência brasileira*, 1 (São Paulo: Culturix, 1976), p. 368.
[33] Cortesão, *Alexandre de Gusmão*.

edition, has eclipsed interpretations of the novel itself, calling attention to a possible male authorship rather than to the openly feminist, abolitionist and anti-absolutist content of the book. In fact, existing interpretations of *Máximas de virtude e de formosura* tend to assume a universal core or norm that produces a hierarchy of subjects and themes. This is attested, for example, by the manner in which critics commonly refer to the novel as *Aventuras de Diófanes*, which encourages immediate comparison with *Les Aventures de Télémaque*, by Fénelon, and thus prevents readings that go beyond those mediated by the centre.

In Brazil, the novel was only published for the first time in 1945, under the title *Aventuras de Diófanes*.[34] This is also the first time that the real name of the author, Teresa Margarida da Silva e Orta, appears on the book cover. The edition is prefaced by Rui Bloem, who reads the book as Brazilian:

> O primeiro romance brasileiro surgiu [...] em 1752. É brasileiro no sentido de ter sido escrito por uma romancista nascida no Brasil, porque pertence à fase da nossa literatura em que apenas se começava a esboçar uma consciência de nacionalidade nos homens da pátria que mal surgia e em que, portanto, os escritores brasileiros não se preocupavam em situar a acção dos seus livros no ambiente da Colônia paupérrima e oprimida. Nem por isso, contudo, deixa de ser um livro brasileiro, e não pode nem deve ficar esquecido em nossa história literária.[35]

> [The first Brazilian novel appeared [...] in 1752. It is Brazilian in the sense that it was written by a novelist born in Brazil, because it belongs to the moment in our literature when a national consciousness was beginning to take shape among the men of the fatherland, which was about to emerge, and during which Brazilian writers were not concerned with situating the action of their books in the setting of the extremely poor and oppressed Colony. That does not mean, however, that this is not a Brazilian book, and it must not, and should not, be forgotten in our literary history.]

In 1952, Ernesto Ennes described it as 'o primeiro romance brasileiro, precursor do romance nacional' [the first Brazilian novel, forerunner of the national novel].[36] Ivana Versiani would later apply the expression 'escritora luso-brasileira' [Luso-Brazilian writer] to define Orta's position as a writer.[37] It is only towards the end of the 1960s and 1970s, with the rise of the black consciousness movement and the growth of women's politicization in Brazil, that those readings of Orta as Brazilian and her novel as Luso-Brazilian begin to be challenged. For example, in 1969, Nelson Werneck Sodré argued that Orta cannot be considered part of the universe of Brazilian letters because 'de

---

[34] Teresa Margarida da Silva e Orta, *Aventuras de Diófanes* (Rio de Janeiro: Imprensa Nacional, 1945).
[35] Rui Bloem, 'O primeiro romance brasileiro: retificação de um erro da história literária do Brasil', in *Aventuras de Diófanes* (Rio de Janeiro: Instituto Nacional do Livro, 1945), p. 222.
[36] Ernesto Ennes, *Dois paulistas insignes: Teresa Margarida da Silva Orta e o primeiro romance brasileiro* (São Paulo: Companhia Editorial Nacional, 1952), p. 15.
[37] Ivana Versiani, 'Teresa Margarida e as *Aventuras de Diófanes*', *Kriterion*, 67 (1973/74), 293–310, cited in Santa Cruz, 'Crítica e confluência', p. 77.

brasileira, tivera apenas o acidente do nascimento' [the only Brazilian aspect of her life is the incident of birth].[38]

Despite more recent repudiations, it is fair to say that *Máximas de virtude e de formosura* has been valued more in Brazil than in Portugal. The complete works of Orta were compiled and published in 1993 in Brazil under the title *Obra reunida: Teresa Margarida da Silva e Orta*.[39] In 2006, Conceição Flores published the first book dedicated to Orta's novel, titled *As Aventuras de Teresa Margarida da Silva Orta em terras de Brasil e Portugal*, based on a PhD dissertation from 2004.[40]

In Portugal, on the other hand, the novel has been mostly dismissed as mediocre, or ignored by canonical literary criticism. In the 1960s, João Gaspar Simões considered the novel to be Portuguese but of little importance: 'Vale a pena, em verdade, reclamar o seu nome para a história do romance nacional, embora ela não nos tenha proporcionado uma obra novelística de vulto' [Truth be told, it is worth claiming her name for the history of the national novel, although she did not leave us a major work of literature].[41] In *História da literatura portuguesa*, António José Saraiva and Óscar Lopes sum up Orta's achievements rather disparagingly by describing her as:

> Mulher de temperamento irrequieto, que casou contra vontade dos pais, foi deserdada, odiada pelo irmão, aprisionada pelo Marquês de Pombal e que escreveu *Aventuras de Diófanes* (4 edições, 1752, 1777, 1790, Rio de Janeiro 1945), romance [...] de conteúdo mais ou menos discretamente feminista e liberal.[42]
>
> [A woman of restless character, who married against her parents' will, was disowned, hated by her brother, imprisoned by the Marquis of Pombal and who wrote *Aventuras de Diófanes* (4 editions, 1752, 1777, 1790, Rio de Janeiro 1945), a more-or-less discreetly feminist and liberal novel.]

In 1980, Maria Ondina Braga dedicated a chapter of *Mulheres escritoras* to Orta, describing her as 'uma escritora feminista no século das luzes' [a feminist writer of the Enlightenment] and 'primeira romancista luso-brasileira' [first Luso-Brazilian novelist].[43] But it is only in 2002 that a new edition of the novel came out in Portugal, edited by Maria de Santa-Cruz, author of the first and only PhD thesis dedicated to Orta's novel completed in Portugal (within a Brazilian studies department), in 1990.[44]

---

[38] Nelson Werneck Sodré, *História da literatura brasileira* (Rio de Janeiro: Editorial Sul Americana, 1969), p. 110.
[39] Orta, *Obra reunida*, ed. by Ceila Montez (Rio de Janeiro: Graphia, 1993).
[40] Conceição Flores, *As aventuras de Teresa Margarida Silva e Orta em terras de Brasil e Portugal* (Natal, RN: Opção Gráfica, 2006).
[41] João Gaspar Simões, *História do romance português* (Lisbon: Estúdios Cor, 1967), p. 212.
[42] António José Saraiva and Óscar Lopes, *História da literatura portuguesa* (Porto: Porto Editora, [1955] 1979), pp. 509–10.
[43] Maria Ondina Braga, *Mulheres escritoras* (Lisbon: Bertrand, 1980), p. 170.
[44] Orta, *Aventuras de Diófanes*, ed. by Maria de Santa-Cruz (Lisbon: Caminho, 2002); Maria de Santa-Cruz, 'Crítica e confluência em *Aventuras de Diófanes*' (unpublished PhD dissertation, Faculdade de Letras da Universidade de Lisboa, 1990).

None of the studies I have encountered so far attempts to read it alongside Afro-Brazilian literature by women. Typically, the novel is compared to the work of Orta's brother Matias Aires and other men of letters. One example of this may be found in Tânia Furquim's master's thesis, which sets out to compare the novel to:

> outros textos com os quais, de alguma forma, dialoga: os romances *Aventuras de Telêmaco* (1699), de François Fénelon, *O Feliz Independente do Mundo e da Fortuna* (1779), do padre Theodoro de Almeida, o livro de máximas: *O Casamento Perfeito* (1630), de Diogo de Paiva Andrada; e os tratos filosóficos *Reflexões sobre a Vaidade dos Homens* (1752), de Matias Aires, *O Verdadeiro Método de Estudar* (1746), de Luiz Antônio Verney, e *A Educação das Moças* (1687), também de Fénelon.[45]

> [other texts with which, in some way, it engages: the novels *Les Aventures de Télémaque* (1699), by François Fénelon, *O Feliz independente do mundo e da fortuna* (1779), by the priest Theodoro de Almeida, the book of dicta: *O casamento perfeito* (1630), by Diogo de Paiva Andrada; and the philosophical tracts *Reflexões sobre a vaidade dos homens* (1752), by Matias Aires, *O verdadeiro método de estudar* (1746), by Luiz Antônio Verney, and *Traité de l'éducation des filles* (1687), also by Fénelon.]

Challenging existing criticisms from both sides of the Atlantic that have read Orta as either Brazilian, Portuguese, or Luso-Brazilian, this study proposes a new understanding of this novel as a minor transnational contribution to literature in Portuguese that links the struggles and writings of pioneering Afro-descended women writers in a lateral and non-hierarchical way. My goal is not to dethrone Reis in favour of Orta as a literary forerunner, but to argue for the urgency of putting forward a transnational understanding of Orta's work and mobility that may, in time, be supported by much needed research on Orta's maternal Afrodescendancy, so that the emphasis lies as much on the multiple specific margins of the transnational as on the hegemonic powers and knowledge that structure that space of contact.

Máximas de virtude e de formosura: Geographical Mobility and the Normativities of Gender

Beyond the scope of her Brazilian birth, Orta's under-researched African genealogy, via her mother, and the inevitable ethnic and community identification with Portugal, via her father, transform her into the consummate example of the transnational subject. It is in this light that I set out to discuss her very audacious defence of the end of slavery, as well as her engagement with notions of transnational space and ideas of feminism in her novel. In order to

---

[45] Tânia Magali Ferreira Furquim, 'Aventuras instrutivas: Teresa Margarida da Silva Orta e o romance setecentista', master's dissertation (Campinas: Universidade Estadual de Campinas, 2003), p. 8.

challenge the hermeneutical script that surrounds *Máximas de virtude e de formosura*, and in the current absence of biographical material on the author's mother, I turn to the mother–daughter relationship between Hemirena and Clymenea, both of whom present a strong awareness of their multivocality and a kind of diaspora consciousness.

Máximas de virtude e de formosura is set in Ancient Greece and is divided into five books. The plot focuses on the fate of the rulers of Thebes, Diófanes and Clymenea, and their two children, Almeno and Hemirena. Whilst travelling to Delos for the wedding of Hemirena to her fiancé Arnesto, they encounter a storm and are driven off route, which leaves them exposed to the assault of their enemies from Argos. The brother Almeno dies in the fight; the rest of the family survives but is separated and enslaved: Diófanes is sold and sent to Corinth; Hemirena is taken as a slave to the house of Hortelio, the captain of one of the enemy ships; and Clymenea is able to escape and finds shelter in a cave.

From the start, the gender-neutral narrative voice privileges the viewpoint of Hemirena, and her relationship with her mother. This is a point made by Braga, for whom 'A princesa Hemirena, e não Diófanes, é a figura mais importante do romance. Inconscientemente, Teresa Margarida deve ter-se identificado com ela' [Princess Hemirena, rather than Diófanes, is the most important character in the novel. Unconsciously, Teresa Margarida must have identified with her].[46] Because of her beauty and moral integrity, Hemirena is despised by Hortelio's daughter Anchizia, but is helped by Anchizia's brother Carmindo, who sells her to the Princesses of Athens, Beraniza and Argenea. In Athens, Hemirena is treated fairly for four years, but after the death of Beraniza, the advances of Prince Iberio lead her to plan her escape from Athens, which she describes as a pilgrimage away from the dangers of love and the excesses of the royal court. In order to preserve her life and her honour in foreign lands, Hemirena changes her name and her gender, answering from here onwards by the name of Bellino:

> recommendando ao silencio da noite o livralla dos tumultos da Corte, sahio com vestido de homem, disposta com aquele fingimento a vencer os maiores assaltos de sua cruel fortuna.[47]

> [hoping the silence of the night would keep her away from the turmoils of the Court, she left dressed as a man, determined to overcome, through this disguise, the greatest difficulties of her cruel fate.]

Hemirena's performance of gender, the result of her imagination of what a young transnational should look like, raises questions about the relationship between geographical mobility and the normativities of gender. The disguise as a young man will suit her needs, by keeping her sexually safe as she roams the unknown lands in search of her family and allowing her to experience the consequences of displacement from a more empowered position. By imagining

---

[46] Braga, *Mulheres escritoras*, p. 175.
[47] Orta, *Máximas de virtude e de formosura*, pp. 43–44.

herself as Bellino, Hemirena demonstrates an understanding of the diasporic space as a profoundly gendered one, experienced differently by both men and women.[48] She justifies her gender dissimulation to her mother by drawing on men's impunity:

> Não me culpeis o haver usado da dissimulação de taes vestidos, porque como os maiores trabalhos, e desgraças, que acontecem às mulheres, são originados pelos enganos dos homens, que ou cegos de amor, ou dos seus desordenados costumes, lhes prendem a liberdade, e as encaminhão aos precipicios, pareceu-me que só escondendo-me assim aos seos olhos, caminharia com menos risco.[49]

> [Do not blame me for having disguised myself in men's clothing, since the greatest troubles and disgraces that fall upon women come from the falsehoods of men, who, either blinded by love or by their uncontrolled habits, take women's freedom away and lead them down precipices; as such, it seemed that only by hiding like this from their eyes could I move about more safely.]

Although this technique is perceived by her mother as a sign of modesty ('a modestia he o mais preciso adorno das mulheres' [modesty is women's most precious adornment]), in reality Hemirena's gender change allows her to walk freely amongst men in foreign lands, go to war, and even jump out of windows to save her mother, whilst simultaneously denouncing male double standards ('sendo nellas infame desaire, o que he nelles timbre da mocidade' [what is perceived as a sign of youthfulness in men is viewed as infamous misfortune in women]). The identitarian coherence of the other characters is also put on the line, as they become multiply coded in their attempts to escape slavery, via a change in names, and physical appearance. Diófanes answers by the name of Antionor and adopts the appearance of a leper; Clymenea presents herself as a much older woman called Delmetra; Hemirena's fiancé Arnesto, in search for his lost bride, leaves Delos disguised as Albenio.

But it is Hemirena's gender change that best exemplifies the manner in which the novel destabilizes the production of meaning from a single locational and gendered standpoint. By dressing as Bellino outside of national borders, Hemirena poses a challenge to both national and sexual identification. Her dissimulation troubles not only the primacy of the national as the main category of identity but also the conventional boundaries of gender, inviting the reader to 'consider the transnational as a dimension of trans space'.[50] While she does not embrace masculinity indefinitely, and is not transgender in the terms dictated by Western contemporary models of transgender identity,

---

[48] In this article I understand 'diaspora' not simply as the direct result of migration but also as a phenomenon that encompasses other kinds of travel and displacement, such as the one described in *Máximas de virtude e de formosura*.

[49] Orta, *Máximas de virtude e de formosura*, p. 241.

[50] Jessica Berman, 'Is the Trans in Transnational the Trans in Transgender?', *Modernism/Modernity*, 24.2 (2017), 217–44 (p. 223).

Hemirena is, in many ways, a trans figure, taking a male name, dressing in male clothing, and challenging traditional expectations for women. Her movement outside of national/gender borders, which serves to defy fixed categories, has implications not only for the transnational space she inhabits, which becomes marked by open-ended forms of gender performance, but also for the reading practices it incites. Hemirena's gender dissimulation abroad encourages the reader to understand the text within a transnational frame of reference, and to challenge assumptions about national belonging via the focus on gender mis-identification. Without losing sight of the nation, *Máximas de virtude e de formosura* effectively ties together the instability of both gender and normative citizenship as a trans text that, in the words of Jessica Berman, 'challenges the normative dimensions of nationality and disrupts the systems of embodied identity that undergird them'.[51]

When Hemirena, disguised as Bellino, encounters her mother, also in disguise, she finds it hard to believe that this feeble-looking woman, who appears to be in her seventies, has managed to survive on her own for six years among wild beasts inside a cave: 'fazes tão boa sociedade com as féras, que te respeitão' [you live so peacefully with the beasts, who respect you].[52] Displaying extreme emotional and physical endurance, Delmetra explains the hardships posed by the situation of having to share a place of hiding with wild animals, noting that their peaceful coexistence is the result of daily efforts to conquer her space. As an eccentric female subject surviving in isolation, away from home and family, Delmetra's newly discovered ability to coexist with wild beasts unveils diasporic experience as an always-gendered experience. The episode emphasizes the impact of enforced dislocations on gendered bodies, and brings out the double pain that afflicts women in diasporic situations: the physical/material and mnemonic insecurities of living away from home. Feeling simultaneously at home and away from home, both here and there, and, in the words of Clifford, living 'loss and hope as a defining tension',[53] Delmetra exclaims, 'Onde está a que então era, e donde veio a que hoje sou?' [Where is the one I used to be, and where did the one I am today come from?].[54]

The narrative does not solely highlight the dangers of the gendered diasporic experience, but also points to ways in which women are empowered by life outside home. Without recognizing each other, Bellino and Delmetra decide to move from the cave to a nearby village of shepherds, where they live in relative peace for four years. In the borderline space of the village where they find provisional refuge, mother and daughter take part in a wedding, during which Delmetra gives a much applauded speech where she calls for equality between men and women:

---

[51] Berman, 'Is the Trans in Transnational', p. 218.
[52] Orta, *Máximas de virtude e de formosura*, p. 73.
[53] Clifford, 'Diasporas', p. 312.
[54] Orta, *Máximas de virtude e de formosura*, p. 209.

Eu não intento louvallas contra justiça, pois tem sido o meu empenho advertir-lhes os defeitos, que em muito poucas se acharão; mas não haverá quem lhes negue a Gloria de que a mais rude está em mais alto gráo que todos elles, só em conservar a sua moderação, e constancia em desprezallos. [...] Estes discursivos se não dizem que as almas tem sexo, para que forjão distinções, que não tem mais subsistencia que na sua corrupta imaginação, pois forão igualmente creadas, e a disposição dos orgãos (de que dizem provém a bondade do espirito) he tão ventajosa nas mulheres, como nos homens? Alguns ha tão faltos de espirito, e capacidade, que se lhes tirarem hum só gráo, não lhes faltaria nada para brutos; assim como são inumeraveis as heroinas, que se tem visto tão intelligentes, que humas tem parecido milagre nas artes, e outras tem dado a entender que eles julgam ignorancia, o que são effeitos da modestia. Não resplandece em todas a luz brilhante das sciencias; porque eles occupão as aulas, em que não terião lugar, se ellas as frequentassem, pois temos igualdade de almas, e o mesmo direito aos conhecimentos necessarios.[55]

[I do not wish to praise them unfairly, for it has been my plight to point out their flaws, which may be found in many; but no one can deny them the Glory that even the rudest woman is of a higher standard than all of them [men], just by keeping with her moderation and by consistently despising them. [...] These wordy subjects, if they are not busy arguing that souls have a sex, why do they forge distinctions, which have no substance except in their corrupt imagination, for they were equally created, and the position of bodily organs (from where the kindness of spirit comes from, they say) is as advantageous in women as it is in men? Some of them [men] are so devoid of spirit and ability that, if a single grain was to be taken away from them, they would turn into brutes, just as there are countless heroines who are so intelligent that some have been like miracles in the arts, and others have pretended to be what they [men] take as ignorance, when they are simply modest. The resplendent light of sciences does not shine through all of them [women]; because they [men] occupy the classrooms, in which they would not find a place to sit if they [women] attended them, for we have equality of souls, and the same right to necessary knowledge.]

The feminist tone of the speech is enhanced by its position in the narrative: the reader has just read about Delmetra's problematization of the dichotomy between civilized and wild spaces in the provisional home of the cave, where she is found by her trans daughter living gracefully amongst the beasts. This reveals the extent to which, in *Máximas de virtude e de formosura*, gender difference and place are closely tied together, as the former is of significance to geographical constructions of the latter.

It is important to note that the final return home in the novel is structured through a direct protest against slavery. When the family finally reaches the end of their forced peregrination, the return to Thebes is celebrated by a decree that frees all slaves: 'deo-se liberdade a todos os escravos, que alli se achárão' [all slaves that were there were freed] (p. 350). From Thebes, they travel to Delos for

[55] Orta, *Máximas de virtude e de formosura*, pp. 92–93.

the wedding festivities, and on the island they commit to ending slavery: 'Depois de jurarem os Principes, e grandes, que jà mais naquella Ilha se consentiria, que houvessem escravos, porque seriam restituidos à inteira liberdade os que, como cativos, alli chegassem' [The Princes and the greatest swore that slavery would no longer be allowed on that Island, since the entire freedom would be restored to all those who arrived there as slaves].[56] The book thus not only describes the trauma of imprisonment and enslavement but also proclaims the need to put an end to slavery — in 1752, this meant the end of the enslavement of black people from Africa — a very audacious proclamation that needs to be understood also in the light of the author's putative Afro-descended matrilineality.

Conclusions

The fact that Orta is not fully recognized by existing Afro-Brazilian criticism as representing a transatlantic (Afro-descended?) identity across differentiated nation spaces confirms the extent to which Afro-Brazilian literary studies, in contrast to the Afro-Brazilian musical, religious and culinary fields of study, have yet to offer inventive combinations of minor voices across national borders to negotiate the diaspora in transnational terms.[57] Whilst the translocal and the transnational have been allowed to thrive as an oppositional practice in other fields of study, Afro-Brazilian literary studies, and black women's writing in particular, are arguably still trapped within the politics of binary oppositions produced by internal colonialism, understood here as the continuation in Brazil of external colonialism, but this time led by national elites over domestic subaltern groups.[58] Although applying the lens of postcolonial theory to Brazil is, as several critics have noted, a complicated task, it is possible to argue that the fight against the act of incorporation of difference into the same proposed by internal colonialism is close to the binary model advanced by postcolonial critique — which emphasizes the common and collective use of strategies of resistance by minority cultures in their subjection and opposition to a dominant culture.[59] This binary, which lies at the heart of the postcolonial dialectic has, to

---

[56] Orta, *Máximas de virtude e de formosura*, p. 353
[57] To give one example, the story that James Matory tells in his book *Black Atlantic Religion* is that of the transnational dialogues involving 'West African, Afro-Brazilian and Afro-Cuban priests, alongside European and American slave traders, European imperialists, postcolonial Latin American and African nationalists, black transatlantic merchants, and an international community of ethnographers', without which religious identities, leaderships and sacred values could not be explained. Matory's understanding of religion emerges in the context of dynamic politics, economics, and long-distance communication that disrupts nation-state boundaries. James Lorand Matory, *Black Atlantic Religion: Tradition, Transnationalism, and Matriarchy in the Afro-Brazilian candomblé* (Princeton, NJ: Princeton University Press, 2005), p. 3.
[58] Letícia Maria Costa da Nóbrega Cesarino, 'Brazilian Postcoloniality and South-South Cooperation: A View from Anthropology', *Portuguese Cultural Studies*, 4 (2012), 85–113 (p. 91).
[59] For examples of how turning the lenses of postcolonial studies to Brazil is not a simple task, see: Walter Mignolo, *Local Histories / Global Designs: Coloniality, Subaltern Knowledges and Border Thinking* (Princeton, NJ: Princeton University Press, 2000); Bill Ashcroft, 'Latin America and

a large extent, safeguarded the emphasis on birth, life-long residency in Brazil and, I would argue, a sense of authenticity that, as noted by Lee, may be defined as a relation between 'embodiment, experience of a culture and knowledge of a culture'.[60] This sense of authenticity arguably continues to define literary Afro-Brazilianness. The field therefore requires a new understanding of Afro-Brazilian contributions to literature in Portuguese that links the struggles and writings of pioneering Afro-descended women writers in a lateral and non-hierarchical way. This calls for a major methodological shift, from the national location of specific women writers to their transnational way of remembering and imagining movement within and beyond their nation's borders.

Postcolonial Transformation', in *On Postcolonial Futures: Transformation of Colonial Cultures* (New York: Continuum International Publishing Group, 2001), pp. 22–35.
[60] Lee, 'The Epistemology of the Question of Authenticity', p. 265.

The Empires Write Back: Tracing Transnational Indias in the Work of Maria Ermelinda dos Stuarts Gomes

HILARY OWEN

University of Manchester / University of Oxford

> Transnational cross-currents were also at the heart of colonialism, slavery, and other forms of exploitation by globalized capital involving the violent asymmetrical entanglement of racialized communities; this shadow side of national progress has been largely occluded from memory.[1]

In her 1905 feminist manifesto, *Às mulheres portuguesas*, the first wave writer and activist Ana de Castro Osório (1872–1935) uses her chapter on 'Ser Português' [Being Portuguese] as a national rallying call for women. Aiming her comments specifically at the nation's mothers, she accuses them of trying to shirk their patriotic duties and 'conservar-se na abstenção culposa em que tem vivido até aqui a mulher portuguesa' [keep up the shameful inactivity in which Portuguese womanhood has lived until now].[2] This is particularly significant for her, in relation to Portugal's territories overseas. In the context of this imperialist rhetoric, in the aftermath of the Berlin Conference (1884–85) and the Ultimatum crisis of 1890, it becomes a woman's individual patriotic duty to ensure that no pieces of the Portuguese empire are cut off, through her lack of maternal vigilance or interest in national affairs, as she remarks: 'ao seu espírito desocupado passa tão desapercebido que um pedaço das colónias seja retalhado à pátria, como um novo empréstimo ou uma sobrecarga de impostos' [to their indifferent minds, a piece of the colonies being cut off the fatherland is no more noteworthy than a new loan or over-taxation].[3] Castro Osório's work provides the canonical cornerstone of Republican Feminism from the turn of the last century, building a strong pedagogical imperative for women's education and civic duty. As Ana Paula Ferreira points out in her foundational analysis, 'Nationalism and Feminism at the Turn of the Nineteenth Century: Constructing the "Other" (Woman) of Portugal', Castro Osório's brand of feminist thinking saw a woman's duty as being to learn and transmit to her

---

[1] Chiara de Cesari and Ann Rigney, eds, *Transnational Memory: Circulation, Articulation, Scales* (Berlin: De Gruyter, 2014), p. 7.
[2] Ana de Castro Osório, *Às mulheres portuguesas* (Lisbon: Ed. Viúva Tavares Cardoso, 1905), p. 68. All translations into English are my own unless otherwise indicated. The original Portuguese spelling has been retained in all archive materials cited.
[3] Castro Osório, *Às mulheres portuguesas*, p. 68.

children a rational model of loyal and healthy Portugueseness for the good of empire and nation, with a strong emphasis on rehabilitating a now diminished image of historic national virility.[4]

At the same time, Castro Osório's prolific correspondence with feminists and women activists abroad and her own period of residence in Brazil (1911-14) formed a famously extensive web of exchange and debate on women's roles, rights and political duties during this period. Of particular interest to me here is the question of how, given the centrality to her feminism of this patriotic imperial teleology, Castro Osório engaged with those few feminist women from the far corners of Portugal's empire who were, at this time, beginning to 'write back'. They were not yet, I would argue, writing back from positions of open resistance, but they were in some instances adopting strategically double-voiced subjectivities in which the cracks of non-conformity were starting to be discernible. For them, a very different, proto-independent vision of their 'pedaço das colónias' [piece of the colonies] was central to their thinking on women's rights. One such example of a person who entered into direct dialogue with Castro Osório on the issues of empire, colonialism and women's rights was Maria Ermelinda dos Stuarts Gomes (1889-1937), an educated, Goan Catholic who also travelled, published, lectured and taught in Portugal.[5]

Gomes was born in Chandor, Salcete, belonged to the Chardo caste, and came from an eminent Indo-Portuguese family.[6] She eventually settled in Portugal in 1933 and became a secondary school teacher in Moura, in the Alto Alentejo. She worked for the Ministério das Colónias [Colonies Office] and ultimately died in Portugal in 1937.[7] Gomes wrote, taught and lectured extensively in Goa and Portugal about history, ethnography, gender, women's education, political rights and social roles. According to Natividade Monteiro, between 1933 and 1934 Gomes headed the Education Section of the Conselho Nacional das Mulheres Portuguesas (CNMP) [National Council of Portuguese Women], which had been set up in 1914.[8] Her writings also appeared in the

---

[4] Ana Paula Ferreira, 'Nationalism and Feminism at the Turn of the Nineteenth Century: Constructing the "Other" (Woman) of Portugal', *Santa Barbara Portuguese Studies*, 3 (1992), 123-42. See also Silvia Bermúdez and Roberta Johnson, eds, *A New History of Iberian Feminisms* (Toronto: University of Toronto Press, 2018), especially Deborah Madden, 'Feminist Thought in Portugal, 1900-1926', pp. 205-12.

[5] My sincere thanks are due to Claire Williams for our collaborative archive research and her always valuable discussion during our research trip to Panaji in 2009.

[6] Rochelle Pinto has described the chardos as 'a powerful but subordinate caste among Catholics [who] had long opposed the monopolistic hold of brahmins over the church and the bureaucracy under the Portuguese'. Rochelle Pinto, *Between Empires: Print and Politics in Goa*, SOAS Studies on South Asia (New York: Oxford University Press, 2007), p. 45.

[7] Aleixo Manuel da Costa, *Dicionário de Literatura Goesa* (Macau: Instituto Cultural de Macau-Fundação Oriente, 1997), pp. 61-63. See also Zília Osório de Castro and João Esteves, dir., António Ferreira de Sousa et al., coord. *Dicionário no Feminino (séculos XIX-XX)* (Lisbon: Livros Horizonte, 2005), pp. 662-63.

[8] Natividade Monteiro notes that Gomes took on this role with the CNMP after she came to live in Portugal. This places it after 1933. See Monteiro, 'Mulheres e Cidadania na Iª República: Mobilização e Migração na Guerra de 1914-1918', *Tertúlia da Diáspora*. Blog. 2 October 2014. <http://tertuliadadiaspora.blogspot.co.uk/2014/10/mulheres-e-cidadania-na-irepublica.html> [accessed 2

journal *A Semeadora*, and in publications such as *Alma Feminina*, the official organ of the CNMP, and *Portugal Feminino*.[9] As Filipa Lowndes Vicente notes in her highly informative 'roadmap' of Portuguese-speaking women writers in Goa (1860–1940), Gomes, specifically, 'needs to be studied in the international context of the intersection of colonialism and feminism, in order to better understand the ways in which her discourse on Indian women's empowerment was intertwined with the European colonial presence'.[10] Indeed, Vicente has described Gomes as 'the first case of a Goan woman identified as "feminist" even if the term has historically multiple and contested meanings'.[11] Disclosing the hitherto rather muted transnational crosscurrents of the Portuguese first wave, Gomes's Indian nationalist sympathies would have conflicted with the imperialist stance of her friend and mentor, Ana de Castro Osório.

By demonstrating how the less canonical, 'peripheral', raced and colonized voices of women's rights entered into dialogue with the hegemonic feminist voices of the metropolis, Gomes exemplifies the shifting and at times contradictory political subjectivities this created, as well as the discursive possibilities opened up by reviewing 'empire' and 'nation' as plural transnational phenomena. Chiara de Cesari and Ann Rigney, drawing on Benedict Anderson in their work on memory, have significantly noted the transnational character of the ideal of 'nation' itself, producing 'transnational cross-currents which were operative at the height of nationalism but which were subsequently written out of national narratives. These cross-currents included the transnational character of nationalism itself.'[12]

If Portugal's late nineteenth-century national image was conditioned by its reactions to imperial rivalry and decline, this had, as Ferreira points out, significant implications for the patriotic disciplining of naturalized gender roles, making Portugal 'obsessively preoccupied, and especially after the 1890s, with recuperating its self-image of heroic masculinity'.[13] As a corollary of this, Castro Osório's liberal feminist vision of the ideal 'wife-mother' was wholly bound up with the imperial mission of maintaining and transmitting the nation's virility, both reproductively and culturally. As we will observe shortly,

---

April 2018]. A similar dating of 1933–34 is given by João Esteves, 'Conselho Nacional das Mulheres Portuguesas', *Faces de Eva. Estudos Sobre a Mulher*, 15 (2006), 113–35. <http://www.fcsh.unl.pt/facesdeeva/eva_arquivo/revista_15/eva_arquivo_numero15_g.html> [accessed 3 April 2018]. Monteiro classifies Gomes along with Adelaide Cabete and others who brought their feminist politics to Africa and India, but she does not bring out the fact that Gomes's feminism was, unlike that of many of her peers in the Portuguese colonies, increasingly imbricated in anti-colonial nationalism too.

[9] See Natividade Monteiro, 'Mulheres e Cidadania na Iª República'. Gomes had sent articles from Goa to be published in *A Semeadora* in 1917 and 1918, in *Alma Feminina* at various points between 1931 and 1936, and in *Portugal Feminino* in 1931. For the dates of Gomes's journalism in Portugal, see Castro and Esteves, *Dicionário no Feminino*, p. 663.

[10] Filipa Lowndes Vicente, 'Portuguese-speaking Goan Women Writers in Late Colonial India, 1860–1940', *Portuguese Studies Review*, 25.1 (2017), 315–45 (pp. 338–39).

[11] Vicente, 'Portuguese-speaking Goan Women Writers', p. 338.

[12] De Cesari and Rigney, ed., *Transnational Memory*, p. 7.

[13] Ferreira, 'Nationalism and Feminism', p. 126.

Gomes's principal writings on the condition of women and the imperative of women's education to make them the complementary maternal helpmate, but never usurper, of men are not radically divergent from Castro Osório's.[14] Indeed, in her *Assuntos Pedagógicos* of 1932, Gomes references less overtly 'militant' Portuguese feminist reformists than Castro Osório, such as Emília de Sousa Costa, Virgínia de Castro e Almeida and the educational campaigner Maria Amália Vaz de Carvalho, for whom she reserves particular admiration.[15] One way in which her educational reformist feminism and her views on the political role of women do take a progressively different, and potentially 'dissident', turn, however, relates to the way in which Portugal's late nineteenth-century declinist narrative and its patriotic reaction play out in the Portuguese empire in India, influencing the idealized justificatory ends to which women's independence and education should be put in this context.

The late nineteenth- and early twentieth-century preoccupation with recuperating Portugal's 'self-image of heroic masculinity'[16] in relation to more successfully advanced and progressive imperial powers was felt in acute and specific ways in the direct contra-distinction it posed to British empire in India. As the print historian Rochelle Pinto observes, 'if there was a dominant perspective through which Goa's [Indo-Portuguese] Catholic elite viewed their nineteenth century, it was as a condition to be mourned. The defining condition (and its predicament) of colonial Goa as the elite saw it was its dual location within the economic twilight of the Portuguese empire and the political fringe of British India'.[17] Drawing on Partha Chatterjee's *The Nation and Its Fragments*, Pinto goes on to use the history of print in colonial Goa as a means to 'grasp the multiple locations of its colonial elite and the nature of the colonial state' as they were submitted to 'the pressure of alternate temporalities generated by Portuguese and British colonialisms, and alternate narratives of conquest and liberation'.[18]

This nineteenth-century decline narrative, based largely on dwindling economic pre-eminence, was countered by Goan elite self-representations and political discourses, drawing, as Pinto notes, on three compensatory forces, all of them relevant to Gomes's writings: the overarching historical narratives and

---

[14] See Maria Regina Tavares da Silva, 'Feminismo em Portugal na voz das mulheres escritoras do início do século XX', *Análise Social*, 19.77/78/79 (1983), 875–907.

[15] Maria Ermelinda dos Stuarts Gomes, *Assuntos Pedagógicos* (Nova Goa: Imprensa Gonçalves, 1932), pp. 139–40 and p. 182. Emília de Sousa Costa was a particularly strong proponent of an essentialized maternal 'Feminismo Verdadeiro' against the denatured masculinization designated 'Feminismo Falso'. See Tavares da Silva, 'Feminismo em Portugal', p. 880. Castro Osório's views on the differences between 'Feminismo Verdadeiro' and 'Feminismo Falso' did circulate in Goa in the women's journal *Mascotte. Jornal para Mulheres e Crianças*, 18 (6 August 1933), p. 1. As Gomes was also a contributor to *Mascotte*, during this period, and she and Castro Osório had clearly known each other at least since 1925 (the date of Castro Osório's preface to Gomes's *Sumário Geral da História da Índia. Livro 1*), it is quite possible that Gomes sought to disseminate Castro Osório's ideas in Goa.

[16] Ferreira, 'Nationalism and Feminism', p. 126.

[17] Pinto, *Between Empires*, p. 1.

[18] Pinto, *Between Empires*, p. 16 and p. 24.

historiographies of British India; British scholarly and Romantic orientalism; and the putative rise of Indian nationalism in the early twentieth century. At the same time, however, Goa's writers and intellectuals, with access to print media, also frequently felt the need to assert their Portuguese identity, loyalty and patriotic vigour, not least as a defence against the frequent strictures of censorship and suspicion that greeted periods of political unrest.[19] These alternate and competing temporalities, along with the alternate narratives of conquest and liberation that they imply, are clearly discernible forces shaping the intersectional cross-weave that characterizes Gomes's principal published works, as well as their points of tension with Castro Osório.

Gomes began her public career in 1924, publishing lectures on topics such as women's work, teaching practices, and the suppression of alcoholism, but her principal educational, historical and political writings are her *Sumário da História Geral da Índia* (Livro 1 and Livros 2–5, in two separate volumes dated 1926 and 1930 respectively), her *Assuntos Pedagógicos* in 1932, and a public lecture, entitled 'A Mulher Indiana', delivered for India Day in Portugal in 1934.[20] The *Sumário da História Geral da Índia* comes endorsed with a commendatory preface or 'Apreciação' written by Ana de Castro Osório. This preface is dated 20 December 1925 and is included in the Livro 1 publication in 1926, that deals with 'Os Portugueses na Índia' [The Portuguese in India]. However, it was also reproduced unaltered for the second part of the work, Livros 2–5, published in 1930, where volume 5 deals with the history of 'outros europeus na Índia' [other Europeans in India]. In ordering events in this way, Gomes separates Portuguese history off, achronologically, from the rest of what follows. She puts the fifteenth-century Portuguese sea voyage to India and the conquests of Goa up front in her Livro 1, before the later Livros 2–5 that cover the fuller historical span, extending on either side of the fifteenth century, from pre-Vedic antiquity, Vedic and medieval India, to the colonial conquests by other European powers (France, Denmark, Holland and Britain), culminating powerfully with the rise of Gandhian Indian nationalism and anti-colonial resistance in the present 1920s.[21] Gomes clearly performs here a very overt form of Portuguese loyalty and patriotism, at the same time as she promotes her reformist visions of Indian women as instrumental to the

---

[19] Pinto, *Between Empires*, p. 38 and p. 45.
[20] Maria Ermelinda dos Stuarts Gomes, *Sumário da História Geral da Índia, Livro 1. Os portugueses na Índia. História resumida da sua acção extraída de vários autores* (Nova Goa: Imprensa Gonçalves, 1926); *Sumário da História Geral da Índia. Livros 2–5* (Bastorá: Tipografia Rangel, 1930); *Assuntos Pedagógicos* (Nova Goa: Imprensa Goncalves, 1932) and *A mulher indiana* (Pôrto: Guedes Lda, 1934). As she makes clear in the introduction to her second volume in the *Sumário da História Geral da Índia*, entitled 'Explicando...' the five sections that make up her *Sumário* have been designated as 'Livros' [Books]. These Livros (themselves subdivided into 'partes' [parts]) are published across two printed volumes, the first containing only Livro 1 in 1926, and the second with the remaining four Livros in 1930. For a full bibliography of Gomes's works, see Costa, *Dicionário de Literatura Goesa*, pp. 62–63.
[21] See Pinto, *Between Empires*, p. 55, where she refers to a 'distinctly Hindu antiquity, a medieval Muslim age and a debilitated present'.

progress of Indian nationalism.²² As she explains in her own 'Palavras Prévias', dated 1924 and prefacing the 1926 Livro 1 of the collection, her rationale for locating 'em primeiro lugar o último, os Portugueses na Índia' [last things first, the Portuguese in India], was largely patriotic and pedagogical, a necessary correction to the fact that Goan school children are only given small, isolated 'trechos dessa História' [passages of that History], i.e. of Portuguese Indian history in their school primers.²³ However, although she starts with the classic heroic trajectory of the 'Ínclita Geração' [Illustrious Generation] and Vasco da Gama's voyage to India, Afonso de Albuquerque, the Old Conquests in Goa, and the role of the religious orders and Christianization, she nonetheless progressively shifts into a standard British, and Goan anglicized, historiography of decline and disaster, summarizing a series of acknowledged historical sources, such as Vincent Smith, her own brother Benedito Gomes, and Teixeira Pinto.²⁴

Furthermore, when this rather doom-laden Livro 1 is set alongside Livros 2–5, particularly Livro 5, the effect is dramatically to relegate Portugal's history in Goa to the role of a placatory set piece in relation to the liberal evolutionary and regenerative thrust that characterizes Livro 5 and its references to women's changing role in modern India and Indian nationalist struggle. She thus makes Portugal a token mythical backcloth to a genuinely 'future oriented' proto-Indian nationalist, and evolutionary narrative, whose epicentre is definitely elsewhere than Portugal, albeit strongly felt in Goa. Hence, the concluding sections of Livro 5 detail the Indian nationalist politics of non-cooperation, the 1920s campaigns of Mahatma Gandhi and the importance of Indian nationalism's founding feminist and poet Sarojini Naidu (1879–1949), who is pictured in Gomes's book. Indeed, she and Gandhi's wife Kasturba are the only women who figure among the images. The visual narrative created by tracing the images that head each chapter evokes an evolutionary history culminating in the necessary present-day elevation of women, typified by Sarojini Naidu and by the fact of Gandhi being pictured alongside his wife. The last word in the book is given to Goa, but in a hesitant, questioning tone set against the massive and growing uncertainties arising from further non-cooperation strategies, and the ongoing actions of the Home Rule or 'swarajista' movements, as Gomes asks, 'vingará o Estatuto do Domínio? Vingará a independência? São prematuras todas as previsões sobre o futuro político da Índia. E o que será da nossa Goa?' [Will the Statute of Dominion remain in force? Will independence be victorious? It is too early to make any forecasts about the political future of India. And what will become of our own Goa?].²⁵

---

²² Pinto has referred to the 'schizophrenic' identifications often produced by this ostensible, strategic duality of political allegiances. See *Between Empires*, p. 46
²³ Gomes, *Sumário. Livro 1*, p. ix.
²⁴ The main English-language history she refers to is Vincent Arthur Smith, *The Oxford History of India, from the Earliest Times to the End of 1911* (Oxford: Clarendon Press, 1919).
²⁵ Gomes, *Sumário. Livros 2–5*, p. 271.

This narrative of Portugal's decline in Goa, located within a proto-nationalist evolutionary historiography of India, was certainly not patriotic enough for Ana de Castro Osório, nor did it escape her correction. In the 'Apreciação' that is included in both volumes of the *Sumário Geral*, Osório tries to reframe Gomes and her work in a suitably imperialist pedagogy. Osório thus responds critically to two aspects of Gomes's account as she writes: 'uma coisa falta para que aos alunos não seja dada uma falsa ideia da acção portuguesa na história da civilisação moderna' [something more is needed if our pupils are not to be given a false idea of Portugal's role in the history of modern civilization].[26] The something that is missing is the view that the rise of other European powers in India, particularly the British, occurred for no other reason than that Portugal transferred its attentions to Brazil. Gomes has effectively refused to conform to Castro Osório's 1920s imperialist mandate first by embracing an anglicized historiography of Portuguese India and second by failing to situate the decline of Goa in a properly global, Luso-centric perspective. Indeed, Gomes's characteristically Goan early twentieth-century view of the decadence of a twilight Portuguese empire finds itself contradicted at the outset by Osório, who counters:

> O enfraquecimento do nosso domínio e acção no Oriente tem de ser explicado aos estudantes de hoje, que serão os portuguêses de amanhã, homens e mulheres que formarão o conjunto da Nação forte e gloriosa, que fomos e queremos continuar a ser, não como a demonstração da derrota e da decadência do povo, mas como o abandôno duma ideia exclusivamente comercial por uma acção maior e mais bela perante a vida mundial, que foi a criação do imenso país lusíado, que é o Brasil.[27]

> [The weakening of our dominion and activity in the East has to be explained to today's students, who will be the Portuguese of tomorrow, men and women who will make up the entirety of that strong and glorious Nation, which we were and which we wish to continue to be, not as the demonstration of the defeat and the decline of a people, but rather as abandoning an exclusively commercial idea in favour of a greater and finer role in the life of the world, namely, the creation of the vast Lusitanian country that we know as Brazil.]

Nothing daunted by Osório's rather double-edged affirmation, Gomes's introduction to her *Assuntos Pedagógicos*, published two years later in 1932, and comprising a collection of diverse pieces originally published in various journals, takes the anti-imperial challenge even further and strikes at the relevance and reach of the Portuguese language:

> O único paiz que nos pode server de modêlo é a Índia Britânica. Nenhuma Colónia Portuguesa oferece semelhança com a nossa, visto que África e Timor são regiões na sua maior extensão ainda bastante atrazadas que

---

[26] Castro Osório, 'Uma apreciação', *Sumário. Livro 1*, p. xxiv.
[27] Castro Osório, 'Uma apreciação', *Sumário. Livro 1*, p. xxv.

Portugal se empenha em absorver civilizando-as. [...] [O insistir] no contrasenso de exterminar a vernácula e popularizar a língua portuguesa, dentro do régime político de descentralização reconhecido, é uma utopia que jamais logrará realização.[28]

[The only country that could provide a model for us is British India. No Portuguese Colony is similar to ours, since Africa and Timor are, for the most part, still fairly backward, and Portugal is trying to absorb them by civilizing them. [...] [Insisting] on the nonsense of exterminating the vernacular and popularizing the Portuguese language, within a political regime that is renowned for decentralization, is a utopia that will never be realized.]

In the same vein, she moves to exalt 'o grande Triunfo obtido pela Índia na sua luta contra o Imperialismo' [the great Triumph achieved by India in its struggle against Imperialism] as being attributable largely to the women.[29] For Gomes, women's 'tendência natural para a abnegação e para o sacrifício' [natural tendency to abnegation and sacrifice] aligns them specifically with anti-colonial nationalism and campaigns of civil disobedience.[30] Adhering assiduously to the complementarity of naturalized male and female roles, Gomes echoes Castro Osório's emblematic defence of maternal femininity as the true source of women's national, political and pedagogical power.[31] She goes on to praise Indian woman precisely because 'não é grato registar que ela não se distingue, em sendo concorrente do homen [sic], mas sim a sua colaboradora' [it is worth noting that she does not distinguish herself by competing with man but rather by collaborating with him].[32] She then extends this universal naturalization to the specific situation of India, to value the feminized nature of *ahimsa* (the virtue of non-violence towards others and respect for living things, upheld by the Hindu, Buddhist and Jainist religions, and espoused by Gandhi), of which women were, for Gandhi, the particularly privileged exponents.

In 1933, a year after the publication of *Assuntos Pedagógicos*, Gomes left Goa to go and settle in Portugal when she was placed in an official position with the Ministério das Colónias. A couple of interesting letters to Ana de Castro Osório survive from this period, addressed from Moura, in the Alto Alentejo, and from Porto.[33] In the first letter, dated 2 November 1933, Gomes refers resignedly to her decision to live in Portugal as 'exílio voluntário' [voluntary exile] as she worries about the probable loss of her teaching pension and her precarious financial situation, while also suffering from the cold weather during her first full winter in Portugal. She talks of the fatalism needed to 'aguardar os

---

[28] Gomes, *Assuntos*, pp. xvii–xviii.
[29] Gomes, *Assuntos*, p. 172.
[30] Gomes, *Assuntos*, p. 173.
[31] Tavares de Silva, 'Feminismo em Portugal', pp. 878–80.
[32] Gomes, *Assuntos*, p. 123.
[33] The two letters cited here are in the Coleção de Castro Osório, Espólio no. 12/22, in the Biblioteca Nacional de Portugal.

acontecimentos' [await further events], although not with 'braços cruzados' [arms folded], indicating a political resolution not to remain inactive in exile, a view reinforced by an oblique allusion to various 'contratempos' [setbacks] that have occurred in Lisbon.[34] She makes it clear that she experiences living in Portugal as exile and hates the cobbled streets of small-town Moura that ruin the heels of her shoes. Her second letter, from Praça da República in Porto, 28 August 1934, records her difficulties in obtaining a teaching job as she is not 'diplomada' [a graduate] and reinforces her dislike of having to live at a distance from Lisbon. It is clear in her letters that she is responding to correspondence with Castro Osório, although sadly these letters to Gomes do not appear to have survived. A fairly strong friendship, in addition to Gomes's subordinate and partly supplicant situation, might explain Gomes's addressing the older woman as 'minha muito prezada amiga' [my dearest friend] in the 28 August 1934 letter. Here it emerges that she has been introduced to some Porto friends of Castro Osório, Dona Filomena, Sr. Lemos and his wife, and has had the opportunity through them to visit Viana do Castelo, the rural Minho (her favourite province of Portugal), and the Santuário de Bom Jesús and shrines of Braga. Only at the end of this missive does Gomes remember her real news as she writes:

> Vou-me esquecendo, fui convidada pela Comissão da Exposição para fazer uma Conferência no dia 11 de Setembro, dia dedicado à Índia. Ainda não escolhi o assunto pois estou bastante atrapalhada porque todos os elementos de consultas e citação estão em Lisboa. Em todo o caso vou ver o que faço.
>
> [I nearly forgot to say that I was invited by the Comissão da Exposição to deliver a lecture on the 11 September, India Day. I have not chosen a topic yet, indeed it is rather inconvenient that all the materials I want to consult and quote from are in Lisbon. Anyway, I will see what I can do.]

Perhaps the lack of access to more formal sources such as books, notes and academic citations goes some way toward accounting for the very direct and forthright discourse of appeal that characterizes the public lecture that she went on to deliver on India Day, 11 September, for the Exposição Colonial Portuguesa [Portuguese Colonial Exhibition] held in Porto, from 19 June to 30 September 1934. In this speech, Gomes proceeds to develop her elevation of women as both rhetorically and pragmatically central to the Indian nationalist cause, with much more explicit reference to women's political role.[35] This speech is ostensibly produced with a view to her direct participation, albeit in 'native informant' mode, in the Portuguese colonial project, as this was emerging by the mid-1930s. She effectively uses the 'woman question' to gloss

---

[34] Censorship was formally imposed in Portugal after the right-wing coup that brought the Republic to an end in 1926. It increased in scope and severity over the following decade, becoming officially enshrined by the state in the *Estado Novo* Constitution of 1933 and coming under the centralized Direção Geral dos Serviços de Censura in 1936, which mandated prior censorship of books and press.

[35] Maria Ermelinda dos Stuarts Gomes, *A mulher indiana* (Pôrto: Guedes Lda., Edições da Primeira Exposição Portuguesa, 1934).

the 'schizophrenic' nature of her own national loyalties, apparently praising Portugal as offering a platform from which to expound her views on Indian nationalism. Here she describes India as 'o país onde a mulher, com mais razão do que nenhuma outra, pode empregar o têrmo *a reivindicação dos seus direitos*' [the country in which woman, with more justification that in any other, may use the phrase *demanding her rights*].[36] Using a romantic and clearly Orientalist-influenced vision of Indian history, which goes back to pre-historic antiquity, pre-Vedic India and ancient matriarchal goddesses in religion and folklore, she effectively places women's contemporary emancipation, rights and subject identities on a natural, evolutionary continuum with a glorious, natural and matriarchal past that was defeated by the patriarchal rise of Brahmins and Islam.[37] As Sangheeta Ray observes in *En-gendering India*, with reference to the construction of Indian women in the competing discourses of British Imperialism and Indian Nationalism:

> The rhetoric of benevolence extended toward the subjugated 'native' woman by the English nation highlights the paradoxical position of the Indian woman in an imperial economy. [...] The Indian woman became a further contested site of appropriation when Indian nationalists sought to advance their agenda by fusing their desire for an independent nation with the independence of the Indian woman, who, they argued, could never achieve her 'pure' status as an equal participant in the domestic or public spheres within the boundaries of a spurious [British] imagined community.[38]

In her 1934 lecture, Gomes rushes to join this imperial competition to save and reform the native woman, by stressing Portugal's comparatively progressive achievements in securing the abolition of *sati* and the prohibition of child marriage in Goa, ahead of British India. In this context, Gomes clearly idealizes the pacifistic, romantic and famously feminized discourse of Gandhi's civil disobedience in her 'Contemporânea' section, where she notes the 'factos lamentáveis ocorridos nos anos de 1930 e 1931' [the terrible events of 1930 and 1931]. Gandhi's famous Salt Marches of 1930 and 1931, with their peaceful resistance to mass violence against protestors, had drawn world media attention. These references to the Civil Disobedience movements and the violently suppressed

---

[36] Gomes, *A mulher indiana*, p. 10.
[37] Thus Gomes remarks: 'já viram a forma como ela [a mulher indiana] sucessivamente foi despojada da liberdade, dos direitos e da personalidade, e transformada de ser pensante e activo em um autómato, sem vontade própria, coisa do senhor possuidor' [you have seen the way she (the Indian woman) has been successively deprived of liberty, rights and personality, and transformed from an active, thinking being into an automaton, with no will of her own, a thing possessed by her master]. See *A mulher indiana*, p. 18. On one level, in so far as Gomes (herself of Chardo caste, not Brahmin) blames male Brahmin culture for Hindu women's oppression, she also invites further class and caste-specific analysis in the context of anti-Brahminist thinking, along the lines propagated by the Indian social reformer Jotirao Phule in the nineteenth century, which had a significant influence on women's struggle. See Kumari Jayawardena, *Feminism and Nationalism in the Third World* (London: Zed Books, 1986), p. 84.
[38] Sangheeta Ray, *En-gendering India: Woman and Nation in Colonial and Postcolonial Narratives* (London and Durham, NC: Duke University Press, 2000), pp. 8–9.

Salt Marches, which witnessed the substantial participation of Indian middle-class women in public demonstrations for the first time, wrest the initiative of women's 'rescue' firmly away from colonial benevolence, giving priority instead to the opportunities opened up by Indian nationalist liberation struggle. This enables Gomes to shift the centre of gravity for her own authorizing discourse. She thus praises and idealizes Indian women's fortitude, value and equality as part of her importance as the 'personalidade da pátria' [personality of the fatherland].[39]

As Gomes inserts this Indian liberation discourse into the rhetorical machinery of the Portuguese colonial state in 1934, her position on women's rights takes her thinking dialectically beyond the two forms of colonial nationalism that had authorized her work to date, in a transnational sleight of hand that ultimately permits her a much more overtly anti-imperial position.[40] As a further corollary of this, the ancient feminine pre-Brahmanic values that Gomes's concept of the 'Indian Woman' embodies are not only the rationale for Indian women's elevation, trapped in an ongoing reformist rivalry between the Portuguese and the British; they are also central to Gomes's real preoccupation, namely the rhetorical feminization of Indian nationalist pacifism itself, as manifested in Gandhi's non-violent campaigns of passive resistance. If Ana de Castro Osório, as the Portuguese Republican Mother, advocated the type of reinvigoration and virility that would be useful to a patriarchally rehabilitated empire, the ideal woman of Indian nationalism, as Gomes perceived her, was Sarojini Naidu, the romantic poet and political campaigner, who led the march on the Dharasana Salt Works.[41] Her authority, like Gandhi's, lay in peaceful public submission to the colonial police beatings in the Salt Protests and Civil Disobedience campaigns of 1930–31.[42] In this context, she takes Naidu as the

---

[39] Gomes, *A mulher indiana*, p. 20.

[40] See Pinto, *Between Empires*, p. 57, on the legitimacy bestowed by this discourse of antiquity. See also Lina Fruzzetti and Rosa Maria Perez, 'The Gender of the Nation: Allegoric Femininity and Women's Status in Bengal and Goa', *Etnográfica*, 6.1 (2002), 41–58.

[41] For historical sources on Naidu published in India, see Tara Ali Baig, *Sarojini Naidu* (New Delhi: Rakesh Press, 1974) and Padmini Sengupta, *Sarojini Naidu*, Makers of the Indian Literature Series (New Delhi: Sahitya Akademi, 1974). For more recent criticism of the poetry and political writings of Sarojini Naidu, see Chapter 5, 'The Voice of India: Sarojini Naidu's "Nationalist Poetics"', in Ellen Brinks, *Anglophone Indian Women Writers, 1870–1920* (Farnham: Ashgate, 2013), pp. 171–207. As Brinks notes in the Introduction to this study: 'The debates about women's education and gender roles, so vigorous in the late nineteenth century, were gradually overshadowed by anti-colonial nationalism. Many reformers sought to enfold the woman question into the question of the nation. For example, Sarojini Naidu, [...] argued that India's women were the spiritual "mothers" of the nation; they had proven their right to citizen status by protesting side-by-side with India's men. These actions, according to Naidu, had already fully "nationalized" them, guaranteeing their right to the franchise. Yet despite the efforts of Naidu and other feminists — indeed, all social reformers of the time — the struggle for independence eclipsed the momentum of women's rights: [...] Indeed, Indian feminists have noted how nationalism effectively "resolved" the woman question by sidelining it' (p. 10). See also Elleke Boehmer, *Women, Gender and Narrative in the Postcolonial Nation* (New York and Manchester: Manchester University Press, 2005), especially Chapter 6, 'East is East: Where Postcolonialism is Neo-orientalist — The Cases of Sarojini Naidu and Arundhati Roy', pp. 158–71.

[42] By 1936, positions such as Gomes's identification with Sarojini Naidu became more broadly

'expoente máximo' [greatest exponent] of feminist values in this 'evolução social da mulher até os tempos presentes' [social evolution of women up to present times].[43] In a clearly anti-assimilationist move, she claims that Indo-Portuguese women like herself have a greater degree of equality in India than they do in the metropolis. In the final section of her speech, she describes the different trajectories of Goa's women in relation to the Christianized Old Conquests and the Hindu New Conquests, implying a particularly advantaged transimperial status for the women who combine both, namely the Westernized Indo-Portuguese who can now be found in 'todos os campos, quer na Índia portuguesa quer na inglesa' [all fields, either in Portuguese or English India]. In paying tribute to her Indo-Portuguese feminist compatriot Propércia Correia Afonso de Figueiredo, for winning the second colonial literature prize, and in praising Sarojini Naidu and her circle in the Indian Renaissance, she further displaces the initiative of tutelary feminism away from Ana de Castro Osório and the other 'Mães Republicanas' [Republican Mothers].[44]

Her femininized, matriarchal vision of Indian woman's history and ancient history relativizes the assimilative pull of a Europeanized Portuguese modernity, implicitly placing the latter further back on an evolutionary continuum in which Indian civilization has become the more progressive force, leading the next cycle of development and making women's emancipation simultaneously the necessary condition and the inevitable result of British Indian independence. Certainly, Gomes's feminism was no less likely than Castro Osório's to fall prey to what Ferreira calls 'the equivocal, though seductive, alliance between nationalist interests and feminist demands', as she tries to push feminism and anti-colonial nationalism into dialogue, as early as the 1930s.[45] However, with the beginning of the end of British Empire in India just over a decade away, in 1947, it is Portugal here and not India that is being called upon by Gomes to learn. Taking a dissonant, if not actively dissident, feminine stance and betraying the anxiety of divided origins already present in her clashing

---

discernible in Goa. In the Goan women's newspaper *Mascotte. Jornal para Mulheres e Crianças*, Ano IV (26 April 1936), pp. 1-2, an unsigned article appeared entitled 'A independencia economica da mulher' [sic] reporting on a Women's Conference in Lucknow. Its author praises the efforts of Sarojini Naidu, 'o Rouxinol da Índia' [the nightingale of India] and cites a Miss Maniben (probably the well-known independence activist, Maniben Patel) as stating, 'não somos uma mera maquinação de fabricar crianças mas temos um maior e mais útil papel a desempenhar, sobretudo temos de dar a nossa contingente para a independência da Índia. [...] Cada uma de nós pode ser uma Sarojini Naidu' [We are not simply machines for making babies but rather we have a greater and more useful role to fulfil, above all we must make our contribution to the independence of India. [...] Every one of us can be a Sarojini Naidu] (p. 2).

[43] Gomes, *A mulher indiana*, p. 21.

[44] Propércia Correia Afonso de Figueiredo (1882–1944), from Benaulim in Salsete, was Gomes's noteworthy Goan contemporary and also a teacher at the Escola Normal de Goa. She too was an exponent of Indian nationalism and women's rights during this period. Her most significant work was her history of Indian and Indo-Portuguese women, *A mulher na Índia Portuguesa* (Nova Goa: Tipografia Bragança & Ca., 1933). For a full bibliography, see Aleixo Costa, *Dicionário de Literatura Goesa*, pp. 233-37.

[45] Ferreira, 'Nationalism and Feminism', p. 138.

transnational inspirations — Ana de Castro Osório and Sarojini Naidu — Gomes's writings allow us to trace the counter-weave of an always transimperial Portuguese India that was already coming under pressure in the 1930s, even as the rhetorical rehabilitation of this imperial ideal in the metropolis was barely beginning at the Primeira Exposição Colonial Portuguesa of 1934.

Early Twentieth-Century Portuguese Feminist Writers as Transnational Cultural Mediators: Virgínia de Castro e Almeida and Ana de Castro Osório

Chatarina Edfeldt

Dalarna University

Introduction

In 1905, the Portuguese writer and prominent intellectual, Ana de Castro Osório (1872–1935), sent a copy of her book *Às mulheres portuguesas* [*To Portuguese Women*], considered to be the first Portuguese feminist manifesto, to a friend and colleague in Sweden. The book was accompanied by the dedication: 'provando-lhe a minha admiração e eterna estima e denunciando ao seu espírito os grandes males do meu país' [as proof of my admiration and eternal appreciation and denouncing to you the great flaws of my country].[1] The friend to whom she was writing this dedication was Göran Björkman (1860–1923), a leading figure within the Swedish cultural establishment. Björkman was a special advisor on literature in Portuguese to the Nobel Committee and a translator of Romance languages into Swedish. The correspondence that took place between these two prominent cultural figures reveals an ongoing productive dialogue, an exchange of ideas on Portuguese culture and literature, as well as (Western) cross-cultural concerns (political and social) of their time.

This article will consider the role of Portuguese feminist writers and intellectuals of the early twentieth century as important transnational cultural mediators, who functioned both as promoters of Portuguese culture and literature across national borders, as well as importers of ideas that were in circulation at that time. The article will trace how the correspondence between Ana de Castro Osório and Göran Björkman, together with Virgínia de Castro e Almeida's 1874 reception and dissemination of the feminist thinker Ellen Key (1849–1926), illustrates the cross-cultural exchange between Portugal and

---

[1] Ana de Castro Osório, *Às mulheres portuguesas* (Lisbon: Editora Viuva Tavares Cardoso, 1905). Handwritten dedication in the copy held by the Royal Library in Stockholm. The original spelling is respected in citations and titles of primary sources. All translations from Portuguese to English are my own unless stated otherwise.

Sweden, thus highlighting how these Portuguese intellectuals functioned as transnational beacons for the circulation of ideas.

The feminist writers of the First Republic have scarcely been recognized in Portuguese literary historiography, either in terms of their full literary achievement or as significant transnational mediators, responsible for shaping Portuguese culture and society at the beginning of the twentieth century. Furthermore, their intellectual activities have mostly been considered within a national framework, which fails to do full justice to their dynamic position as participants in the transnational movement known as first-wave feminism. Therefore, this article wishes to place the discussion in the context of Transnational Literary History, for its capacity to break away from a narrow national perspective while simultaneously broadening its scope through the inclusion of crucial sociological aspects of literary activity into literary historiography.

Recent literary studies that aspire to revitalize the research areas of literary history and criticism have made a transcultural and/or transnational turn in an attempt to move away from the narrow scope of conceptualizing literature and authors within an exclusively national framework. This trajectory towards a global understanding of literary texts as (inter)relational also includes a shift in attention from the literary text as an exclusive representative of the literary field towards an inclusion of a sociological approach, focusing on locations and mediators involved in cultural contacts and in the exchange of ideas. This also calls for an interdisciplinary approach that intertwines literary history research with book history, translation studies, sociology of literature and literary markets, literary didactics, and so forth.[2] A recent international project, *New Portuguese Letters 40 Years Later*, is worth mentioning in this context, as an example of this new interdisciplinary way of performing transnational literary history.[3] The project encompasses a broad, cross-cultural transnational network of researchers from more than fifteen countries, covering research on the national and international reception and circulation of the iconic second-wave text *Novas cartas portuguesas* [*New Portuguese Letters*] (1972). This innovative research combines a wide range of perspectives: cultural and literary studies, translation studies, book history, reception studies, the circulation and intercultural exchanges of ideas, among others.[4]

---

[2] See Venkat B. Mani, *Recoding World Literature: Libraries, Print Culture, and Germany's Pact with Books* (New York: Fordham University Press, 2017); Gisèle Sapiro, 'The Sociology of Translation', in *A Companion to Translation Studies*, ed. by Sandra Bermann and Catherine Porter (Chichester: Wiley Blackwell, 2014), pp. 82–94.
[3] Coordinated by Ana Luísa Amaral, Faculty of Letters, Porto University. Project funded by the Portuguese national funding agency for science, research and technology (PTDC/CLE-LLI/110473/2009). Web page <http://www.novascartasnovas.com/en/index_en.html >.
[4] See *Novas cartas portuguesas: entre Portugal e o mundo*, ed. by M. Freitas and A. L. Amaral (Alfragide: Dom Quixote, 2015) and *New Portuguese Letters to the World: International Reception*, ed. by A. L. Amaral, A. P. Ferreira and M. Freitas (Oxford: Peter Lang, 2015).

The sociological approach to literary production and circulation of symbolic goods and ideas shifts the focus to the role of literary magazines, public speakers, salons, translation activities and, not least, cultural and literary mediators. By focusing on how the Portuguese feminist writers of the First Republic worked as cultural agents (rather than on their literary text production as such), this article will argue for the importance of fostering an intertwined sociological and transnational perspective in emerging modes of studying literary history subjects. The article's overarching aim is to highlight the role played by these women writers as mediators in the transnational processes of cultural exchange, which underpinned and shaped the modernization of Portuguese early twentieth-century culture.

Feminists of the First Republic as Transnational Cultural Mediators

The writing and socio-political activism of the feminist intellectuals of the Portuguese First Republic in the early twentieth century was preoccupied with all the major questions and reforms of its time, in particular the reformulation of citizenship and women's role in society, women's right to vote, and education.[5] These women formed the first feminist and suffragist movements, organized lectures, directed literary and cultural magazines, and functioned as mediators and disseminators of Portuguese literature and culture through their international activity and networking. Accordingly, their textual production is diverse and covers various genres: fiction for children and adults, poetry, educational material, essays, scholarly and press articles, pamphlets and lectures, among others.

Even though their work forms a rich transnational literary and cultural history, there is still a lot of research to be done for them to be properly incorporated into dominant Portuguese literary and cultural discourses. To historicize is to contextualize, and one reason why these women writers continue to be marginalized in, for example, mainstream Portuguese literary history is because their activities were not properly contextualized in the first place, be it in literary, socio-political or cultural terms. This, in turn, derives from the manner in which institutional processes of Portuguese canon-formation conceptualized *modernity* itself, as carried out in masculine terms, confining 'woman' to its opposite pole, and thus creating an incompatibility between the sign 'woman writer' and *modernity*.[6] One hundred years later,

---

[5] The number of women writers (in various genres) of this period is extensive. Some of the authors who were engaged both in the first wave of Western feminism and in the construction of the Portuguese First Republic (1910) were: Angelina Vidal (1853–1917), Cláudia de Campos (1859–1916), Alice Pestana (1860–1929), who also published under the pseudonym Caïel, Alice Moderno (1867–1946), Maria Veleda (1871–1955), Beatriz Pinheiro de Lemos (1871–1922), Ana de Castro Osório (1872–1935), Maria O'Neill (1873–1932), Olga Moraes Sarmento (1881–1948) and Virgínia Quaresma (1882–1973).

[6] For an example of this regarding literary history writing see Chatarina Edfeldt, *Uma história na história: representações da autoria feminina na história da literatura portuguesa do século XX* (Montijo: Câmara Municipal do Montijo, 2006).

it is obvious that this discursively constructed 'incompatibility' between 'woman', on the one hand, and *modernity* and the *public sphere* on the other, sprang from the gender-biased ideological thinking of the last century.[7] From today's perspective, the very central claim of these women intellectuals, which was to reformulate and emancipate the female political and social subject as part of a new social order and nation-building endeavour, inscribes them as protagonists at the very heart of the development of Portuguese modernity in their time.

Correspondingly, their literary fiction and feminist periodicals worked as forums for contesting definitions of *modernity* that fit perfectly into the Western cosmopolitan context of their time. Just like their European counterparts, these Portuguese women writers explored themes related to the role of the new modern woman in the formation of the modern nation, society and family. By writing about such topics as 'love', 'marriage', 'divorce', and by promoting women's education, often through the portrayal of the drawbacks of an 'ignorant woman' as spouse and mother, their work relates directly to the transnational image of the 'Modern Woman' or the 'New Woman'.[8] For all these reasons, the multifaceted activism and emancipatory literature of these women intellectuals would greatly benefit from being read and studied within a broader Western cosmopolitan context, which, in short, was the transnational movement of first-wave feminism.

A first step in this direction is the recently published edited collection *A New History of Iberian Feminism* (2018), which brings together research on feminist activity and writing from all the different geographical areas of the Iberian Peninsula and incorporates them into a coherent overview of feminist thinking and development.[9] In the Portuguese context, the social sciences have provided interesting research on these Portuguese feminists' activities and main concerns, writing them into the history of ideas and culture. Especially rich and revealing, from a cultural transfer and networking perspective, is the research conducted by João Esteves and others on the journals of these women's organizations.[10] Ana de Castro Osório, Maria Veleda and Alice Pestana

---

[7] See Rita Felski, *The Gender of Modernity* (Cambridge, MA: Harvard University Press, 1995).
[8] Although some countries, for example England and Sweden, can be argued to have a more solidly conceptualized genre of New Woman's novels than Portugal, these Portuguese novels nevertheless dispute old gender roles and present a view of the new woman's role in a modernized society. This is something that still needs to be recognized and could benefit from being researched in a transnational perspective, namely in the context of its European counterparts. For instance, in a pioneering study Graça Abranches analyses the literary production of Ana de Castro Osório and recognizes sketches of the 'new woman' in Osório's narratives. Graça Abranches, 'Verlernen um zu Sprechen: Politik und Poetik Portugiesischer Frauen im 20. Jahrhundert', in *Portugiesische Literatur*, ed. by Marina Spinu and Henry Thorau (Frankfurt am Main: Suhrkamp, 1997), pp. 204–35.
[9] *A New History of Iberian Feminisms*, ed. by Silvia Bermúdez and Roberta Johnson (Toronto: University of Toronto Press, 2018).
[10] See João Esteves, 'Historical Context of Feminism and Women's Rights in Nineteenth-Century Portugal', in *New History of Iberian Feminism*, pp. 101–10. For extensive and in-depth research on the feminist mobilization and organization processes, members, activities and the main social questions

(Caïel), among other feminists, invested a lot of effort in creating, writing and editing a variety of periodicals. Their feminist press functioned as a major channel for the transnational exchange of ideas and, just as in other countries, their periodicals had sections monitoring the events of, and adhesions to, international associations, such as the International Women Suffrage Alliances created in 1911, and the International Council of Women in 1914. These publications offered a record of the cultural exchange of ideas and contacts with international women's periodicals, covering Germany, Austria, Spain, Finland, France, Holland, England and Sweden.[11]

In line with their international profiles, Virgínia de Castro e Almeida and Ana de Castro Osório, among others, worked, albeit in different ways, to disseminate their emancipatory texts and ideas, as well as male (canonical) Portuguese literature abroad.[12] As the main aim of this article is not to explore the literary output of these authors, but rather their importance as intellectuals and mediators of cultural ideas crossing borders, the next two sections will provide case-studies on cultural mediation by focusing on these two feminist thinkers.

Virgínia de Castro e Almeida and Feminism in Sweden

As documented by Tavares da Silva, Virgínia de Castro e Almeida lived much of her life abroad, in Switzerland and France, and she published critical works on distinguished Portuguese writers such as Camões and translations of Portuguese canonical works, such as historical chronicles, into French. Almeida also translated Dickens, Cervantes, Erich Kästner and George Sand into Portuguese.[13] Other facts about Almeida point to an interesting life filled with contradictions and pioneering positions. Almeida was among the first women to get a divorce under the new divorce legislation, passed in Portugal in 1910. She later lived in a lesbian relationship with the modernist sculptor Pamela Boden, in Paris, where she worked as a governmental representative for the

---

of the Portuguese first-wave feminism, see João Esteves, *As origens do sufragismo português* (Lisbon: Editorial Bizântico, 1998) and Maria Regina Tavares da Silva, *Feminismo em Portugal na voz de mulheres escritoras do início do século XX* (Lisbon: Comissão para a Igualdade e Direitos das Mulheres, 1992).

[11] Esteves observes a diversity of contacts established by the Portuguese feminists and their European counterparts, which increased after Carolina Beatriz Ângelo succeeded in voting in the First Republic, in May 1911, in a unique event that was internationally publicized. This caused a scandal following which the Portuguese constitution was rewritten to prevent women from voting. Among the international feminist periodicals that reported on the event was the Swedish periodical 'Rösträtt för Kvinnor' [Voting Rights for Women]. See Esteves, *As origens do sufragismo português*, p. 157. For a record of the events related to Ângelo's voting see Deborah Madden, 'Historical Context in Portugal', in *A New History of Iberian Feminism*, pp. 199–203.

[12] For an extensive portrait of these authors' translation and publishing activities, see Maria Regina Tavares da Silva, *Mulheres Portuguesas, Vidas e Obras celebradas — Vidas e Obras ignoradas* (Lisbon: Comissão para a Igualdade e Direitos das Mulheres, 1991).

[13] Tavares da Silva, 'Virgínia de Castro e Almeida (1874–1945)', in *Mulheres Portuguesas*, pp. 83–88.

repressive Portuguese fascist regime — the *Estado Novo*. In 1922, she became a film producer in France and created her own company, Fortuna Films.[14]

Almeida also had a vast, diversified and rich literary production and her transnational mediating activity bears witness to an author with an outstanding knowledge of European literary and cultural matters, as well as Western contemporary social and political issues. This is evidenced in her book, published in 1913, *A mulher: história da mulher, a mulher moderna — educação* [Woman: Woman's History, the Modern Woman — Education].[15] The book is an ambitious study based on empirical research on the curriculum and the system of women's education in Switzerland, informed readings in a variety of academic areas (such as history and philosophy), and international literary works. The text is divided into three parts, linked together by the overarching ambition of empowering women through the dissemination of knowledge about women's history (from antiquity to the nineteenth century), the new modern woman's situation in other countries, and new educational systems, as well as through the presentation of exceptional female role models.

This text is of relevance to the present analysis as a revealing example of how major Western ideas and thinkers on women's emancipation and their new role in society and nation were brought into the Portuguese cultural arena. Almeida introduces the second part of the text, in which she investigates feminism and 'the modern woman's situation' in some developed countries, with a claim that inscribes the woman in modernity and relegates man's prejudice to a prehistoric era:

> As troças, os sarcasmos e as perseguições dos anti-feministas perdem gradualmente, em frente da luctadora grave e obstinada, o seu caracter por assim dizer classico, e cahem a pouco e pouco na cathegoria de imbecilidades. O homem que estuda e observa, o pensador moderno, já não pode mostrar desdem pelo movimento feminista. (p. 165)
>
> [The ridicule, sarcasm and persecution by anti-feminists are gradually losing their so-called classic character; when confronted by the serious and perseverant [feminist] combatant, they are slowly falling into the category of idiocies. The modern thinker, a man who studies and observes, can no longer show contempt for the feminist movement.]

This section of her text provides facts, figures and descriptions about women's

---

[14] For a more comprehensive study of Virgínia de Castro e Almeida, see Isabel Lousada, 'Anatomia de uma autora: Virgínia de Castro e Almeida em trânsitos atlânticos', in *Gênero e literatura: resgate, contemporaneidade e outras perspectivas*, ed. by Edilene Ribeiro Batista (Fortaleza Ceará/CE: Expressão Gráfica e Editora, 2013), pp. 275–96.

[15] Virgína de Castro e Almeida, *A mulher: história da mulher, a mulher moderna — educação* (Lisbon: Livraria Clássica Editora, 1913). This work is discussed in Madden's article covering Portuguese feminist thought of the first wave in the volume *New History of Iberian Feminism* (2018). However, as Almeida's text is scarcely analysed and its content is considered only as representative of, and within, the Iberian context, this analysis does not encompass various interesting qualities, such as its larger European and transnational content and context. Deborah Madden, 'Feminist Thought in Portugal, 1900–1926', in *New History of Iberian Feminism*, pp. 204–12 (pp. 210–12).

contemporary civil (political, economic and legal) status and cultural situation in a number of different countries (USA, Great Britain, Russia, Sweden, Finland, Italy, Spain and France). Addressing positions open to women in the labour market, educational opportunities, and legal, social, political and property rights, these countries represent good examples, in contrast to Portugal and Spain, which, according to Almeida, only experienced feminism in an 'embryonic state' (p. 206).

The chapter on Sweden distinguishes itself in this context, for additionally supplying very well-informed portraits of the internationally recognized thinker and cultural critic Ellen Key, as well as of the Nobel Laureate Selma Lagerlöf. The chapter evidences Almeida's in-depth insights into Key's work and readings of her texts and cultural ideas, alongside explicit praise and admiration for her. Incidentally, there are many affinities between the ideas developed by Key on the new woman's role and emancipation, love, marriage, feminism and the 'social mother', and those fostered by Almeida and by Portuguese feminism. These are affinities that could lead one to regard Ellen Key as a possible major influence on Portuguese first-wave feminism. However, this is something that needs more investigation to confirm, and I will limit the present analysis to Key's impact on Almeida as revealed in her chapter.

Just as Almeida points out, Ellen Key was one of the most influential personalities and cultural critics in Europe at the beginning of the twentieth century. Her work consists of over forty books and hundreds of scholarly articles and essays, much of it translated into major European languages. Almeida mentions in her text Key's 1896 work *Falso emprego das forças femininas* [Misused Female Power] (p. 192).[16] In this text Key also develops, alongside her ideas on atheist, naturalist and socialist views of love and emancipation, the idea of 'motherliness' which she foregrounds as central to the new woman's femininity and emancipatory project.[17] Almeida also refers to Key's lecture tours, which attracted thousands of people and were often published, as an example of noble educational acts.

Almeida's chapter starts with one of the first Swedish feminist thinkers, Fredrika Bremer,[18] and goes on to state: 'O feminismo sueco deve sem dúvida muito a Ibsen, cuja obra inteira tão ardentemente defende a causa da mulher;

---

[16] The Swedish title of this work by Key is *Missbrukad kvinnokraft* (1896). I could not find any evidence of Ellen Key being translated into Portuguese. However, Key's literary production was translated into German, Spanish, French, English and Italian, giving Almeida no problem in accessing her major works.
[17] See Claudia Lindén, *Om kärlek: Litteratur, sexualitet och politik hos Ellen Key* [On Love: Literature, Sexuality and Politics in Ellen Key] (Stockholm: Symposium, 2002), p. 305.
[18] Fredrika Bremer (1801–1865) was a pioneering Swedish thinker on women's rights and a novelist of international renown. She is considered the introducer of the modern novel into Sweden and her large number of novels and travelogues reached an international audience through translations. Her work and ideas influenced, and had a crucial impact on, subsequent suffragist and feminist movements in Sweden and abroad. For instance, she gave her name to the Fredrika-Bremer Förbundet (1884–1921) [Fredrika Bremer Association], the leading association working for women's rights at the turn of the twentieth century.

e muito tambem à guerreira intrepida e genial que é Ellen Key' [Swedish feminism undoubtedly owes much to Ibsen, whose entire work so ardently defends the cause of woman, and also to the fearless and genius warrior that is Ellen Key] (p. 189). This utterly surprising statement concerning the Norwegian playwright Ibsen as being important for the development of Swedish feminism can only be understood if we trace the claim back to a lecture organized by Ellen Key in 1898, in honour of Ibsen's seventieth birthday. Key convened the conference in the name of Swedish women, something that was strongly criticized by more radical Swedish feminists and added more fuel to the conflict Key had with them at the time.[19]

Not only is Almeida familiar with the contents of the lecture (where Key defines Swedish feminism), she is also familiar with the ideological conflicts that permeated Swedish feminism. Almeida takes sides with Key and describes the outcome of the first period of Swedish feminism as an exaggeration and excessiveness of rights for women that went beyond the boundaries of common sense (p. 192). Her defence of Key mirrors her own (and Ana de Castro Osório's) standpoint and, accordingly, Almeida identifies with her struggle: 'Ellen Key teve a coragem que ninguém usava ter. Ella, defensora, ardente adepta do feminismo, insurgiu-se francamente contra o exagero; a sua voz forte chamou a mulher sueca ao lar, ao amor, à maternidade' [Ellen Key had boundless courage. She, a defender and ardent follower of feminism, openly stood up against this exaggeration; her strong voice called the Swedish woman back to the home, love and motherhood] (p. 192). This division between a moderate and an exaggerated feminism echoes the strategic rhetorical use, noted by Tavares da Silva, whereby Portuguese feminist writers defined themselves as upholding 'verdadeiro feminismo' [true feminism], as opposed to another 'falso feminismo' [false feminism].[20]

In every paragraph, Almeida lavishes praise on Ellen Key, bestowing on her superlatives. Hence, her text stresses Ellen Key's exceptional personality as a feminist role model, at the expense of really engaging with the content of her feminist ideas. In defending Key as an exceptional character who displays honesty and high morals, it also becomes evident that Almeida strongly identifies with her difficult dissident position. When analysing Key's style, Almeida finds that: 'sua argumentação cerrada e independente tem todas as qualidades da sinceridade e do talento. O seu estylo é brilhante e forte, as suas phrases incisivas, a sua vehemencia e o seu enthusiasmo inexcediveis' [her cohesive and independent argumentation has all the qualities of sincerity and talent. Her style is brilliant and strong, her phrases incisive, her vehemence

---

[19] Lindén, *Litteratur, sexualitet och politik hos Ellen Key*, p. 24.
[20] See Tavares da Silva, *Feminismo em Portugal*, pp. 15–34. Likewise, the motto 'Only a true emancipation can save us from a false one' was also frequently used strategically by the Swedish feminist Fredrika Bremer Association (1884–1921). In Ulla Manns, *Den sanna frigörelsen, Fredrika-Bremer-förbundet, 1884-1921* [True Emancipation: The Fredrika Bremer Association, 1884–1921] (Stockholm: Symposium, 1997), p. 251.

and her enthusiasm unsurpassed] (p. 191). This is a style that echoes Almeida's own voice in the volume, especially in the preface, where she establishes a (surprisingly) personal and honest tone, describing her personal path to maturity and intellectual development. In a voice filled with firm confidence and solemnity, as she describes the role of women, Almeida expresses how these new feminist forces of unstoppable knowledge have the potential to lead to major social change: 'forças invenciveis destinadas a mudar a face do mundo' [invincible forces destined to change the face of the world] (p. 14).

For this to become real, women have to rise up to the level of wonderful exceptions and follow moral ideals, which echo the ideas of Ellen Key:

> As missões mais nobres da mulher são sem duvida o amor, a maternidade, e a educação; mas para comprehensão déstas missões delicadas e hoje em dia complexas e cheias de graves responsabilidades, é necessario que a mulher se eleve a uma altura de onde a sua vista possa abranger toda a extensão dos seus deveres e dos seus direitos. (p. 21)
>
> [The noblest duties of a woman are without a doubt love, motherhood and education; but to comprehend these subtle missions, which today are complex and full of serious responsibilities, it is necessary for women to rise to a vantage point from where they can survey the full extent of their duties and their rights.]

The need for a modernized education for women emanates as the main issue for all these feminist intellectuals and was regarded as the strategic path for women in achieving dignity and true emancipation. The question of women's education is equally debated in literature and magazine articles, both by female and male writers, in Portugal as well as in other Western societies at the time. Caïel, Almeida and Osório were also pioneers in writing and editing literature for children and developing a new pedagogical field — for youngsters and adults — and, as such, they performed extremely important work for literacy and education in the Portuguese society of the First Republic.[21]

Ana de Castro Osório in Correspondence with Göran Björkman

Shifting our attention to the feminist Ana de Castro Osório, there is no question about the prominent role and impact she held in her time as a respected intellectual both in Portuguese society and abroad. Osório is also the most recognized figure from this first-wave feminist generation in contemporary Portuguese national discourse.[22] Her vast and diversified textual production

---

[21] The literature for children produced by Ana de Castro Osório and Virgínia de Almeida is still being republished today. Ana de Castro Osório's books were also translated into various languages.

[22] Besides the increasing scholarly interest in Osório, a specialist library in her name has been created in Lisbon, which focuses on documentation on gender equality issues, Osório's major works, and some correspondence. These documents have been made available through digitalization, accessible through the website of the Portuguese National Library/Biblioteca Digital/Obras de Ana de Castro Osório <http://purl.pt/index/geral/aut/PT/29996.html>. The recently established publishing house

is listed in the following three sub-categories, which appear in the paratext of several of her publications from 1918 onwards: firstly, Novels, Short Stories and Theatre; secondly, Social Questions (including her lectures); and thirdly, Educational Works and Children's Literature.[23] Osório became famous for her pedagogical ideas and sociological texts and received letters from many countries about her social ideas, opinions, publications and translations, although, arguably, the most solid connection was the transatlantic alliance with Brazil. She lived in São Paulo from 1911 to 1914 and was connected to the Brazilian feminist movement, publishing articles, books and pedagogical manuals on and in Brazil. In 1923, she performed a lecture tour of many Brazilian cities, the results of which later were published in *A grande aliança* [The Great Alliance].[24]

Osório's correspondence in itself constitutes indisputable evidence of her intellectual status as a transnational mediator of ideas, and of Portuguese culture and literature. The very rich Coleção Castro Osório (N12), held at the National Library in Lisbon, encompasses literary manuscripts and family correspondence.[25] The majority of the hundreds of letters in the collection are addressed to Ana de Castro Osório and include correspondence from many of the main figures of cultural importance at that time.[26] Many of these correspondents are from abroad, and the topics covered range from Republican politics, feminism, pedagogy, education, culture, literary and publicist issues to personal matters, revealing how Osório supported other female writers, family members and friends, both economically and emotionally. An example of the latter is found in the letters from Virgínia de Castro e Almeida to Osório, evidencing their deep friendship and how Osório emotionally supported (and assisted) Almeida in a difficult custody dispute after Almeida had divorced.[27]

The letters have received attention in studies within a national framework. Furthermore, since the material offers a really interesting insight into the networking of cross-cultural travelling of ideas, some attention has been given to Osório's correspondence with international feminists in the context of transnational alliances and the exchange of ideas. Besides the studies by João

---

Publicações Sibila has republished two of Osório's novels: *O Mundo Novo* (2018) and *Ambições* (2019).

[23] Osório founded the collection 'Para as crianças' [For Children], constituting the first collection of books, both moral and educational, directed at children.

[24] See Maria José Lago dos Remédios, 'Ana de Castro Osório e a construção da grande aliança entre os povos: dois manuais da escritora adoptada no Brasil', *Faces de Eva*, 12 (2004), 91–107, and Isabel Lousada and Angela Laguardia, 'Maria Lacerda de Moura e Ana de Castro Osório: correspondência em trânsitos atlânticos e feministas', *Navegações*, 6.1 (2013). <http://revistaseletronicas.pucrs.br/ojs/index.php/navegacoes/article/view/14680> [accessed 13 July 2018].

[25] Research in the 'Coleção Castro Osório N12' was conducted during October 2016.

[26] Many of the major Republican personalities are represented in the letters, for example, Presidents Teófilo Braga and Manuel de Arriaga. Deeply rooted in Republican politics, Osório drafted the new progressive legislation on divorce law in 1910, in collaboration with Minister Afonso Costa.

[27] The letters bear witness to Virgínia de Castro e Almeida's agony over the legal process. Ana de Castro Osório had valuable personal contacts, which offered her insights into the process. See letter to Osório from Castro e Almeida, 2 November 1914. BNP, N12/152.

Esteves already mentioned, Rosa María Ballesteros García has examined the correspondence between Ana de Castro Osório and the Andalusian feminist Carmen de Burgos (1867–1932),[28] confirming their friendship and a common feminist struggle for women's education and civil rights. García stresses the development of an Iberian feminism, upheld through a mutual cultural exchange between Osório and the feminists in Spain, which led to lectures and texts published in each other's periodicals and book markets.[29] It is, however, revealing to explore the material within a broader transnational context. Among the letters addressed to Osório, there are four extant letters from the Swedish Lusophile Göran Björkman (1860–1923), who was a prominent figure within the Swedish cultural establishment at the turn of the twentieth century.[30] The available evidence of the correspondence between Osório and Björkman consists of these four letters, as well as five personal handwritten dedications in books by Ana de Castro Osório; these are held at the Royal Library in Stockholm.[31] The material is dated between 8 September 1905 (dedication in *Às mulheres portuguesas*) and 24 October 1921 (letter from Björkman to Osório).

Göran Björkman was a translator of literature, mainly poetry from the Romance languages, and at the time was the main translator from Portuguese into Swedish. In 1894, he was awarded a PhD from Uppsala University for a thesis on Antero de Quental.[32] He published several anthologies of translated Portuguese and Brazilian poetry, which contain mainly male poets, with the exception of some poems by Alice Moderno and a short story by Maria Amália Vaz de Carvalho.[33] Some interest has been shown by Portuguese

[28] Coleção Castro Osório, Letters from Carmen de Burgos, BNP, N12/123. See also the biography of Carmen de Burgos by Concepción Núñez Rey, *Carmen de Burgos, Colombine en la Edad de Plata de la literatura española* (Seville: Fundación José Manuel Lara, 2005).
[29] Alongside these feminist publications, Osório was also asked to publish a chapter on education in a Pedagogical Dictionary [Diccionario pedagógico] in Madrid. See Rosa María Ballesteros García, 'Cartas a una amiga portuguesa (Carmen de Burgos y Ana de Castro Osório)', in *Actas del III Congreso de Historia de Andalucía* (Córdoba: Publicaciones Obra Social y Cultural Cajasur, 2002), pp. 21–38. This crucial alliance between Burgos and Castro, in the context of the development of Iberian feminism, is briefly addressed in some of the articles in the *New History of Iberian Feminisms*. See, for example, Madden, 'Feminist Thought in Portugal, 1900–1926', p. 205.
[30] Three letters are in the Coleção Castro Osório, BNP, N12/382, and one in the Camilo Pessanha collection, BNP, N1/97. The latter was accompanied by a translation of one of Pessanha's poems by Björkman.
[31] The five books originated from the personal library of Björkman and all contain a hand-written dedication addressed to him; they are *Às mulheres portuguesas* (1905), *Les Femmes Portugaises* (translated into French by Henry Faure in 1906), *Quatro novelas* (1908), *Em tempo da guerra* (1918) and *De como Portugal foi chamado à guerra* (1918).
[32] Göran Björkman, *Anthero de Quental — Ett skaldeporträtt* [Portrait of a Poet]. The dissertation includes a panoramic survey of Portuguese literature and its context, with literary analysis of Quental's poetry based on his own translations into Swedish.
[33] Björkman published several anthologies of Portuguese poetry in translation: António Feijó, *Fallna blad: madrigaler* (1893), *Dikter* (1895), *Ur Portugals samtida diktning: poetiska öfversättningar* volume 1 & 2 (1894–1895), *Ekon från Portugals parnass* (1899). He published a volume on Portuguese short stories: *Lilla Rosa och andra berättelser* (1895). He also regularly translated poems from Brazilian and Portuguese authors and published them in literary magazines, such as, for example, *Vår tid*, a periodical produced by the literary society Samfundet De Nio.

scholars in Björkman's translation activity: Júlio Eduardo dos Santos, for example, has published an article analysing the anthology *Ur Portugals samtida diktning* (1894) [From Portugal's Contemporary Poetry], where he stresses the professional merits of Björkman as recognized in Portugal.[34] Björkman became a personal friend of the diplomat and poet António Feijó, who was Portugal's *chargé d'affaires* in Stockholm from 1895. Björkman was elected to prestigious academies and literary associations, both in Portugal and Brazil.[35] Furthermore, he translated work by the French poet, Sully Prudhomme, who was awarded the very first Nobel Prize in Literature, in 1901. That same year, Björkman became special advisor to the Swedish Academy, as a specialist on Literature in Portuguese, though he never succeeded in persuading the Academy to reward an author working in the Portuguese language in his lifetime.[36] In 1904, Björkman received funding from the Academy to embark on a journey to Spain and Portugal, where he most likely met and established his friendship with Ana de Castro Osório.

Interestingly, Björkman was one of the first members of a prestigious Swedish literary society, Samfundet De Nio [The Nine Society], founded in 1913, with nine chairs (members) elected for life. This literary institution was created out of the estate of Lotten von Kramer, an activist in the Swedish women's and suffragist movement. Kramer stipulated in her will (which went on to constitute the association's statutes) that a woman should hold every other chair in the society and that a woman and a man should alternate in holding the position of President.[37]

In accordance with Kramer's will, Göran Björkman was appointed Secretary and among the other members were the internationally known cultural personalities, Ellen Key and Selma Lagerlöf. The overarching aim of The Nine Society was to promote Swedish fictional literature, peace and 'kvinnosaken' [best translated as 'feminism']. The main activities associated with the Society were awarding prizes and publishing a journal (or yearbook) *Vår tid* [Our Time], covering the subject of literature, peace and women's matters.[38] Little

---

[34] Santos lists all the Portuguese poets appearing in translation and praises Björkman for his in-depth knowledge and recognition of the work of Lisbon poet Júlio de Castilho. Santos also credits Björkman with being not just a skilled translator, but also a writer and critic of merit (who is not recognized in Sweden). See Júlio Eduardo dos Santos, 'Poemas de Júlio de Castilho e de outros portugueses, dos quais sete lisboetas, traduzidos em sueco', *Olísipo, Boletim grupo amigos de Lisboa*, 130 (1970), 61–67.

[35] Björkman was elected as corresponding member of both the Academia Brasileira de Letras [Brazilian Academy of Letters] and the Academia Real das Ciências de Lisboa [Lisbon Royal Academy of Sciences]. In Santos, 'Poemas de Júlio de Castilho', p. 65.

[36] Ulla Åkerström, 'Göran Björkman 1860-1923', in *Svenskt översättarlexikon*, <http://www.oversattarlexikon.se> [accessed 6 January 2017].

[37] The society is still operating and could be considered as an alternative 'sister' to the Swedish Academy. Many prestigious women writers and intellectuals have been among its members and, as a whole, gender equality is better represented, in both activities and awards, than is the case for the Nobel Prize of the Swedish Academy.

[38] Inge Jonsson, *Samfundet De Nio, 1913-2013: hundra år av stöd till svensk litteratur* (Stockholm: Norstedt, 2013).

wonder then that, between 1916 and 1923, *Vår tid*, edited by Ellen Key, published essays on women's emancipation and peace, alongside translations of Portuguese literature into Swedish made by Björkman. It seems reasonable to suggest that one had to be an intellectual in favour of women's emancipation and their new role in society in order to be considered for membership of The Nine Society.

The five books authored by Ana de Castro Osório found at the Swedish Royal Library, originating from the private library of Göran Björkman, all fell under the category of social questions, with the exception of *Quatro novelas*. It is possible that Osório sent Björkman more than these five items, but available evidence indicates that she chose the books dedicated to theories of how to develop society and nation. The very fact that Osório sent Björkman the publication *Às mulheres portuguesas*, a pioneering feminist sociological overview of women's role in contemporary society, with the dedication 'revealing to you the great flaws of my country' (as quoted in the introduction to this article), points to a mutually felt closeness in their thinking and opinions.

Both the letters and the dedications reveal a close and personal friendship between them. From the second dedication onwards, Osório includes Björkman's wife, Ebba, and addresses them both with variations of: 'Aos meus queridos amigos e irmãos em ideal' [To my dear friends and brothers in ideals].[39] In every letter, Björkman talks in detail about his children's lives and activities (school, skating, etc.), and signs all his letters with the names of his wife Ebba, daughter Signe, and son Göran junior alongside his own. Likewise, he starts every letter addressing Osório in an affectionate and respectful way: 'Ex. ma Senhora e prezadíssima amiga' [My Lady and dearest friend] and ends with: 'tenho a honra de subscrever-me seu amigo e admirador muito dela e obra' [I have the honour to call myself your friend and the admirer of you and your work] (N12/382-3). Björkman also refers to Osório's sons, João and José.

The letters reveal a constant dialogue on literature, culture and social questions, as well as family matters, such as the well-being of family members. Tellingly, Björkman writes about a mutual exchange of books, thanking her for books and discussions on translations. In a letter dated 3 October 1909, Björkman explains his difficulties in finding a suitable book in French, matching the request Osório had made for an all-inclusive reference book on Sweden (which led Björkman to send her a reference book in English). In the same letter, he explains that he had not yet received the books she mentioned from Brazil, followed by a long discussion on taxes on books.[40] The question of lost books is a recurrent problem described in the letters.

[39] Osório, *Em tempo de guerra* (1918).
[40] Björkman complains of the high Swedish taxes on books compared with Denmark and writes: 'Não é por nada que d'aqui emigram tanto...' [It is not without reason that so many are emigrating from here...] (N12/382-1). Maybe this should be interpreted as a sign of Björkman's sense of humour; however, between 1850 and 1920 one in four Swedes (1.5 million) left Sweden, mainly for the USA, because of poverty and starvation.

Osório also functions as a mediator in personal contacts, connecting Björkman with other writers. In a letter from 1918, he asks her to help him pass on an offprint of his translation of *Kardinalernas supé* [The Cardinals' Supper] to the writer himself, Júlio Dantas. Dantas's play was published in The Society of Nine's yearbook in 1918.[41] In a letter from 1920, Björkman includes a translation of Camilo Pessanha's poem 'Crepuscular' ('Skymning' in Swedish)[42] and a description of the task as 'um empenho bastante difícil, no mesmo tempo que interessante, apanhar e reproduzir as subtilezas da jóia que é o original. Era como transpôr em língua falada uma peça de música' [quite a difficult endeavour, though interesting, to capture and reproduce the subtleties of this jewel that is the original. It was like transposing a piece of music into spoken language].[43] Another example of discussions on translation is to be found in the last letter from 1921, although the content is difficult to interpret, considering its lack of context. Nevertheless, Osório had sent Björkman the Portuguese folk tale 'Os dez anõezinhos da Tia Verde-água' [Aunt Verde-água's ten dwarfs], and in the letter they discuss the translation of 'Tia' into Swedish.[44]

There is a long break in the preserved documentation between the first letter from 1909 and the letter from 1918. During these years, Osório lived in São Paulo, Brazil (1911–14), while, simultaneously, Björkman held the office of Brazilian Consul in Stockholm (from 1909), which gives reason to believe in a continuation of their correspondence during these years. The First World War (1914–18) troubled the world, causing a major impact on the European women's movements, as well as fostering patriotism and nationalistic currents in society. The nationalistic tone is something that is present in their further correspondence, both in subject matters and in choice of language. In a letter from 13 December 1918, Björkman thanks Osório for sending him a picture of the national monument to Torre de Belém, which he had framed and put up on his wall. He continues: 'Ha de lembrar-me sempre um paiz cuja intellectualidade, ha já muitos annos, tornou-se-me familiar, ha de lembrar-me também uma mulher na qual tenho aprendido a admirar um modelo de enthusiasmo cívico' [It will forever remind me of a country whose intellectuality, for many years now, has been so familiar to me, and of a woman in whom I have come to admire a model of civic enthusiasm] (N12/382–2). In this same letter, Björkman addresses the war as 'aquelle flagello da humanidade' [that scourge of humanity] and blames it for causing yet another loss of publications that Osório had sent to him. This time, it was the book *Em tempo da guerra: aos homens e às mulheres do meu*

---

[41] *Vår tid 3: Årsbok* (Samfundet De Nio: 1918), pp. 108–25.
[42] The Swedish translation of the poem was never published.
[43] The letter and the translated poem are filed in the Pessanha collection, at the BNP, N1/97, N1/86 respectively. These are both digitalized and accessible at <http://purl.pt/index/geral/aut/PT/6110.html>
[44] Incidentally, there are two sources claiming that Osório was translated into Swedish, although my research has not found any evidence of this. Santos claims in his article that Björkman made a translation of Osório's *Contos*, but he provides no reference (p. 61). Rosa María García also claims this, likewise without a reference, in 'Cartas a una amiga' (p. 23).

país [In Wartime: To the Men and Women of My Country], and publications of the association Cruzada das Mulheres [Women's Crusade]. The latter was a patriotic association founded by Osório in 1916 in support of Portugal's entry into the First World War.

Nevertheless, the missing book, together with *De como Portugal foi chamado à guerra: história para crianças* [How Portugal Was Called to the War: A History for Children] (1918), are among the books she sent to Björkman in 1919. They both have dedications addressing the Björkmans as 'amigos em ideal humano' [friends in human ideals]. The personal dedication to Björkman in *De como Portugal foi chamado à guerra* is written on the same page that features the printed dedication: 'Aos Soldados Portugueses que erguem tão alto a bandeira gloriosa da Pátria, para que saibam o que aos seus filhos ensinamos da hora em que mais uma vez a nossa raça cumpriu o seu nobre destino' [To the Portuguese Soldiers, who raise high the glorious flag of the Fatherland, so that they may know what we teach their children about the time when our race once more fulfilled its noble destiny]. This shows evidence of how, for Osório, women's emancipatory ideals are intertwined with the patriotic and nationalistic values of defending, creating and educating a vigorous nation.

Indeed, a strong ideological dividing line amongst the feminists of the first wave was established precisely around the question of how they regarded and handled the war situation and the question of peace. For instance, already in a letter from Setúbal dated 7 December 1899, from Osório to Alice Pestana (Caïel), Osório responds negatively to the request by Pestana to join the Liga Portuguesa da Paz [The Portuguese League of Peace], with the explanation: 'não estou de acordo com o objectivo de paz a qualquer custo. Que lindo sonho' [I do not agree with the objective of peace at any cost. What a beautiful dream].[45] That the women's movement was putting on hold its suffragist demands and peacework in favour of patriotic nationalistic support was something that could be seen in Sweden and all over Europe at the outbreak of the First World War.

As mentioned before, Björkman was elected to prestigious academies in Portugal and Brazil and a letter from 1921 indicates that Osório helped him in some of these processes: 'tenho de agradecer-lhe [...] sua iniciativa para a minha admissão no seio do tão symphatico Instituto Historico do Minho' [I have to thank you [...] for your initiative for my admission into the very friendly Historical Institute of Minho] (N12/382–3). Likewise, in a letter from 1920, Björkman thanks Osório for her role in securing him a Portuguese decoration:

> Minha prezada amiga, Muito e muito obrigado pela affectuosa carta de Vossa Excellencia de 21 de Setembro assim como do diploma e dos livros que a acompanhavam. Assim pois poderei desde agora ostentar no meu peito, ao lado da minha placa Hespanhola, também uma Portuguesa, preciosa lembrança de simpathias reciprocas luso-suecas. [...] Ora, a minha gratidão para com a nação que distinguia-me, a quem endereça-la senão a essa brava

[45] Letters between Alice Pestana ('Caïel') and Ana de Castro Osório, BNP, N12/188.

> personificação da Pátria Portuguesa quem é Vossa Excelência? Oxalá que me sejam dados tempo e força para manifestar-lhe mais concretamente a sinceridade dos meus sentimentos. (N1/97)
>
> [My dear friend. Thank you so very much for the affectionate letter from your excellent self, of 21 September, as well as for the diploma and the books that accompanied it. I can now display on my chest, next to my Spanish decoration, a Portuguese one, a precious reminder of reciprocal Luso-Swedish friendship. [...] Now, to whom would I address my gratitude to the nation that has distinguished me, if not to the brave personification of the Portuguese Fatherland, which is your good self? I hope I will be given the time and strength to manifest to you more concretely the sincerity of my sentiments.]

The respectful and friendly tone is accompanied by a discourse on society that is inflected by transnational ideals of nationalism and patriotism prevalent at the time. This nationalistic tone increases in the correspondence between Björkman and Osório after the end of the First World War. It is the Portuguese nation and the Latin race that are highlighted and celebrated through their cultural and literary expressions. Nevertheless, Björkman shows no sympathy for the war, and writes at the end of 1918: 'Esperemos que a fraternização heróica entre as nações latinas, representadas por França, Italia, Portugal e Brasil, e os anglosaxões, tenha inaugurado uma nova era, alheia a perturbações devidas a factores tão brutais como a força physica' [Let us hope that the heroic fraternization between the Latin nations, represented by France, Italy, Portugal and Brazil, and the Anglo-Saxons, has inaugurated a new era, beyond the disturbance caused by such brutal factors as physical strength] (N12/382–2). Björkman keeps expressing the idea that Osório personifies Portuguese high morals, spirit and nationhood. Tellingly, he ends his last letter in a way that echoes the ideas of the social mother proposed by Ellen Key: 'À boa Mater Patria quem é D. Ana de Castro Osório' [To the good Mater Patria who is Mrs Ana de Castro Osório] (N12/382–3). At a time when women were still relegated to the private sphere, there is great emancipatory potential in 'Mater Patria' (the social mother) as a political metaphor for the new woman's role in public life and society.[46]

Simultaneously, the nationalistic overtones in the letters also suggest the prevalent elitist thinking which values different social groups differently in the new nation-building. Deeply rooted in Portuguese Republican ideologies and nationalist ideas, Osório embraces the idea of the formation of the bourgeois mother as an educator who will ensure the preservation (and hygiene) of the Portuguese race and identity. Célia Cordeiro conducts a convincing interpretation of this important strand of Osório's ideas.[47] Indeed, the

---

[46] Claudia Lindén, *Om kärlek*, pp. 184–85.
[47] Célia Cordeiro, *Ana de Castro Osório e a Mulher Republicana Portuguesa* (Bela Vista: Fonte da Palavra, 2012). The book is a published version of Cordeiro's master's thesis on Ana de Castro Osório. The following quotation comes from the thesis: 'Castro Osório emphasizes the role of bourgeois

nationalistic understanding of society as a biological organism, a decadent body that needed to be protected from degeneration by racial control (eugenics) and medical intervention, were transnational Western thoughts that grew stronger in the first decades of the twentieth century. These ideas are also highly relevant for understanding Swedish society and academic discourse at the time.[48]

Although there was a complicity amongst feminists on racial-biological thinking, there was, nevertheless, a dividing line between male-oriented eugenics promoted by academics and doctors, which advocating sterilization or extinction as regulating measures, and feminist social reformers, who promoted education and information as solutions. Furthermore, the same set of principles for organizing society also developed into social reforms of crucial importance, building contemporary Western democratic societies and paving the way for women's rights and equality. Cordeiro's analysis of Osório's texts is accurate and important, although by mainly highlighting a strand of racial hygiene, together with adopting an exclusively Portuguese framework, she risks reducing the complexity of Osório's crucial contribution to women's emancipation of her own time. While Portugal in the 1930s ended up with a fascist regime, Sweden, despite its Institute of Eugenics, ended up with a democratic one. The complex role of the early twentieth-century women's movements, both as major driving forces for increasing social equality and as part of the history of Racial Biology, warrant further investigation from a transnational perspective.

Final Remarks

The overarching purpose of this article has been to highlight the transnational cultural-transfer activities of Portuguese feminist intellectuals of the early twentieth century. Through translations, publications and international networking, Virgínia de Castro e Almeida and Ana de Castro Osório (among others) were very active participants in the dissemination of Portuguese literature and culture abroad, as well as importers of international ideas on women's rights and society-building. Hence, these feminist intellectuals were instrumental in shaping Portuguese modernity and the cultural history of their time. Almeida and Osório are, in their own right, examples of this 'new Western

---

women being the educators of the future generations and being able to maintain the nation's identity by preventing racial and distinctive national traits from deteriorating. In her view, this would ensure that strong, healthy Republican citizens of the future would better represent the nation. Specifically, Castro Osório argues that bourgeois mothers should organize campaigns against illnesses, illiteracy, and crime in order to save the poor by imposing bourgeois values on them.' In Célia Cordeiro, 'Ana de Castro Osório and the Portuguese Republican Woman: Vehicle of Regeneration of the Nation and of Preservation of the National Identity' (unpublished master's thesis, Faculty of the Graduate School, University of Minnesota, 2012), p. iii. < http://hdl.handle.net/11299/121039> [accessed 14 July 2018].

[48] Sweden was the first country in the world to formalize a State Institute of Eugenics, created in Uppsala in 1922. Professor Herman Lundborg fostered a close contact with German eugenicists, whose theories would develop into the Nazi ideology of race biology. Between 1935 and 1975, Sweden had a state subsidized sterilization programme.

modern woman' at the turn of the twentieth century. They were emancipated intellectuals and cosmopolitan polyglots who lived abroad during part of their life, and whose ideas made a strong impact in the public sphere. With the publication of *A mulher*, Almeida introduced major European thinkers, such as Ellen Key, to Portugal, as well as promoting ideas about women's emancipation and the modernization of the role of woman as wife, mother and educator, aspects considered to be crucial for the development of a new society. Likewise, the correspondence between Björkman and Osório shows Osório's role as a disseminator of Portuguese literature and culture in Sweden at that time. The correspondence between these two cultural figures contains a juxtaposition of family matters together with nationalistic and social issues that mirrored the international social climate of the period.

Despite the fact that the cultural and literary activities of these feminist writers and intellectuals belong to a larger transnational movement, that of Western first-wave feminism, this palpable truth has received very little recognition as such in traditional Portuguese literary historiography and literary studies. The recent broadening of perspective in the study of literature, from a transnational and global standpoint, could benefit from the inclusion of a re-reading of the production and viewpoints of these writers as an important part of collective and transcultural memory. In this context, a sociological approach, focusing on mediators involved in the cultural exchange of ideas could offer a productive frame of reference, shedding further light on feminist literary and cultural history.

Finally, the worldview of these Portuguese intellectuals encompasses both transnational nationalism (including racial thinking) and radical emancipatory strategies and thoughts on the redefinition of the role of women in society and in the nation at large. Further research placing the ideas and thinking of these feminists within a transnational framework of emancipatory struggle and first-wave feminism may in future pave the way for important discussions on, and insights into, the formation of cultural history and the circulation of ideas.

'Nem uma coisa nem outra':
Nomadic Subjectivity in the
Crónicas of Ilse Losa

ROSA CHURCHER CLARKE

Universidade de Lisboa

Quando me é posta a pergunta: 'sente-se mais portuguesa ou mais alemã?' respondo: 'Nem uma coisa nem outra'. Como podia sentir-me portuguesa se todos os portugueses vêem em mim a alemã ou a judia alemã? E como me podia sentir alemã se os alemães vêem em mim a portuguesa? Cito de cor Jorge Luís Borges: Todos nos parecemos com a imagem que os outros fazem de nós.

[When people ask me: 'do you feel more Portuguese or German?' I respond: 'Neither one thing nor the other'. How could I feel Portuguese when Portuguese people see in me a German or German-Jewish woman? And how could I feel German when Germans see the Portuguese in me? I quote from memory Jorge Luis Borges: We all resemble the image that others make of us.][1]

Ilse Losa — *née* Lieblich — was born to a Jewish family in Germany in 1913, and came to Portugal as a refugee in 1934. Like the great majority of the tens of thousands of other northern Europeans who fled the Nazis via this route, it was expected that she would travel on across the Atlantic, with Portugal merely serving as a 'sala-de-espera' [waiting room][2] — a stepping stone on the way. However, marriage to architect Arménio Losa in 1935 brought the twenty-one-year-old Ilse to settle in Porto, where she would later have children and establish a long and successful literary career in Portuguese letters, as well as an active role in northern left-wing intellectual groups.

Whilst Ilse Losa received significant praise and prizes for her writing during her lifetime and after her death (as well as having been included on the Portuguese school curriculum continuously for decades now), she is to some

---

[1] Ilse Losa, *À Flor do Tempo* (Porto: Afrontamento, 1997), p. 9. Further references to this edition are given in the text of the article. Except where stated otherwise, all translations into English are my own.

[2] Losa herself refers to 1930s Portugal in these terms in the first *crónica* of the collection (*Flor*, p. 8); the metaphor has also been repeatedly used in the same way by a number of other authors and historians. Cf. Erika Mann quoted in Margarida de Magalhães Ramalho, *Lisboa, uma Cidade em Tempo de Guerra* (Lisbon: Imprensa Nacional–Casa da Moeda, 2012), p. 24; Daniel Blaufuks, 'Sob Céus Estranhos', available at: <http://www.danielblaufuks.com/webnew/film/strangeskies/portugues.html> [accessed 22 August 2018]. A sense of how the interstitial — a key notion for Braidotti — is paradoxically central to Losa's experience is already palpable here.

extent 'uma estrangeira eterna' [forever a foreigner] — forever marginalized — considered apart from her Portuguese colleagues. One indication of this neglect is the relatively scarce academic production on her life and work, with only a couple of Portuguese researchers — namely Ana Isabel Marques and Karina Carvalho de Matos Marques — having maintained their focus on the author beyond a single article or master's thesis.[3] An extensive biography by Ramiro Teixeira from 2013 is a further exception to this rule of neglect or only scant attention.[4] Such a relative dearth of material on Ilse Losa is particularly pronounced in relation to her *crónica* writing, in keeping with the general tendency for the *crónica* form to be side-stepped in discussions within Portuguese academia, as I will go on to discuss.

At the same time as Losa can be said to have been somewhat overlooked, it is my suggestion that she in fact holds a unique dynamizing potential as an individual whose complex identity is neither here nor there, and as such opens up a space in-between, not only for herself but also for her readers.[5] It is here that we arrive at the relevance of Rosi Braidotti's theory of the nomadic subject — first formulated in 1994 — as a challenge to traditional (male-dominated) philosophical approaches to subjectivity.[6] The nomadic subject is, I suggest, a concept which could be useful for an assessment of Losa's ill-defined place in Portuguese literature.

> I am interested only in systems of thought or conceptual frameworks that can help me think about change, transformation, living transitions [...]. I want a creative, nonreactive project, emancipated from the oppressive force of the traditional theoretical approach. I see feminist theory as the site of such a transformation from sedentary logocentric thinking to nomadic creative thought. (pp. 63-64)

Declaring her passion for critical thought but also, as a feminist, her deep frustration at the phallologocentric, exclusionary limitations of philosophy as a discourse, Rosi Braidotti, in *Nomadic Subjects*, calls for the 'philos' to be returned to the academic act of thinking, and thus for a more empathic and inclusive conceptual framework within which to work as a thinker, and a

---

[3] See: Ana Isabel Marques, *As traduções de Ilse Losa no período do Estado Novo* (Coimbra: Minerva Coimbra, 2014); Karina Carvalho de Matos Marques, 'De l'écriture personnelle à l'écriture de l'histoire: questions d'identité dans l'œuvre de Ilse Losa et de Samuel Rawet' (unpublished doctoral thesis, University of Paris Sorbonne, 2014; abstract at <https://tel.archives-ouvertes.fr/tel-01143977>); Karina Marques (ed.), *Ilse Losa: estreitando laços. Correspondência com os pares lusófonos (1948–1999)* (Porto: Edições Afrontamento, 2018).

[4] Ramiro Teixeira, *Ilse Losa: Vida e Obra: Sob Céus Estranhos* (Porto: Associação dos Jornalistas e Homens de Letras, 2013).

[5] For fuller introductions to Losa's life and work see: Ana Isabel Marques, *Paisagens da memória: identidade e alteridade na escrita de Ilse Losa* (Coimbra: Minerva, 2001); Teixeira, *Ilse Losa: Vida e Obra*; Karina Marques, 'De l'écriture personnelle à l'écriture de l'histoire'; Rosa Churcher Clarke, 'Ilse Losa and the Portuguese Literary Establishment: Finding the Nomad a Home?' (unpublished master's thesis, Universidade Nova de Lisboa, 2016).

[6] Rosi Braidotti, *Nomadic Subjects*, 2nd edn (New York: Columbia University Press, 2011). Further references to this edition are given in the main text.

female feminist thinker at that. Contained in the quotation cited above is one illustration of the double-edged sword that she would seem to use to carve out her original new model — one edge formed by a fierce criticism of the present system, the other aimed at mapping out a creative alternative to that which is being dismantled. The emphasis on creativity — on the breathing of fresh life into an old and decrepit body — is something Braidotti repeats throughout: 'Nomadic subjects are capable of freeing the activity of thinking from the hold of phallocentric dogmatism, returning thought to its freedom, its liveliness, its beauty' (p. 29).

She attempts to open up what she terms a 'point of exit' from the entrenched, male-dominated philosophical system to which we are accustomed, and which, it would seem, remains reluctant to admit female subjects — amongst other marginal identities — on an equal footing. To do this, Braidotti takes aim at the rigid, exclusionary, dualistic structures traditionally used to define individual identities and suggests these be uprooted and replaced with an approach to subjectivity based on flexibility, fluidity and mutability.

In making her case for the nomadic subject, Braidotti gives two important clarifications of points which otherwise might be misconstrued. One is that such nomadism does not imply any absolute negation of belonging and community but rather of the absolutism and exclusivity of any such connection (p. 64); the other is her emphasis upon the fact that the nomadism she promotes need not be literal — one need not be de-territorialized in physical, geographical terms. Rather, it is a mental breaking out from, and cultivation of, a new and active disregard for boundaries, that is in question here. That is to say, it is about a general approach — a will to bring down the walls we are used to thinking within:

> The nomadism in question here refers to the kind of critical consciousness that resists settling into socially coded modes of thought and behaviour. Not all nomads are world travellers; some of the greatest trips can take place without physically moving from one's habitat. Consciousness-raising and the subversion of set conventions define the nomadic state, not the literal act of travelling. (p. 26)

Specifically, it is Braidotti's suggestion of an 'affirmation of fluid boundaries, a practice of intervals, interfaces, interstices' (p. 28) and her defiance of conventional binaries via an acknowledgement and celebration of marginal zones — those 'areas of silence, in between the official cacophonies' (p. 44) — that I see as the principal elements reflected in Ilse Losa's work. Emphasis upon the act of tracing — geographic, linguistic or cultural trajectories, for example — as an ethical tool for activating nomadic consciousness (p. 46), is a further aspect of Braidotti's theory and approach that I will highlight in my discussion of Losa's *crónica*-writing.

At this point, and before moving on to consider the neither/nor, 'hybrid' characterization of the *crónica* form and how this fits with Braidotti's proposal of a nomadic mode and perspective, it is worth recalling how Ilse Losa, whilst not a self-proclaimed feminist *per se*, should certainly be considered a transgressive female author and citizen, whose literary and broader civic activity habitually crossed multiple boundaries. She challenged established divisions and power dynamics in a number of fields, consistently giving particular attention to the position and rights of women.

In terms of her socio-political activity, it has been noted by various researchers[7] that Losa held relatively central roles in two important women's associations during, and in opposition to, the *Estado Novo*'s repressive and patriarchal rule, which saw 'as mulheres portuguesas [...] privadas de espaços organizativos próprios' [Portuguese women [...] denied their own organizational spaces].[8] As early as 1942, Losa co-founded the Porto wing of the *Associação Feminina Portuguesa para a Paz* [Portuguese Association of Women for Peace] and later also took on an active role in the *Comissão Nacional de Socorro aos Presos Políticos* [National Commission for Aid to Political Prisoners]. In the words of Manuela Tavares, who studied the development of feminism in Portugal from 1947 to 2007, 'a luta pela Paz era, deste modo, um espaço de luta das mulheres' [The struggle for Peace was thus a women's space for struggle].[9] Indeed, as has been noted by historian Irene Flunser Pimentel, the non-explicit political nature of these organizations belied their proximity to other more overtly anti-regime groupings, such as the Portuguese Communist Party (PCP),[10] and somewhat obscured the commitment of its members to wider political demands, including a greater role for women in society.[11] As Ana Isabel Marques puts it:

> as atividades realizadas pela AFPP vão no sentido da valorização do papel social das mulheres [...]. Refira-se, no entanto, que o apartidarismo programático do movimento, mormente vocacionado para a formação e

---

[7] See: Ana Isabel Marques, *As traduções de Ilse Losa no período do Estado Novo*, pp. 96–105; Karina Marques, 'De l'écriture personnelle à l'écriture de l'histoire', p. 319; Manuela Tavares, 'Feminismos em Portugal (1947–2007)' (unpublished doctoral thesis, Universidade Aberta, 2008), p. 93. Available at: <https://repositorioaberto.uab.pt/bitstream/10400.2/1346/1/Tese%20de%20doutoramento%20Manuela%20TavaresVF.pdf>.

[8] Tavares, p. 87.

[9] Tavares, p. 93.

[10] Pimentel describes the AFPP as 'criada provavelmente sob o impulso do Partido Comunista Português (PCP), em 1936, em pleno período da guerra civil espanhola para apoiar, discreta e clandestinamente, os republicanos espanhóis' [probably created under the influence of the Portuguese Communist Party (PCP), in 1936, at the height of the Spanish Civil War, to discreetly and clandestinely support the Spanish Republicans]. Irene Flunser Pimentel, *História das organizações femininas do Estado Novo* (Lisbon: Temas e Debates, 2001), p. 117.

[11] Alexandra Losa noted of her mother's involvement in the AFPP: 'Ainsi, elle a fini par faire la connaissance de Maria Lamas et d'autres femmes qui ont créé ces mouvements féministes. Ma mère s'intéressait à tout ce qui était culturel et d'avant-garde' [And so she ended up getting to know Maria Lamas and other women responsible for starting these feminist movements. My mother was interested in all that was cultural and avant-garde], K. Marques, 'De l'écriture personnelle à l'écriture de l'histoire', Annexe I. The curious suggestion made in that final reflection is that Ilse Losa's association with the feminist movement, amongst other causes, was somewhat superficial, reducible to a mere interest in the avant-garde.

valorização da mulher, cuja inocuidade teria permitido a sua ratificação legal, concretizar-se-ia ao arrepio das orientações do regime — assente numa sociedade patriarcal em que é reservado à mulher um papel passivo e submisso.

[the AFPP's activities aimed at gaining greater recognition of the role of women in society [...]. It is worth noting, however, that the movement's programmatic non-partisan approach, principally aimed at the training and greater recognition of women — its innocuous nature having surely permitted its legal ratification — would take shape at odds with the regime's outlook — based as this was on a patriarchal society in which women were required to be passive and submissive.][12]

Regarding Losa's literary activity, the prevalence and privileging of female figures across the whole of her *oeuvre*, from a range of social classes and positions, also serve to reinforce an idea of the author's commitment to her fellow women. Karina Marques, tracing precisely this strand of interest in Losa's writing, puts it thus:

les textes de Ilse Losa dénoncent la séparation culturelle entre femmes pauvres et femmes riches, ce qui va de pair avec les revendications du mouvement *gender studies* américain à partir des années 1975-1980. Au contraire de l'identité unitaire et univoque de la femme prônée par le mouvement féministe des années 1960 et 1970, les textes de Ilse Losa essaient de rendre compte des questions socio-politiques (différence de classe, de nationalité et d'ethnie). Ainsi, au lieu de prêcher une identité féminine contre une identité masculine, cette œuvre propose de briser les oppositions binaires sur lesquelles la notion de genre a été construite (public/privé, culture/nature, associées à homme/femme).

[Ilse Losa's texts criticize the cultural separation of poor women and rich women, which goes hand in hand with the demands of the American *gender studies* movement from the years 1975-1980. Unlike the single and unambiguous female identity advocated by the feminist movement of the 1960s and 1970s, Ilse Losa's texts try to take account of socio-political questions (differences of class, nationality and ethnicity). Instead of preaching a feminine identity against a masculine one, this body of work seeks to break down the binary oppositions on which the notion of gender has been constructed (public/private, culture/nature, associated with man/woman)].[13]

With these brief examples of Losa's broad activity in the name of women's rights — both literary and civic — the relevance of Rosi Braidotti's feminist theory of nomadic subjectivity, with its celebration of flow, transition and a multiplicity of perspectives and identities, as well as the solidarity with marginalized figures that it promotes, seems increasingly appropriate.

As an ambiguous genre treading a number of fine lines — perhaps most

---

[12] Ana Isabel Marques, *As traduções de Ilse Losa no período do Estado Novo*, pp. 103-04.
[13] Karina Marques, 'De l'écriture personnelle à l'écriture de l'histoire', p. 322.

obviously that between literature and journalism — the *crónica*, a generally literary style, in contrast with the journalistic tone of daily news reporting, inhabits the kind of peripheral and in-between spaces that Braidotti brings to our attention in her theory. As Ana Filipa Prata contends in her thorough doctoral study of three *cronistas*, the genre:

> se apresenta como uma forma marginal, oscilando constantemente entre vários tipos de discurso: entre história e literatura, entre jornalismo e literatura, e entre ensaio, poesia ou conto [...] tentar definir a crónica segundo os critérios formais tradicionais atribuídos aos géneros literários leva-nos a uma mesma conclusão: a crónica é um género híbrido e impossível de identificar com um paradigma genealógico, ocupando frequentemente uma posição marginal no sistema literário.
>
> [presents itself as a marginal form, constantly oscillating between various different sorts of discourse: between history and literature, between journalism and literature, and between the essay, poetry and the short-story [...] any attempt to define the *crónica* according to the same traditional formal criteria attributed to literary genres brings us to the same conclusion: the *crónica* is a hybrid genre and cannot be identified with a genealogical paradigm, often occupying a marginal position within the literary system.][14]

By mixing everyday events with more removed philosophical, historical and socio-political reflections, serving as a regular invitation for lyricism in the otherwise principally fact-focused context of a newspaper, the form seems to be inherently 'nomadic', naturally incorporating the 'repetitious, cyclical moves, rhythmic displacement' with which Rosi Braidotti characterizes the nomadic mode (p. 58). Indeed, the description, in Américo Oliveira Santos's postface to *À Flor do Tempo*, of the way 'a crónica moderna se bandeou com armas e bagagens do campo da historiografia para as margens da literatura' [the modern *crónica* upped sticks from the field of historiography and moved into the margins of literature] (*Flor*, p. 133) echoes precisely the idea of migration and marginality that Braidotti uses for her core image.

Whilst the 2004 comment by Portuguese literary critic Fernando Venâncio that no history of the *crónica* had yet been written still stands true today,[15] and as such serves as an indication of the relative neglect to which the genre has been subjected in more general terms, it is worth noting that it has received some attention in certain geo-cultural spheres, namely in Brazil and wider Latin America. Ana Filipa Prata, who has directly compared the Portuguese and Brazilian contexts in this respect, emphasizes the disparity, highlighting how, if in Brazil the *crónica* is considered a:

---

[14] Ana Filipa Prata, 'Práticas narrativas da cidade: crónicas urbanas de Carlos Drummond Andrade, Maria Judite Carvalho e Jaques Réda' (unpublished doctoral thesis, University of Lisbon, 2010), p. 218. Available at <http://repositorio.ul.pt/bitstream/10451/3048/1/ulsd60208_td.pdf>.

[15] 'Não existe, nunca tal se fez, uma história da crónica no século XX em Portugal' [A history of the *crónica* in twentieth-century Portugal doesn't exist — one's never been written]. *Crónica Jornalística: Século XX. Antologia*, ed. by Fernando Venâncio (Lisbon: Círculo de Leitores, 2004), p. 12.

género fundador da literatura nacional e bastante estudado pela crítica, em Portugal a sua classificação é mais complexa [...] a integração da crónica no cânone literário não é pacífica. O trabalho crítico sobre o género da crónica é esparso e pouco sistematizado, em parte por ser um género limítrofe e aglutinador de várias formas discursivas, muitas vezes relegadas para o domínio da paraliteratura.

[founding genre of the national literature, and has been greatly studied by critics, in Portugal its classification is more complex [...] the *crónica*'s integration into the Portuguese literary canon is not straightforward. Indeed, critical production on the *crónica* is dispersed and quite unsystematic, in part because it is a fringe genre which binds together various discursive forms, themselves often relegated to the area of para-literature.][16]

Beyond Prata's more recent contribution, key references in the existing literature on the form include, from the Latin American sphere, works by veteran Brazilian literary figures Massaud Moisés and Antonio Candido, from 1985 and 1992 respectively, and *La invención de la crónica*, by the Argentine researcher Susana Rotker, also from 1992.[17] Portuguese publications, which, Venâncio aside, typically take the form of article contributions to wider-themed collections, include: 'O outro lado da ficção — diário, crónica, memórias, etc.', by Maria Alzira Seixo in her *A palavra do romance: ensaios de genologia e análise* (Lisbon: Livros Horizonte, 1986), and Maria Helena Santana's article 'A crónica: a escrita volátil da modernidade', in *Rumos da narrativa breve*, ed. by Maria Saraira de Jesus (Aveiro: Universidade of Aveiro, 2003). An upcoming contribution to the field is the volume organized and introduced by Carina Infante do Carmo, *A Visagem do Cronista: antologia de crónica autobiográfica portuguesa. Séculos XIX-XXI* (Editora Arranha Céus, in press). In Anglophone academia, Tania Gentic's 2013 book *In the Everyday Atlantic: Time, Knowledge and Subjectivity in the Twentieth-Century Iberian and Latin American Chronicle* (Albany: State University of New York Press) is a rare example of an in-depth discussion of the genre.

With Prata's assessment of the *crónica*'s lesser 'limítrofe' [fringe] status in Portugal in mind, use of the form by Ilse Losa, herself a multiply marginal figure — as a transnational Portuguese-language woman writer and former refugee — offers itself for discussion. Deploying various literary techniques to express something of her mobile personal and professional identity, Losa here, as well as elsewhere in her *oeuvre*, can be seen to illustrate practically the nomadic consciousness that Braidotti outlines in more theoretical terms.

À Flor do Tempo [At the Surface of Time], published in 1997, was Ilse Losa's last new book before her death in 2006. Its fifty-one pieces, collected from five

---

[16] Prata, p. 222.
[17] Massaud Moisés, 'Crônica', in *A criação literária: Prosa* (São Paulo: Editora Cultrix, 1985), pp. 245–58; Antonio Candido, 'A vida ao rés-do-chão', in *A crônica: o gênero, sua fixação e suas transformações no Brasil* (Rio de Janeiro: Fundação Casa de Rui Barbosa, 1992), pp. 13–22; Susana Rotker, *La invención de la crónica* (Buenos Aires: Letra Buena, 1992).

decades-worth of regular and semi-regular contributions to various Portuguese press publications (including *Seara Nova, Vértice, Diário de Notícias, Jornal de Notícias, O Jornal, Público*) earned her the Associação Portuguesa de Escritores's 'Grande Prémio de Crónica' [Great *Crónica* Prize] in 1998. In fact, it is worth noting that the texts in this collection were selected and arranged not by the author herself but between her granddaughter, Ana Losa, and Marcela Torres, then director of Edições Afrontamento, Ilse Losa's main publisher from the late 1980s onwards. Beyond the question of the 'shape' of the anthology — how the various individual *crónicas* interact across its course — this compositional detail is relevant to an assessment of the significance of the book's title, which comes not as a citation from any individual text in the collection but perhaps rather reflects the editors' perception of the collection as a whole, and/or of its author's particular, peripheral position.

Whilst it may not have come directly from Losa,[18] the idea of liminality in the book's title echoes an element common to many of the individual texts, which, in their totality, foreground and fuse multiple marginal identities. Throughout the collection, our attention is repeatedly drawn to figures and social issues generally scorned or ignored, such as: refugees in 1930s Porto, Jews in 1920s and '30s Nazi-occupied northern Europe, various destitute women and children, a series of *mulheres-a-dias* [domestic servants], a retired tram-driver, and anonymous economic migrants involved in re-building post-war Germany, to list just some of the most vivid and deliberate portraits in the collection.[19]

As well as a variety of social types, Losa's texts move between different geographies, including London, New York, Amsterdam and Zurich, but most frequently Porto and various named and un-named German locations. As Américo Oliveira Santos says of the collection in his postface (whose title, 'Na orla do bosque' [At the forest's edge], also evokes a peripheral position): 'poderíamos tomar estas crónicas mais como um roteiro de lugares do que como um inventário de tempos' [these *crónicas* might be considered more of a tour of places than an inventory of eras] (*Flor*, p. 134). Through her *crónicas*, Ilse Losa guides her predominantly Portuguese (and often Porto-based) readers around landscapes which would have been a mixture of foreign and

---

[18] It would be interesting to know more about the process by which the collection was put together, given that Losa was already suffering from the onset of Alzheimer's at the time. The absence of any reference to the original publication details of each *crónica* (date, source, etc.) seems an unfortunate editorial oversight for a genre so thoroughly tied up with time and embedded, in its original context, in the news of the day. Indeed, the broader question of how anthologization alters the text — how the *crónica*'s removal from its original context and insertion in a book, amongst other *crónicas*, affects it — is an interesting one to be explored elsewhere.

[19] See, respectively: 'O cine-teatro' [The Cine-Theatre], 'O Porto e os estranhos' [Porto and the Outsiders], 'Um entre muitos' [One Among Many], 'Ai Kafka!' [Oh Kafka!]; 'Gretchen Wohlwill: Retrato' [Gretchen Wohlwill: A Portrait], 'Amsterdão' [Amsterdam], 'Ameaça' [Threat]; 'Chapéus e chapéus' [Hats and Hats], 'New York', 'O cara alegre' [Old Happy Face], 'Um entre muitos'; 'O diabo do chapéu' [The Damn Hat], 'Concorrência desleal' [Unfair Competition], 'A prenda de natal' [The Christmas Gift]; 'Vidas' [Lives]; 'Um herói dos nossos dias' [A Hero of Our Time], all in Losa, *Flor*, 1997.

familiar to them,[20] locating herself in frequently shifting physical positions and demonstratively tracing her path, together with the reader's travelling gaze. So we have, for example: 'A pensão da Dona Julieta situava-se no segundo andar da Rua Magalhães Lemos...' [Dona Julieta's guest-house was on the second floor of Rua Magalhães Lemos...] (*Flor*, p. 11); 'Prinsengracht, 263. Caminho entre casas e canais [...] Passo pela Westertoren...' [Prinsengracht, 263. I walk between houses and canals [...] I pass in front of the Westertoren...] (*Flor*, p. 29); 'Ao subir a Avenida dos Aliados...' [As I walk up the Avenida dos Aliados...] (*Flor*, p. 55); 'Andando a passear pelas vielas do lindo bairro velho de Zurique...' [Wandering through the alleyways of Zurich's beautiful historic neighbourhood...] (*Flor*, p. 85).

But if this strong connection to the physical fabrics of the cities which Losa takes as her focus is perhaps predictable for a typically urban genre,[21] what stands out as an indication of a nomadic identity and mode is Losa's merging of landscapes, her approximation of apparently distant and incompatible realities — be they separated in time or space, or both. The examples which follow, selected from four of the collection's *crónicas*, seek to exemplify this superimposition and blurring of various boundaries at Losa's literary hand.

In 'Na Praça da Liberdade' [In the Praça da Liberdade], Losa describes how, as she waits for the number 3 tram to Campo Alegre, in Porto, sometime in the 1960s:

> o meu olhar desviou-se para a Avenida dos Aliados, com os seus edifícios de pretensa monumentalidade, rematando na Câmara Municipal [...] Foi precisamente ela, a Câmara, que de súbito me fez evocar uma rua da minha infância, cujo remate era também a Câmara Municipal [...] A rua chamava-se Rua das Azenhas [...] Era a minha rua. Instalou-se em mim e, de vez em quando, bate-me à porta da memória.
>
> [my gaze floated down the Avenida dos Aliados, with its pretentiously monumental buildings, finally settling upon the town hall [...] It was specifically that, the town hall, that suddenly brought to mind a street from my childhood, the endpoint of which was also the town hall [...] The street was called Watermill Street [...] It was my street. It was embedded in me and, from time to time, it comes knocking on the door of my memory.]
>
> (*Flor*, p. 71)[22]

---

[20] Whilst she also wrote for national and Lisbon-based newspapers such as *Público*, *Diário de Notícias* and *O Jornal*, an initial assessment of Ilse Losa's *crónica* output seems to suggest that the majority of these texts appeared in Porto-produced publications such as *O Primeiro de Janeiro*, *O Comércio do Porto* and *Jornal de Notícias*, the local setting of many therefore being keenly familiar to much of her readership.

[21] 'A crónica, na sua formulação moderna, articula-se com o aparecimento de discursos que têm forte ligação à vida quotidiana e ao desenvolvimento das grandes metrópoles [...] A relação da crónica com a cidade é de natureza intrínseca' [The *crónica*, in its modern form, is connected to the appearance of discourses which are closely tied to everyday life and to the development of large metropolises [...] The *crónica*'s relationship to the city is of an intrinsic nature], Prata, p. 219.

[22] Ilse Losa's reference to the street of her childhood as 'Rua das Azenhas' is of course a domestication of what would have been the original German name. I have chosen to similarly translate this into English to give a sense of the familiarizing effect of Losa's writing here.

As she overlays two locations which are decades and thousands of kilometres apart, linked, at that moment, by the image of their town halls, Ilse Losa grants her Porto-based readers access to the German village of her childhood, with which most will have no first-hand familiarity but whose latent connection is activated and opened up for all by a consciousness imbued with its memory.

As the *crónica* goes on, Losa opens out the map yet further, as she inserts a third geography and mental landscape — that of Paris as experienced by *Estado Novo* exiles. Or rather, it is the Porto which these exiles remember that Losa evokes, providing an alternative, distanced perspective on a cityscape which is in fact entirely familiar and proximate to her local readers:

> Duas dezenas de anos depois encontrei-me em Paris com dois amigos exilados do Portugal de Salazar [...] 'Quem me dera poder descer, só uma vez, a Rua de Sá da Bandeira, no meu vagar, olhando montras, entrar no café da Brasileira, abraçar os amigos. Ai! que saudades!'
>
> [Two decades or so later I found myself in Paris with two friends exiled from Salazar's Portugal [...] 'What I'd give to be able to go down, just once, the Rua de Sá da Bandeira, wandering at my own pace, looking at the window displays, to go into the Brasileira café, to embrace my friends. Oh, how I miss it all!'] (*Flor*, p. 72)

What we have here then is a Paris-based memory of Porto, written (by Losa) and read (by her readers) in Porto, alongside a Porto-based memory of a small German village — an almost kaleidoscopic exploration of memories and feelings detached from fixed geographies in a most nomadic way.

Indeed, in the closing comments of this *crónica*, Losa underlines precisely the idea that, though these landscapes and political, historical settings are separated in time and space, the emotionally active, memory-filled humans that occupy them are capable of closing the gap, bringing the various disparate points together: 'Pois é' [So it is], she says, '*Saudade, Heimweh, Homesickness, Toská...* Soam diferentes, mas o conteudo é o mesmo' [*Saudade, Heimweh, Homesickness, Toská...* They sound different, but their content is the same] (*Flor*, p. 72).[23]

By narrating her own navigation of multiple mental landscapes, Losa invites her readers to roam with her, to watch and learn as she reaches across the boundaries that separate her, in this case (as in many), from her former self. By comparing her own experience of this landscape-based nostalgia to that of Portuguese exiles in Paris, Losa also cleverly engages with a model of exile more readily accessible to her Portuguese readers than that of her own flight from

---

[23] Here, Ilse Losa echoes others — including the German-born philologist Carolina Michaëlis de Vasconcelos and anthropologist António Sérgio — in questioning the supposed 'untranslatability' of *saudade*, a notion thoroughly explored in João Leal, 'The Making of Saudade: National Identity and Ethnic Psychology in Portugal', in *Roots and Rituals: The Construction of National Identities*, ed. by Ton Dekker, John Helsloot, Carla Wijers (Amsterdam: Het Spinhuis, 2000), pp. 267–87. Losa thus challenges the nationalist rhetoric promoted by the *Estado Novo* regime, which, as thoroughly outlined by Leal in his history of the concept, adopted *saudade* as an inherently Portuguese concept to support its essentialist ideology.

the Nazis as a German Jew, inviting them to experience other positions and perspectives on their ever-familiar, ever-present city.

If in that *crónica* Losa crosses landscapes and time-periods via the image and visual memory of the town hall building, in others it is via less solid, physical portals that she travels. In 'Numa manhã de Fevereiro' [On a February morning], for example, it is via two lines by the German poet, Goethe:

> Os versos, as canções e os provérbios que nos foram legados na infância são, para além da paisagem, os laços mais fortes que nos vinculam à nossa terra de origem. Eles vêm ter connosco a cada passo, a propósito disto ou aquilo, como vindos à superfície do mais íntimo fundo do nosso ser. Foi o que me aconteceu há pouco, numa soalheira manhã de Fevereiro, em que, de súbito, emergiu em mim o verso de Goethe 'Não páras de correr mundo? Vê como a beleza está tão perto', do poema *Recordação*.

> [The verse, songs and proverbs handed down to us as children are, apart from landscape, the strongest bonds connecting us to our original homeland. They greet us at every turn, because of this or that, as if rising to the surface from the most intimate depths of ourselves. That's what happened to me, not long ago, one sunny February morning, when, all of a sudden, a line from Goethe resurfaced in me: 'Wouldst thou ever onward roam? Lo, the good lies very near', from the poem *Memory*.] (*Flor*, p. 75)[24]

Losa goes on to describe the northern German countryside about which these lines would have been written by the eighteenth-century poet, with this idyllic scene summoning up the memory of Losa's uncle and his deep attachment to his home's natural setting, as well as his cruel uprooting from that scene when he was deported to a Nazi concentration camp. 'De tudo isso me lembrei nessa manhã de Fevereiro ao caminhar pelas relvas do meu bairro' [I remembered all this on that February morning, as I walked across the lawns of my neighbourhood] (*Flor*, p. 75), she says (of her neighbourhood in Porto).

Losa, seeing the trees burst into bloom in her present, Portuguese surroundings, remembers German verses committed to memory as a child, the words and images of the poem transporting her to the German landscape of both the era in which they were written (by Goethe) and also that in which they were heard (by her), before, finally, she is returned to her immediate, Portuguese environment by the noise of the life around her, which is itself now coloured by the memory it interrupted: 'Na rua os automóveis e as ruidosas motas "não paravam de correr mundo"' [In the street, the cars and noisy motorbikes 'ever onward' roamed and groaned] (*Flor*, p.: 76). With this intertextual insertion of Goethe's words amongst Losa's own Portuguese narration, the various distant realities — modern-day Porto and both eighteenth-century and 1920s/'30s Germany — are interwoven, bound together by the author's own dual perspective and the words she chooses to express this.

[24] English translation of Goethe: Paul Carus, *Goethe, with special consideration of his philosophy* (London: Open Court Publishing Company, 1915), p. 335, in *The Internet Archive* <https://archive.org/stream/goethewithspeciaoocaru#page/334> [accessed 22 August 2018].

Goethe is by no means the only literary figure with whom Losa engages in *À Flor do Tempo*. As Oliveira Santos says in the postface: 'É [...] à Literatura que Ilse constantemente regressa nestas crónicas' [It is [...] to Literature that Ilse consistently returns in these *crónicas*] (*Flor*, p. 136). A quick scan of the index reveals titles such as: 'Lembrando Anna Seghers' [Remembering Anna Seghers], 'Sobre os contos de Anne Frank' [About Anne Frank's short stories], 'Ai Kafka!' [Oh Kafka!], 'Irene Lisboa', 'Ao Eugénio' [To Eugénio], 'Lembrando Camilo e outros' [Remembering Camilo and Others], 'Uma frase infeliz do Eça' [An Unfortunate Sentence by Eça]. Indeed, as this list indicates, Ilse Losa spreads her attention relatively evenly between German-language and Portuguese identities (as well as between men and women, classic and contemporary writers). But where the treatment of these instantly recognizable and apparently locatable individuals would seem to really express a nomadic subjectivity in Losa is in her systematic deterritorialization of them. Rather than simply evoking the landscapes and social, linguistic panoramas we might expect, as the 'natural', national settings for these figures, Ilse Losa uproots and re-grounds them, surrounding them with elements from different, foreign lands — mixing and merging identities and contexts as she goes.

In 'Ai Kafka!', for example, Losa maps her passage through the inefficient and unyielding bureaucratic process of renewing her Portuguese identity card as a foreign-born citizen who came to Portugal as a refugee:

> Fui aos Serviços de Identificação [...] o funcionário propôs-me ir à Conservatória do Registo Civil onde casara [...] Lá fui [...] À tarde dirigi-me às Informações. Mas os turnos eram outros. Voltei, portanto, a contar o meu caso, e o funcionário achou que devia dirigir-me ao guiché do Registo Criminal. O funcionário do Registo Criminal tentou canalizar-me para o guiché onde eram atendidos os estrangeiros e os retornados. Expliquei-lhe que eu não era nem uma coisa nem outra e que tinha a nacionalidade portuguesa. Mesmo assim achou que eu devia ir lá. Já se vê que não fui.
>
> [I went to the Identification Service [...] the official suggested I go to the Civil Registry Office where I had got married [...] There I went [...] In the afternoon I went to the Information Office. But the shifts had changed over. I therefore explained my situation once again, and the official thought that I should go to the Criminal Record department. The official in the Criminal Record department tried to redirect me to the department which dealt with foreigners and returnees. I explained to him that I was neither one thing nor the other and that I had Portuguese nationality. Even so, he thought I should go there anyway. Obviously, I did not go.] (*Flor*, pp. 100–03)

In this humorous but exasperated account, Losa brings an element of her German-language literary heritage — Kafka — into a situation entirely focused on her new Portuguese citizenship, restating in the process the very real, practical complexity of her identity at the same time as she demonstrates the rich cultural baggage she carries with her.

In terms of the Portuguese authors of the *crónica*-titles I mentioned above, these are, together with their words, similarly re-situated by Losa, amongst foreign landscapes and linguistic fields, this time looking and moving over the imaginary Luso-German border from the other side, in the opposite direction.

In 'Ao Eugénio', which in fact begins almost identically to 'Numa manhã de Fevereiro', with its emphasis upon the emotional power of verse learnt in infancy, Losa recalls her discovery of a still emerging Eugénio de Andrade, before reproducing his 'Canção Infantil': 'Era um amieiro | depois uma azenha | E junto um ribeiro. | Tudo tão aberto! | Que devia fazer? | Meti tudo no bolso | Para os não perder' [There once was an alder | then a watermill | and alongside, a stream. | All right there for the taking! | What should I do? | I put it all in my pocket | So as not to lose them] (*Flor*, p. 121). She reflects that while Andrade may have gone on to develop as a poet, 'da sua "Canção Infantil", que abriga o meu amieiro, o meu ribeiro e a minha azenha, eu nunca me quis separar' [from his 'Canção Infantil', which holds my alder, my stream, and my watermill, I never wanted to part] (*Flor*, p. 122). Losa thus takes the Portuguese poet's words and applies them to the German landscape of her childhood — *her* alder, *her* stream, *her* watermill — inverting the process she performed with Goethe's words. Where there she transposed German verse to a Portuguese context, here it is Portuguese verse that Ilse Losa maps onto a German landscape.

It is interesting to note that beyond what I have called this 'deterritorialization' of literary figures, in both 'Ai Kafka!' and 'Ao Eugénio' Ilse Losa also enacts a re-birth of sorts before the readers' eyes, emphasizing her constantly renewed and restructured identity. In thinking about these texts as examples of nomadic subjectivity and thus as feminist theory in literary action, it seems fitting that Losa, as someone concerned with securing better recognition for female experience, should draw on imagery of birth and rebirth — something generally edited out of view by patriarchal society.

In 'Ai Kafka!', the metaphor is more explicit as, having found the requisite two witnesses to (falsely) attest the details of her birth in Germany in 1913, Losa asserts: 'Desta feita renasci. Tornei-me portuguesa pelo casamento' [And with that I was reborn. I became Portuguese by marriage] (*Flor*, p. 100). This re-birth is at once Ilse's original, German birth, re-created via its confirmation and celebration in Portugal thirty-something years after the actual event, and her Portuguese 'birth' (by marriage), as permitted by the falsified testimonies. The two births then, separated in time and space, are merged here, neither apparently any 'truer' than the other, each to some extent a farce, and yet each of great practical as well as symbolic importance to Losa.

In 'Ao Eugénio', the re-birth is of a more lyrical sort. Describing the cultural disorientation encountered upon being uprooted from one's natural setting (and preparing the ground on which the birth will take place), Losa writes:

> Uma vez chegados a outros mundos, procuramos avidamente coisas familiares parecidas com as que deixámos para trás: uma árvore, um cão,

uma música. Mas, pouco a pouco, tentamos aproximar-nos de novo, do até então estranho, para que nos dê apoio na aclimatação.

[When we arrive in foreign lands, we avidly seek out things which are familiarly akin to those we left behind: a tree, a dog, a song. But bit by bit, we try to reach out again, to the hitherto strange, so that it can support us as we acclimatize.] (*Flor*, p. 120)

It seems that in Eugénio de Andrade's verse Losa found a route by which to move towards her new, strange reality in 1940s Portugal: 'Certo dia, comprei um livro de poesias com o título *Pureza*. [...] Fiquei logo presa, na primeira página, à "Canção Infantil"' [One day, I bought a book of poems with the title *Purity* [...] I was immediately hooked, right from the first page, by the 'Child's Song'] (Ibid.).

The specificity of the moment ('one day') and the immediacy of Losa's instinctive attachment ('I was immediately hooked'), together with the poem's own reference to infancy in its title ('Child's Song'), Losa's description of Andrade's development ('cresceu, cresceu' [he grew and grew], she says), the 'birth' of birds at his fingertips (to paraphrase Losa's own citation of the poet), and, finally, the closing sentence — 'São assim as portas que se nos abrem para podermos entrar e conviver numa casa desconhecida' [That's what they're like — those doors which open up to us, allowing us to enter in and live together in an unfamiliar home] (*Flor*, p. 120) — in all this Losa plays out her own birth into that 'unfamiliar home'. One birth, one home, of many, we might assume. Indeed, if on the one hand Ilse Losa's nomadic subjectivity takes the form of repeated shifts across geographies and timeframes, it also acts as a consistent search for and construction of home — not least through literature.[25]

So while renowned figures of Portuguese and German-language literatures are uprooted to territories and contexts not 'naturally', nationally, their own, and landscapes are transposed across temporal and spatial boundaries, Ilse Losa is herself reinvented, re-presented over and over again in multiple different skins, positions and orientations. Through this repeated action and consistent disregard for fixity, Losa thus opens up and demonstrates for her readers the possibility of a more flexible, complex, multi-faceted identity, which is not easily set down and held within a single category, but rather roams nomadically between many. By providing many overlapping images of herself, of her surroundings, of the people she interacts with, of their relations to her and to one another, Losa, across the course of *À Flor do Tempo* (as well as within each individual *crónica*, and indeed, arguably, throughout her entire *oeuvre*) shakes up and releases her identity from any stable points to which it might be forcefully tied, celebrating, as I hope to have demonstrated, a nomadic consciousness and subjectivity actively operating within Portuguese literature.

---

[25] My master's dissertation provides a more thorough discussion of how Ilse Losa's 'nomadism', perhaps paradoxically, allowed her to carve out a place and find a home for herself in Portuguese literature (see, for example, the section 'Neither/nor but not none', in Churcher Clarke, pp. 50–52).

O mapa cor de rosa by Maria Velho da Costa: Migration, Dis-location and the Production of Unstable Cartographies

Maria Luísa Coelho

Universidade do Minho / University of Oxford

Maria Velho da Costa (b. 1938) is one of the most experimental Portuguese writers of her generation, perhaps still best known to an international readership as the co-author of *Novas cartas portuguesas* (1972), along with Maria Teresa Horta and Maria Isabel Barreno.[1] Over several decades, she has produced an *oeuvre* marked by a spirit of de-centring and de-territorialization, be it by creating an array of characters, worlds, realities and dimensions that nevertheless coexist or even mingle, or by consistently pushing the boundaries of literary genres in order to explore the possibilities offered by language and its dialogue with other artistic media such as music, cinema and visual art. This de-centring process also defines, at least to some extent, her life: born in Lisbon, where as a child she attended a convent school run by Spanish nuns, she moved to London in 1980 and lived there till 1987, first as a writer-in-residence and a Fundação Calouste Gulbenkian grant holder and then as a Portuguese *leitora* at King's College London; she was also a cultural attaché in Cape Verde, between 1988 and 1991.[2]

During her time in England, MVC wrote and published, in quick succession, the novel *Lucialima* (1983) and the collection *O mapa cor de rosa: cartas de Londres* (1984) [The Rose-coloured Map: Letters from London], about her life in London in the early 1980s.[3] References to the novel are interspersed throughout the letters from London, suggesting that the transnational experience fostered the writer's creativity: 'esta cidade, este tempo, foi-me fecundo' [this city, this time, was fruitful for me], she concludes rather optimistically.[4] In addition,

---

I wish to thank the Fundação para a Ciência e Tecnologia for their award of a postdoctoral grant, ref. SFRH/BPD/112293/2015, that has allowed me to conduct research on Maria Velho da Costa and other Portuguese writers who have lived in London over the period 1950 to 1986.

[1] I will use the acronym MVC to refer to the writer Maria Velho da Costa.
[2] MVC's move to Africa in the late 1980s was also a return, for she had briefly lived in Guinea-Bissau, in 1973.
[3] Maria Velho da Costa, *Lucialima* (Lisbon: Publicações Dom Quixote, 1983); Maria Velho da Costa, *O mapa cor de rosa* (Lisbon: Publicações Dom Quixote, 1984). This period in London is described by MVC as a re-acquaintance with Britain, for she confesses in a text from *O mapa cor de rosa* entitled 'Já aqui estive' [I have been here] that she had lived in Bromley whilst on an exchange programme from Lisbon University (Costa, *Mapa*, pp. 234–37).
[4] Costa, *Mapa*, p. 196. All translations, unless stated otherwise, are my own.

O mapa cor de rosa and *Lucialima* are united by their author's collaboration with artists. The former is complemented by illustrations by Oscar Zarate, a migrant Argentinian artist who is described in the early pages of the book as 'um latino-americano que não pode *lá* estar' [a Latin-American who cannot be *there*], whereas the writer defines herself as 'um latino-europeu numa passagem pelo Norte de duração imprevisível' [a Latin-European in a passage through the North of unpredictable duration].[5] These two definitions already suggest very different modes of experiencing migration — Zarate more as an exile, MVC as an expatriate or a cosmopolite. Ana Paula Coutinho inserts MVC in a group labelled dislocated writers, sometimes also self-referenced as expatriate writers, and distinguishes that group from two others: writers in exile and travel writers or writing travellers.[6] In my own article, I am using the terms expatriate and cosmopolite in the sense these are described by Ulf Hannerz:

> [C]osmopolitanism in a stricter sense includes a stance toward diversity itself, toward the coexistence of cultures in the individual experience. A more genuine cosmopolitanism is first of all an orientation, a willingness to engage with the Other. It is an intellectual and aesthetic stance of openness toward divergent cultural experiences, a search for contrasts rather than uniformity.[7]

As for expatriates, Hannerz describes them as:

> [P]eople who have chosen to live abroad for some period and who know when they are there that they can go home when it suits them. Not all expatriates are living models of cosmopolitanism; colonialists were also expatriates, and mostly they abhorred 'going native'. But these are people who can afford to experiment, who do not stand to lose a treasured but threatened, uprooted sense of self.[8]

As regards *Lucialima*, the book has an enticing cover by Paula Rego, another Portuguese living in London (since the 1950s); it is easy to imagine how effortlessly Rego must have entered MVC's literary world, given the interest both women have in revisiting and revising (Portuguese) literary tradition, as well as in exploring power relations within the family structure, a polyphony of voices and a new language (visual and linguistic) with which to give emotions and trauma 'a face'.[9] Helena Carvalhão Buescu's description of MVC's work could thus also aptly fit Rego's:

---

[5] Costa, *Mapa*, p. 19.
[6] Ana Paula Coutinho, 'Outras "cartas de Londres": *O mapa cor de rosa* de Maria Velho da Costa (contributos para uma cartografia enunciativa de escritores em "passagem de estar")', *Cadernos de literatura comparada*, 24/25 (2011), 48–68.
[7] Ulf Hannerz, 'Cosmopolitans and Locals in World Culture', in *Global Culture: Nationalism, Globalization and Modernity*, ed. by Mike Featherstone (London: Sage, 1990), pp. 237–51 (p. 239).
[8] Hannerz, 'Cosmopolitans', p. 243.
[9] I am here paraphrasing Rego's now famous words, when interviewed by her friend and fellow Portuguese migrant, poet Alberto de Lacerda: 'Porque é que pinta?' [Why do you paint?], Lacerda asks. 'Para dar uma face ao medo' [To give fear a face], answers Rego. See Alberto de Lacerda, 'Paula Rego nas Belas Artes', *Diário de Notícias*, 25 December 1965, pp. 3–4.

> Maria Velho da Costa pertence à família de escritores que sabem que, debaixo da crosta aparentemente sólida e estável do mundo, vibram forças que sacodem as vidas dos homens [...] Crianças, mulheres, mestiços, famílias, noites/madrugadas, revoluções e invasões, infâncias e sacrifícios, imigrantes — todos eles conhecerão um instante de explosão na história.
>
> [Maria Velho da Costa belongs to that family of writers who know that under the seemingly solid and stable crust of the world there are forces that shake the lives of men [...] Children, women, mestizos, families, nights/dawns, revolutions and invasions, infancies and sacrifices, migrants — all of them will know an instant of explosion in history.][10]

Incidentally, shortly after returning to Portugal, MVC published *Missa in albis* (1988), for which she enlisted another Portuguese artist living in London — Bartolomeu Cid dos Santos — whose printed work featured on the cover of that first edition. These details show that MVC's geographical dislocation was particularly fruitful to the development of inter-artistic dialogues, a circumstance that is common to other Portuguese cultural agents living in London before and shortly after the Carnation Revolution.[11]

Starting with the idea of a dialogic migrant experience, in this article I intend to take a closer look at *O mapa cor de rosa* in order to argue that rather than offering a map where territories and their boundaries are drawn in permanent ink, the book produces an unstable geographic and cultural cartography, through which personal, national and linguistic identities and locations are seen as hybrid and always in transit.

The title of MVC's book is a direct reference to the document presented by Portugal, in 1885, at the Berlin conference, in which the country's claim to sovereignty over a land corridor connecting its East and West African colonies was put forward. In fact, as perceptively observed by Coutinho, *O mapa cor de rosa* was published a hundred years after that conference. The Portuguese claims collided with British imperialism and were crushed by the principle of effective occupation, which prevailed. The end result was the British ultimatum of 1890, accepted by King Carlos I and perceived as a national humiliation and a blow to the monarchy. Therefore, the title of MVC's book not only refers to Portugal's hegemonic dreams in the late nineteenth century, but also to their by-product, i.e., the clash between Portugal and Great Britain, two colonial powers, over African territories.[12]

---

[10] Helena Carvalhão Buescu, 'Maria Velho da Costa: colidir na história', in *Manual de leitura: casas pardas*, ed. by João Luís Pereira (Maia: Departamento de Edições do Teatro Nacional São João, 2012), pp. 43–47 (p. 44) [accessed online 12 May 2018].

[11] See Maria Luísa Coelho, 'Portuguese Artists and Writers in London (1950–1986): Cultural Networks and Identities in Transit', in *Outros mapas: linguagem, migração, diáspora*, ed. by Ana Gabriela Macedo, Carlos Mendes de Sousa and Vítor Moura (Braga: Centro de Estudos Humanísticos da Universidade do Minho, 2016), pp. 143–54.

[12] See also in *O mapa cor de rosa* the text entitled 'Já aqui estive', which describes in humorous and ironic terms an earlier trip to England as a clash of cultures, a clash that is further substantiated by references to the Rose-coloured Map. Costa, *Mapa*, p. 236.

The texts that comprise *O mapa cor de rosa* were originally published between 1981 and 1982 in the Lisbon newspaper *A Capital*, as a series of *crónicas* [chronicles].[13] The first published chronicle was 'Flores, couves-flores, pássaros' [Flowers, cauliflowers, birds] (dated 3 October 1981) and the last one was 'O Tratado de Windsor' [The Treaty of Windsor] (dated 9 June 1982). The latter title establishes a contrast with the title of the book, as it refers to a treaty signed between Portugal and England on 9 May 1386, sealing the diplomatic alliance between the two countries. The references to such crucial historic documents (the Rose-coloured Map and the Windsor Treaty), placed at the beginning and end of the book, point to the complexities of the Luso-British relationship and are symbolic of the book's comparative arch, which reflects not only on what separates but also on what unites the two countries, and thus avoids clear-cut oppositions.

Originally published as *crónicas* and thus suggesting an up-to-date, even if personal, account, the texts that make *O mapa cor de rosa* become *cartas* [letters] in the book. As MVC explains in the introductory text, named 'Alguns anos depois' [Some years later] and written over a year after her last *crónica*, the change was meant to emphasize the intimate dimension of the texts, which were based on absence rather than distance, and to invoke the complicity of the reader: 'um apelo a uma cumplicidade que suplante a estranheza, o alheamento' [an appeal to a complicity that overcomes strangeness, detachment].[14] As with most letters sent to a distant friend, in MVC's letters from England historical events fight for written space with subjective accounts of daily life, descriptions of places, people and situations, which are conveyed in an effort to make the reader *see* and *listen* and hence shorten the distance between the two.[15] The letters engender an intimate, subjective and sensorial voice, with traces of oral exchange, a voice that retells micro-events mingled with thoughts on macro-events, often making associations between these two levels of experience.[16]

The historical backdrop for the letters is the Thatcher years in Britain, which, in the early 1980s, were characterized by economic recession, unemployment, strikes, poverty, socio-cultural contrasts resulting from rapid changes as well as from the disintegration of the British Empire, instances of xenophobia, class and gender violence, the adoption of an American way of life grounded in capitalist and consumerist values, and the Falklands/Malvinas war, the last of these presented as an event with rippling effects in British society. Widening the

---

[13] This is not the case with the first four letters presented in the book — 'Alguns anos depois', 'Restos', 'O jantarinho' and 'O jantarinho (2)'; the first of these is dated London, 5 October 1983 and is presented as a preface that situates and offers some thematic interpretations of what is to follow. The next letter — 'Restos' — is undated, although the text contains references to spring, daffodils and lilies; the other two letters are dated December 1980. After consulting *A Capital*, I could not find these last three texts, which suggests that they were written prior to the first published chronicle and then added to the compilation.

[14] Costa, *Mapa*, p. 15.

[15] See Costa, *Mapa*, p. 16.

[16] Ibid.

scope, the letters also feature references to the situation in Poland (a country that was being affected by strikes, economic collapse and martial law), followed attentively by both the Portuguese and the British media and often compared in MVC's letters to the political turmoil of the post-revolutionary period in Portugal. This engagement with British and European history in the making may be related to the particular moment in which these texts were written and subsequently published, as this was a period during which Portugal was preparing for integration into the European Union (then European Economic Community), thus signalling a new and crucial phase in the country's position in, and relationship with, Europe.[17] The Portuguese reader of *A Capital* would certainly have looked at MVC's *crónicas* with increased curiosity and a renewed interest. In a way, these texts are as much about England (or Europe) as about Portugal, an approach already suggested in their overarching title and recognized by the writer in the book's opening text: 'A uma velocidade compensatória, a escrita destas [cartas] [...] parece-me hoje padecer, ou ao menos dar sinal, de dois males ligados — a ausência de *lá*, a in-presença *aqui*' [At a compensatory speed, the writing of these [letters] [...] today seems to me to suffer from, or at least to signal, two related problems — the absence of *there*, the in-presence *here*].[18]

The title of the book also points to a similarity shared between Portugal and Britain, of which the Rose-coloured Map is a figurative representation; indeed, both countries have colonial and imperial histories, which at the end of the nineteenth century, during the scramble for Africa, became tensely entangled. References to that common history show up in several letters, as in the following one: 'professores [...] aguentam com grandes canecas de café aleitado a estuância do desabar do Império, rodeados de meninos morenos das Antilhas, do Paquistão, do Sul de Londres' [teachers [...] withstand with mugs of milky coffee the deluge originating from the collapse of the Empire, surrounded by dark-skinned children from the Antilles, Pakistan, South London].[19] MVC's and *A Capital*'s readership would certainly not fail to make the connection between the changing demographics in London due to the immigration to Britain from its former colonies and their own experience in a country (and especially in its capital) whose ethnic population had changed considerably with the dismantling of the Portuguese empire. Likewise, when MVC reports the increased visibility of systemic racism in British society, she not only explicitly relates this to the British imperial dream and its aftermath, but also to the Portuguese (post)imperial condition: 'O que tudo isto tem a ver com Portugal não sei bem. Um ardor de catástrofe, finalistas igualmente chumbados de uma desigualmente proveitosa, mas igualmente idealizada prova

---

[17] Portugal formally applied to join the European Economic Community on 28 March 1977 and became a full member on 1 January 1986.
[18] Costa, *Mapa*, p. 15.
[19] Costa, *Mapa*, p. 175.

imperial?' [What all this has to do with Portugal I'm not quite sure. A burning feeling of catastrophe, similarly failed finalists in an unequally fruitful, but equally idealized imperial test?].[20]

Further references to British imperialism are clearly presented in the letters that refer to the Malvinas/Falklands conflict, which MVC witnessed as it unfolded: 'o império tem de novo uma causa' [the empire has a cause again], concludes the writer.[21] Similarly to those Caribbean and Pakistani heritage children described earlier on, for MVC the conflict exposed Britain's post-imperial condition as an unfinished business, a business that is also regarded by the writer as the result of a wider European imperial dream, to which Portugal also contributed: 'Mas são europeus. Como não reconhecer e doer-se deste tão desrazoado fim de Império?' [But they are European. How not to recognize and feel sorry for this ever so irrational end of Empire?].[22] There is an inherent sadness in these words, but also a very fine irony that elsewhere is replaced by blatant mockery, thus suggesting the author's critical position vis-à-vis the colonial enterprise and its muddled conclusion: 'Londres fez-me lembrar Lisboa num dos seus traços delirante — *cá nunca faz muito frio, cá nunca chove muito*. [...] Será coisa de ex-cabeça de império esta de alucinar o próprio clima?' [London reminds me of Lisbon in one of its delirious traits — *it's never very cold here, it never rains much here*. [...] Is it something to do with having been the imperial capital, this thing of hallucinating its own climate?].[23]

On the other hand, the Falklands conflict leads MVC to reflect on the paradoxical position of Portugal in relation to Europe, for whom otherness is not only situated beyond its geographical borders but also at its margins:

> Entretanto resíduos de sonho e transmigração de *vendettas* mantêm-nos presos a esta briga inesperada, inesperadamente antiquíssima, o confronto entre a latinidade e os Bárbaros, entre o império e os gentios. E quem é quem? Não comento mais, são demasiadas ironias para uma só, nacional e pessoal, memória. *Adios muchachos compañeros de mi vida*, The British are coming.
>
> [In the meantime, residues of dreams and transmigration of *vendettas* keep us glued to this unexpected fight, unexpectedly ancient, the conflict between the Latins and the Barbarians, between the empire and the pagans.

---

[20] Costa, *Mapa*, p. 218. See also: 'Enoch Powell afirmou impunemente que a solução para o problema da violência e da marginalidade, a seu, claro!, entender, de origem racial, seja o retorno da população de cor (milhões ora na segunda geração de desempregados, subempregados e outros, todos eles residuais duma prática imperial), para as ex-colónias' [Enoch Powell got away with stating that the solution to the problem of the violence and the delinquency, which in his, obvious!, view had a racial origin, was returning the coloured population (millions now part of a second generation of unemployed, under-employed and others, all of them residues of imperial practices), to the ex-colonies]. Costa, *Mapa*, p. 217.
[21] Costa, *Mapa*, p. 182. The Malvinas (in Spanish)/Falklands (in English) conflict was a ten-week war between Argentina and the United Kingdom over two British dependent territories off the Argentinian coast. It began on 2 April 1982, when Argentina invaded and occupied the Falkland Islands. During the conflict, Portugal supported the British side, making available the facilities at its air base in the Azores.
[22] Costa, *Mapa*, p. 199.
[23] Costa, *Mapa*, p. 95.

And who is who? I'm not commenting any further, there are too many ironies for a single, national and personal, memory. *Adios muchachos compañeros de mi vida, The British are coming.*]²⁴

Boaventura de Sousa Santos describes Portugal as a semiperipheral country in the modern capitalist world system and claims that 'this complex semiperipheral condition reproduced itself until quite recently on the basis of the colonial system'.²⁵ Furthermore, according to Sousa Santos:

> [T]he subalternity of Portuguese colonialism resides in the fact that, since the seventeenth century, the history of colonialism has been written in English, not in Portuguese. This means that the Portuguese colonizer has a problem of self-representation rather similar to that of the British colonized.²⁶

A similar understanding surfaces in MVC's analysis of the Falklands conflict, which allows her to reflect on Portugal's marginal, hybrid and almost paradoxical condition — simultaneously in and out of Europe, imperial and barbarian, producer of alliance treaties and humiliating rose-coloured maps. It is a condition that ultimately makes the writer sympathize with the British whilst identifying with the Argentinians.

In brief, although colonialism is not *O mapa cor de rosa*'s main subject, it does, nevertheless, occupy an important place in the book, as evidenced by the previous examples and as already hinted at in the book's title. In fact, it seems that moving to England further gave MVC the critical distance to reflect on and criticize Portugal's recent past whilst addressing such past within the wider framework of British and, ultimately, European history. In so doing, her *crónicas* from England are also one of the first Portuguese texts to break the silence surrounding that uncomfortable and traumatic side of Portuguese history; the radical and transgressive nature of her texts is even more impressive given their circulation in the Portuguese press of the period.

In *O mapa cor de rosa*, traditional historiographical account and its correlated national spatial imaginary are signalled by textual references to geopolitical events, toponyms and cultural idiosyncrasies; the original form of the texts — chronicles for regular publication in a newspaper — also lends itself to documenting the time of history. However, and in keeping with the fluid status of the Portuguese *crónicas*, such an account overlaps with the presentation of more subjective, sensorial and intimate experiences and, in particular, with the

---

²⁴ Costa, *Mapa*, p. 185. The quote contains a reference to the first words of an Argentinian tango ('Adiós Muchachos'), made famous by singer Carlos Gardel. As for the expression 'The British are coming', it is attributed to Paul Revere, who supposedly alerted his fellow Americans to British troop movements during the American Revolution. Both references are thus uttered from the New World — Latin America and North America, respectively — and connect the Argentinian position with a wider American refusal of British imperialism.
²⁵ Boaventura de Sousa Santos, 'Between Prospero and Caliban: Colonialism, Postcolonialism and Inter-Identity', *Luso-Brazilian Review*, 39.2 (2002), 9–43 (p. 9).
²⁶ Santos, 'Between Prospero and Caliban', p. 11.

writer's feelings for a sensuous and fecund natural world. Take the following excerpt, which presents, in rich detail, Gordon Square, in the Bloomsbury area of London:

> Entra-se por um portão cruzado como o dum presídio. Logo à entrada, os arbustos baixos obrigam-nos a baixar a cerviz como em câmara de infanta. No chão há sempre um casal de melros, mais gordos se arrufados de frio, ele negro com o seu vivo bico lacado, ela caseira, parda. Dão as alegrias, não fogem muito, por migalhas e vício saltarico. E então — aquele espaço abre-se dentro do seu casco de plátanos, gracioso e parado como um momento perfeito o fica na memória. Cada árvore está pensada para estar ali na sua mudança cíclica de cores e volumes [...] Por esse mistério dos solos ou dos amores desta terra, havia ainda nos galhos botões grossos como pálpebras fechadas, sob a neve. Vi um cristal de gelo pender duma que agonizava num vermelho quase negro, queimada e tenaz.
>
> [You enter through a crossed-bar gate, like in a prison. Right by the entrance, the low bushes force us to bend our necks as in a princess's chamber. On the ground there's always a pair of blackbirds, fatter if swollen from being cold, the male black with its bright lacquered beak, the female homely, plain. They give joy, and do not run away much, on account of the crumbs and their hopping habit. And then — that space opens up inside its sycamore shell, graceful and still as a perfect moment that remains in memory. Each tree has been designed to be there in its cyclical change of colours and volumes [...] Due to that mystery of the soils or the lovers in this land, in the branches there were still buds as thick as closed eyelids, underneath the snow. I saw an icicle hanging down from one tree in the throws of agony, whose red hue was almost black, burnt and tenacious.][27]

As the above citation exemplifies, MVC revels in sensorial, sensuous and lush descriptions of parks, romantic gardens and the countryside; to sum up, 'uma natureza pujante *e controlada* e feita a medidas de *promeneur solitaire*, a coberto' [a thriving *and controlled* nature, made to measure for the *promeneur solitaire*, sheltered].[28] If this interest in a controlled nature is perceived as a typically British trait, it also minimizes national differences, since the writer recognizes that same love within herself; initially saying: 'Não é para mim este país' [This country is not for me], she confesses shortly after: 'Traí-me porém na entrega à cena verde' [However, I betrayed myself in my surrender to the green landscape].[29] In addition, there is an explicitly stated rapport between the Portuguese writer's love of a British 'manufactured landscape' and her way of interlacing the text with the threads of the real and the imagined, the physical and the literary worlds, in what is ultimately regarded as a preference for pretence:

---

[27] Costa, *Mapa*, p. 138.
[28] Costa, *Mapa*, p. 16. This quote contains a reference to Jean-Jacques Rousseau, whose unfinished book is precisely entitled *Les Rêveries du promeneur solitaire*.
[29] Costa, *Mapa*, p. 16.

> As mesmas preferências que me alhearam os ledores de prosas abertas e desornadas, me arredam aqui no prazer de descrever [...] o enunciador enuncia aqui o seu prazer, aqui sim síntono com o prazer do autóctone que o gere — a falsa naturalidade do parque e prado desanuviado de campónios, o (bom) gosto romântico.
>
> [The same preferences that alienated the reader of open and plain prose from me, turn me here to the pleasure of describing [...] the enunciator enunciates here her pleasure, here indeed in harmony with the native pleasure that generates it — the false naturalness of the park and meadow clear of peasants, the (good) romantic taste.][30]

Going back to the description of Gordon Square, it is also an example of how rich *O mapa cor de rosa* is in references to the changing of seasons and weather phenomena that mark the passing of time and remind us that life, beings and places entail movement and transformation. On the other hand, the text too draws attention to cyclical time and, as such, to change understood as permanent renovation, a perspective that is similarly conveyed by the natural world.

In its intertwining of linear and national history, on the one hand, and cyclical, natural and fertile events, on the other, *O mapa cor de rosa* echoes one of Julia Kristeva's most famous essays — 'Women's Time' (1979) — published some years before MVC's *crónicas* from London. Emily Apter's summary of Kristeva's understanding of female subjectivity and its relation to time is an operative one in the context of the argument I am putting forward:

> Kristeva argues that female subjectivity is divided between cyclical, natural time (repetition, gestation, the biological clock) and monumental time (eternity, myths of the resurrection, the cult of maternity). These modalities are set off against the time of linear history (defined by project, teleology, progression, *Bildung*) and its territorial correlatives (national spatial imaginaries, supranational cultural and religious memory).[31]

For Kristeva, then, female subjectivity becomes a problem with respect to the time of history, as indeed to national identity, due to those two types of temporality (cyclical and monumental) in which it seems to exist and which ascribe to it a marginal position in the socio-symbolic system.[32]

---

[30] See 'neste país fabricante de paisagem' [in this country, manufacturer of landscape]. Costa, *Mapa*, p. 17; idem.
[31] Emily Apter. '"Women's Time" in Theory', *Differences: A Journal of Feminist Cultural Studies*, 21.1 (2010), 1–18 (p. 3).
[32] Julia Kristeva, 'Women's Time', *Signs*, 7.1 (1981), 13–35 (p. 17). Despite referring to female subjectivity, Kristeva's analysis does not offer an essentialist but rather a corporeal and positional view of gender difference as her emphasis is on the specificity of the female role in society and the symbolic order: 'Sexual difference — which is at once biological, physiological, and relative to reproduction — is translated by and translates a difference in the relationship of subjects to the symbolic contract which *is* the social contract: a difference, then, in the relationship to power, language, and meaning'. Kristeva, 'Women's Time', p. 19.

Her argument is then constructed upon three generations of feminists (understood more as signifying than chronological spaces): the first fought to move women from their marginal position and inscribe them in historical, linear time, which is also the time of rationality and linguistic coherence; the second situated itself within cyclical and monumental temporality in order to assert sexual difference and 'give a language to the intra-subjective and corporeal experiences left mute by culture in the past';[33] and the third, advocated by Kristeva herself, seeks to reconcile the historical and cyclical/monumental modes, both participating in historical time and rejecting its subjective limitation, and ultimately undermining the notion of a fixed, singular identity: 'What can "identity", even "sexual identity", mean in a new theoretical and scientific space where the very notion of identity is challenged?', she concludes in 'Women's Time'.[34] In the context of this third generation, Kristeva addresses aesthetic practices that counterbalance and demystify 'the *community* of language as a universal and unifying tool', in order to bring out 'the singularity of each person' and 'the multiplicity of every person's possible identification'.[35] Such practices, which seem far from the dominant value of rationality and closer to the semiotic level of language, are further described by Apter as posed against epic time and, as such, contrary to the male-authored tradition of the historical novel, in which epic time is conveyed through watershed dates such as wars and revolutions.[36]

In light of Kristeva's radical proposition, could *O mapa cor de rosa* be one example of such transgressive aesthetic practices? While MVC's writing displays several watershed dates (the Falklands conflict, the Polish upheaval, etc.), anchoring the text in epic time, linear history and national imaginaries, these dates coexist with monumental and cyclical time, as well as with a correlated fecund body (and thus a liminal, hybrid and ultimately maternal one), which, in the following example, is conveyed through the metaphor of the mother-earth: 'A terra, que formava lama nos trilhos cheios de traças de animais de cascos ou pata tripartida, galinholas, faisão bravo, perdizes, era de um castanho profundo, quase negro, como o íntimo de um corpo' [The soil, which formed mud in the tracks full of traces of hoofed or tripartite-foot animals, woodcocks, wild pheasant, partridges, was of a deep brown, almost black, like the intimacy of a body].[37] In addition, the workings of 'women's time' are further exposed in the sensuous, rhythmic and fluid nature of the text itself, which disrupts the rationalist/phallocentric paradigm by producing a discourse closer to the body and emotions and bringing to the surface of the text that which has been repressed by the social contract.[38]

---

[33] Kristeva, 'Women's Time', p. 19.
[34] Kristeva, 'Women's Time', p. 34.
[35] Kristeva, 'Women's Time', p. 35.
[36] Apter, '"Women's Time" in Theory', p. 4.
[37] Costa, *Mapa*, p. 68.
[38] See Kristeva, 'Women's Time', pp. 24–25.

If, as I have been suggesting, *O mapa cor de rosa* unravels 'women's time', most notably in those moments when the writer is enraptured by nature, then it may also reveal a diasporic feminine. Such literary entanglement of the feminine and the diasporic conditions represents not only what Avtar Brah calls *the diasporic space*, that is, an interstitial location where 'boundaries of inclusion and exclusion, of belonging and otherness, of "us" and "them" are contested', but also a female subject position that questions linear history and clear cartographic outlines, favouring instead processes of dissemination and transitive, multivocal and plural forms of existence and representation.[39]

In this context, the title of MVC's book acquires a further meaning, as gender connotations are added to its more obviously political and national ones. Suggesting such connotations in the initial pages of the book, the writer comments on her chosen title, connecting it to an earlier text, *Da rosa fixa* (1978), 'De que o título, para quem me conhece os fervores *da rosa*, dá sinal' [Whose title, for those who know my devotion *to the rose*, signals].[40] According to Maria Irene Ramalho, in *Da rosa fixa* 'The rose remains fixed in the middle, at the core where the seeds of life are. So this book is also about the womb-as-origin, about the woman, the mother, the giving birth, the bringing forth'.[41] In *Da rosa fixa* and *O mapa cor de rosa*, the rose is, therefore, a female symbol.

Migration and the subsequent exposure to different geographical, cultural and social realities — in short, to otherness — presented MVC with the necessary and safe distance to revisit and re-assess her subjective and cultural identity. To a certain extent writing becomes a pretext to look back upon oneself, both as an individual and as a nation. Such a purpose is already contained in one of the book's epigraphs, an excerpt of a poem by José Carlos Ary dos Santos, 'Fado do campo grande': 'Aqui no meu país | por mais que a minha ausência doa | é que eu sei que a raiz de mim | está em Lisboa' [Here in my country | no matter how much my absence hurts | I know that the root of myself | is in Lisbon].[42] These verses are rehearsed by MVC in one of her letters: 'Em Londres, em duas línguas, isso digo, muito mais plenamente portuguesa' [In London, in two languages and, I must say, much more completely Portuguese].[43] *O mapa cor de rosa*, not unlike Ary dos Santos's poem, thus seems to propose that losing yourself or your *roots* through *routes* and dislocation is also finding yourself, even if through a violent process of *carência* [lack].[44] This self-reflexive process

[39] Avtar Brah, *Cartographies of Diaspora: Contesting Identities* (London: Routledge, 1996), p. 208.
[40] Costa, *Mapa*, p. 18.
[41] Maria Irene Ramalho, '*Da Rosa Fixa* by Maria Velho da Costa', *World Literature Today*, 54.1 (1980), 85–86 (p. 85).
[42] Costa, *Mapa*, p. 9. The other epigraph included in *O mapa cor de rosa* is by Gastão Cruz and is an excerpt of a poem with references to London. Like MVC, Gastão Cruz was a Portuguese lecturer at King's College London in the 1980s (1980–86).
[43] Costa, *Mapa*, p. 196.
[44] 'Estar longe do chão onde se botou raízes e onde se afinaram as folhas, é violência, é carência' [Being far from the ground where one has laid roots and where the leaves are refined, is violence, is lack]. Costa, *Mapa*, p. 144.

is recurrently suggested in the letters, as in the following one, which discusses different writing styles: 'da eficácia da desfaçatez *naturalista* anglo-saxónica apercebo-me, mais, da pedanteria *cultista* nacional' [from the effectiveness of the Anglo-Saxon *naturalist* impudence I become more aware of the national *cultivated* pedantry].[45]

In her essay 'Art and the Conditions of Exile: Men/Women, Emigration/ Expatriation' Linda Nochlin concludes that the dislocation experienced by artists creates a fertile opportunity for 'new perceptions of place and, in some cases, of the relationship between places', as well as 'personal transformation, which may take the form of "rewriting" the self'.[46] A similar kind of subjective process is central to *O mapa cor de rosa*, which exhibits a productive tension between self and other, location and dislocation: 'Creio-me num fim de uma passagem e de uma concessão de estada, com alguma rebelião a trabalhar-me nesta diferença' [I believe myself to be at the end of a passage and a concession to stay, with some rebellion working its effects on me at this difference].[47] Not only does migration expose identity as something permeable and in transit, but also it gives the territorial and national imaginaries the consistency of an *imagined place*, that is, a place that, according to Ernst Van Alphen, is made of real and imaginary existence and where past and present, here and there, coexist.[48] MVC's migrant letters address British and Portuguese national identities in those very same terms: 'Sempre amei a Inglaterra. Se é que se pode amar outro país, ou até o próprio, sempre projeção tão mais ou menos belamente inventada de um reconhecido' [I have always loved England. That is, if one can love another country, or even one's own, always a projection more or less beautifully invented of something recognizable].[49]

This literary representation of identities in transit and imagined places is matched by the textual form adopted in *O mapa cor de rosa*. Its narrative voice is framed by the characteristics of the chronicle and the epistolary genres, both of which refer to daily events. Nevertheless, the texts that make up this book are seldom entirely factual, as often dreams (a theme within the book itself and one that becomes the focus of scrutiny in the letter entitled 'Já aqui estive' [I have been here]) and fictional elements blend with reality and the stream of an alert consciousness, whose voice, feelings and thoughts flood the text whilst overcoming the distance separating the recipient from the sender of the letters.[50] The intended effects of this mingling of real and

---

[45] Costa, *Mapa*, p. 231.
[46] Linda Nochlin, 'Art and the Conditions of Exile: Men/Women, Emigration/Expatriation', in *Exile and Creativity: Signposts, Travellers, Outsiders, Backward Glances*, ed. by Susan Rubin Suleiman (Durham, NC: Duke University Press, 1998), pp. 37–58 (p. 38).
[47] Costa, *Mapa*, p. 17.
[48] Ernst Van Alphen, 'Imagined Homelands: Re-Mapping Cultural Identity', in *Mobilizing Place: Placing Mobility: The Politics of Representation in a Globalized World*, ed. by Ginette Verstraete and Tim Cresswell (Amsterdam: Rodopi, 2002), pp. 53–70 (p. 67).
[49] Costa, *Mapa*, p. 18.
[50] Most of these characteristics are already found in the *crónica* genre, whose status is situated between journalism and literature.

imaginary journeys are 'acordar a coisa onírica' [awake the oneiric thing], dissolving 'fronteiras de vida e obra e géneros' [boundaries of life and work and genres].[51] This disruption of boundaries is one of the ways of granting *O mapa cor de rosa* the status of unstable written object. The texts turn into literary *mongrels* that were first published as *crónicas* only to become letters and even a diary, as MVC suggests in a section entitled 'Querido Diário' [Dear Diary]: 'Estou hoje um pouco espavorida das escritas e em *mal de crónica*, assim que tenho licenças, de diário' [Today I am a bit anxious about writing and with a *chronicle block*, so I am entitled to write a diary].[52] In so doing, the book not only provides the reader with the account of a Portuguese migrant's experience in England at a time when there was a renewed social and political interest in the relationship between Portugal and its European other, but it also reveals a self-analytical author concerned with the plurality of her own identitarian terms (as a Portuguese, a migrant and a writer). In other words, the malleability and liminality of the form mirrors the subject in transit that the writer seeks to represent.

Similarly to other migrant narratives, *O mapa cor de rosa* interweaves simultaneous dimensions and different times or spaces, through which the text becomes a Borgesian labyrinth, an unstable literary space with a meandering nature and a *contrapuntal voice*, an expression I borrow from Edward Said, who describes those in exile as sharing a plural, contrapuntal vision: 'Most people are principally aware of one culture, one setting, one home; exiles are aware of at least two, and this plurality of vision gives rise to an awareness of simultaneous dimensions, an awareness that — to borrow a phrase from music — is *contrapuntal*'.[53]

A letter entitled 'Square Tolstoi, Gordon Square, Eighth Square' is particularly demonstrative of this process: it starts with a quotation from Lewis Carroll's *Through the Looking Glass and what Alice Found There*, followed by a reference to the book *Square Tolstoi* (1981), by Nuno Bragança (himself another consummate producer of experimental fiction partially developed within the context of a diasporic existence), which then leads to a description of Gordon Square, in the Bloomsbury area of London, and then to Virginia Woolf (a member of the Bloomsbury group who lived in Gordon Square), then back to Nuno Bragança and, finally, back full-circle, to Carroll's Alice.[54] The text overlaps the three locations/squares mentioned in its title — Bragança's Square Tolstoi, Woolf's Gordon Square and Alice's Eighth Square (an imaginary place found in *Alice's Adventures in Wonderland*). Each of these spaces is linked to

---

[51] Costa, *Mapa*, p. 223.
[52] Costa, *Mapa*, p. 81.
[53] Edward Said, 'Reflections on Exile', in *Reflections on Exile and Other Essays* (Cambridge, MA: Harvard University Press, 2000), pp. 173–86 (p. 186). See also Mimi Sheller and John Urry, 'The New Mobilities Paradigm', *Environment and Planning A*, 38 (2006), 207–26.
[54] See an earlier letter, which seems to contain a warning about the circular nature of the book: 'Fecha o círculo'. Costa, *Mapa*, p. 85. See also Maria Irene Ramalho's article in this issue for an insightful discussion of the relationship between Maria Velho da Costa's writing and Carroll's fiction.

specific historical and national sites, but all are embedded in the literary realm, which is, in itself, a central theme in MVC's letters from London. It is therefore literature, along with the narrator's voice, that holds the text together and this is further suggested by Zarate's accompanying drawing for this particular section of the book: depicting Woolf and MVC against each other in Gordon Square, it visually represents the disturbance of linear history and points to the text's intertextual nature, its dialogic and plural vision.

MVC embraces the intrusion of foreign literary elements into her own writing, allowing them to dialogue with each other and overcome barriers of genre, time and space: 'há dias em que nos parece que escrevemos todos uns para os outros, uma feira franca' [there are days in which we all seem to write for each other, an open market];[55] she ruminates on this literary otherness so that it can be incorporated: 'Buscar salvar, *saudar*, alguém que está longe dentro da cabeça, pátria ou ente [...] Ler o Outro, até ao mal. Até ao mal ser comum' [To attempt to salvage, *greet*, someone who is far inside your head, homeland or being [...] To read the Other to the rotten core. Until that core is common].[56] Going back to Carroll, Bragança and Woolf, these were highly experimental, innovative writers, the authors of texts in which dreams, fiction, autobiography and subjective consciousness often coalesce. They are particularly stimulating and inspiring references for MVC's own work, which justifies the special attention they are granted in the letters. The allusion to Lewis Carroll's heroine may even function as a key to enter *O mapa cor de rosa*, in which MVC, qua Alice, explores a strange world, unknown to herself, and sets off on a meandering, sometimes dream-like journey, often wandering from the rational, logical, beaten-track:

> Esta crónica está a sair meândrica como a ria do Nilo, ou pelo menos a da ria de Aveiro — em pequena — mas parece que meândrica, quer dizer, às voltas e voltinhas, costuma ser a minha prosa, e ainda por cima um pouco para nada, isto é para não dizer muito [...] Perdi-me.
>
> [This chronicle is turning out to be as meandering as the Nile, or at least as the Ria of Aveiro — only smaller — but it seems that meandering means twisting and turning, just like my prose usually does, and to make matters worse for nothing much, that is, for not saying that much [...] I lost my train of thought.][57]

Paradoxically, though, the construction of the text as contrapuntal, disruptive and in transit does not place *O mapa cor de rosa* further away but rather closer to life, inasmuch as its words and images 'não *adoçam* mas antes *atiçam* o vivido' [do not *sweeten* but rather *stir up* what is lived].[58] The text and the diasporic existence prompting its creation lead the writer to the conclusion that

---

[55] Costa, *Mapa*, p. 86.
[56] Costa, *Mapa*, pp. 139–40.
[57] Costa, *Mapa*, p. 81.
[58] Costa, *Mapa*, p. 210.

life, and by implication identity, 'é mesmo assim, descosida, feita de farrapos muito difíceis de consertar em peça unida' [is just like that, unstitched, made of rags very difficult to sew up into a single garment].[59] The dream-like journey is then ultimately one of reconnaissance — of others and of oneself.

Not only does *O mapa cor de rosa* assimilate (sometimes anthropophagously) a wide range of writers and texts, it also amalgamates at least two languages.[60] In so doing, it questions linguistic purity, putting in check monolingualism's message of integrity, indivisibility, sovereignty and transposability, and replacing it by processes of linguistic dissemination.[61] Multilingualism is illustrated when MVC refers to her work as a Portuguese lecturer at King's College London, as the writer admits to communicating with her students in a hybrid language, a lingua franca: 'começando a frase numa língua e acabando na outra, que é assim que faço se quero que me entendam' [beginning the sentence in one language and ending it in the other, which is how I do it when I want to be understood].[62] Nevertheless, it acquires a sharper thematic focus in 'Pimlico ou a língua verdadeira' [Pimlico or the real language], a letter that refers to MVC's first lesson to the children of Portuguese migrants: 'a língua, força tão frágil que uma geração basta para a dissolver na *caca das outras*. Ou tão envergonhada. E mista, o que não é muito grave, *a shop, uma pound, a insurança social, os holidays* [...] Tantas línguas' [the mother-tongue, a force so fragile that a generation is enough to dissolve it in *the poo of other languages*. Or so embarrassed. And mixed, which is not particularly serious, *a shop, uma pound, a insurança social, os holidays* [...] So many languages].[63] The linguistic hybridism presented here denotes a practice of dis-location that endows languages with a hyphenated status, particularly when these are placed between roots and routes. It is a practice that also contaminates the writing of *O mapa cor de rosa*, where English words and expressions erupt on the surface of the Portuguese text, transgressing its apparent monolingualism. In his reading of Kafka's relation to mono- and multilingualism, David Gramling describes these 'utterances from the elsewheres of languages' as 'nascent fissures in the myth of monolingualism', an image that could also describe MVC's writing.[64] Gramling's conclusion on Kafka's texts is therefore fitting to my own analysis of *O mapa cor de rosa*:

> They endeavor to perform — not describe — the intrusion of the multi-lingual world into the mythic monolingual significations of literature, reminding us, again and again what is becoming of — and unbecoming in — language under the episteme of monolingualism.[65]

---

[59] Costa, *Mapa*, p. 82.
[60] *O mapa cor de rosa* is a patchwork of references — mostly to writers, but also to film directors.
[61] See David Gramling, 'Getting up onto Monolingualism: Barthes, Kafka, Myth', *Thamyris/Intersecting*, 28 (2014), 15–38 (p. 34), discussed further on in this article.
[62] Costa, *Mapa*, p. 247; see also Costa, *Mapa*, p. 179.
[63] Costa, *Mapa*, p. 159.
[64] Grambling, 'Getting up', p. 35.
[65] Ibid.

In her last letter from London MVC writes: 'a língua é uma passagem para um outro modo de ser e estar' [language is a passage to another mode of being and being-in-the-world].[66] Engendering a literary space for multilingual discourse and linguistic exchange, *O mapa cor de rosa* presents a subject in transit whose cartographic drawings suggest unstable national and cultural identities. It is true that writing had already been described in an earlier text as a de-territorializing phenomenon: 'Porque se escreve sempre em terra alheia, em língua que não é mãe, assim de entre amante e madrasta' [Because one always writes in an alien land, in a language that is not a mother but kind of a mix between a lover and a stepmother];[67] but MVC is well aware that the inherently intertextual, palimpsestic and dialogic nature of writing is exacerbated by her migrant experience, as she embraces the resulting multilingual openness to the other:

> Há quem diga que é mau para o escritor estar longe da pátria. Não sei. Às vezes vai-se pela rua, ao fim de uns meses da ausência dentro de outra língua, e dá-se pelo facto de que aquele palrar íntimo [...] está — pelo menos — invadido, paralingue. Por mim, devo dizer-lhes que não me assusta muito, esse babel achado na mente.

> [Some people say it's bad for the writer to be far from her homeland. I don't know. Sometimes one is going down the street, after some months of absence inside another language, and one realizes that that intimate chatter [...] has been — at least — invaded, paralingual. Personally, I must say that it does not scare me that much, that babel found in the mind.][68]

Certainly, even though a disruptive mongrelization defines to a large extent MVC's *oeuvre* as a whole, the process of dislocation at the heart of *O mapa cor de rosa* strongly contributed to the reconstruction of writing and the rewriting of the self.[69]

MVC concludes her last letter from London with these words: 'Não é a minha cidade, mas dificilmente adoptaria outra para uma tão íntima passagem de estar' [It is not my city, but I would hardly adopt another one for such an intimate passage of being-in-the-world].[70] It seems that the years she spent in London exposed her to moments of being (to paraphrase Woolf), that is, moments of intense and almost intuitive perception that reveal the self in her condition of 'not being here and no longer being there'.[71] As a result, MVC's writing

---

[66] Costa, *Mapa*, pp. 248–49.
[67] Costa, *Mapa*, p. 139.
[68] Costa, *Mapa*, pp. 71–72.
[69] Coutinho, 'Outras cartas', p. 65; See also Nochlin, 'Art and the Conditions', p. 38.
[70] Costa, *Mapa*, p. 249.
[71] 'apercebo-me que não estou aqui, apercebo-me que já não estou lá' [I realize I am not here, I realize I am no longer there]. Costa, *Mapa*, p. 224. See Virginia Woolf, 'A Sketch from the Past', in *Moments of Being: Autobiographical Writings*, ed. by Jeanne Schulkind and Hermione Lee (London: Pimlico, 2002), pp. 78–160, where she refers to moments of being. See also Rui Miguel Mesquita, *A situação e a substância: cinco ensaios sobre a ficção de Virginia Woolf e de Maria Velho da Costa* (Porto: Edições Afrontamento / Instituto de Literatura Comparada Margarida Losa, 2016) for a comparative discussion of Virginia Woolf's and Maria Velho da Costa's writing.

during her London period meditates upon an experience of dislocation and addresses an existential hybridity made clearer through physical, cultural and literary journeys. Contrary to the original Mapa Cor de Rosa, which outlined Portuguese hegemonic dreams and delineated with geographic precision African possessions, MVC's rose-coloured map is the product of an unstable cartographic process that, despite mapping subjective, national, literary and linguistic boundaries, ultimately represents these very same boundaries as complex porous zones of connection and inter-relation between self and other.

Éukié: Maria Velho da Costa's Alice and the Absurd

Maria Irene Ramalho

Universidade de Coimbra

Aprender o absurdo. A coisa mais natural. — *O livro do meio*, p. 386

It is often said that Maria Velho da Costa's books appear to be written in a foreign language. Perhaps not in Proust's sense that 'Les beaux livres sont écrits dans une sorte de langue étrangère', though I would subscribe to it as regards Maria Velho da Costa.[1] No wonder. More than transnational, Maria Velho da Costa is a cosmopolitan writer. She is widely read and moves easily among many different languages and cultures; her writing is peppered with foreign words and adaptations of striking foreign phrases or passages; her epigraphs are often taken from works written in languages other than Portuguese; and she even resorts frequently to comically fake translations with absurdist purposes. Maria Velho da Costa's handling of the absurd is close to Lewis Carroll's, but while the author of the *Alice* books uses the absurd comically to depict the incongruities of Victorian society, Maria Velho da Costa uses the absurd to denounce the unfairness and pretentiousness of Portuguese society, before and after the Carnation Revolution. The absurd has been part of Maria Velho da Costa's art of fiction since the very beginning of her career.

Early on in *Maina Mendes*, the novel, Maina Mendes, the character, is said to go through life honouring 'the right to the absurd', hers and everybody else's.[2] The scene, close to an initiation rite, is worth revisiting. Maina Mendes, who in the previous chapter had learned an obscene gesture from a street boy she watched from the window of her room, is now in the kitchen with Hortelinda, the family's maid. Maina Mendes is enjoying the rich domesticity of the scene, as Hortelinda grudgingly sweats over the laborious cooking she has been ordered to do. The somewhat cryptic narrative beautifully conveys the contrast between the world of the masters and the world of the servants, a

---

[1] Marcel Proust, *Contre Sainte-Beuve* (Paris: Gallimard, 1954) 361: 'Les beaux livres sont écrits dans une sorte de langue étrangère. Sous chaque mot chacun de nous met son sens ou du moins son image qui est souvent un contresens. Mais dans les beaux livres, tous les contresens qu'on fait sont beaux' [Beautiful books are written in a kind of foreign language. To each word each one of us gives his or her sense, or at the very least image, which is often a non-sense. But in beautiful books all non-senses forged are beautiful].

[2] Maria Velho da Costa, *Maina Mendes* (Lisbon: Moraes, 1969), p. 26. Pages included in the text from now on.

contrast that Maina Mendes is beginning to perceive. The child, fully realizing she is transgressing, clearly enjoys the vibrant sights, strong smells, pungent tastes, and vernacular sounds of Hortelinda's world, which contrast with the cold, sugary and repressive sluggishness of the world in which her mother wants to bring her up. Particularly important in Maina Mendes's country-folk instruction are the Portuguese proverbs and vulgar songs to which Hortelinda resorts generously to mask her impotence against her oppressed condition. The proverb 'Albarde-se o burro à vontade do dono' [do as the master wants (no matter what)] helps her to fulfil her hardest chores; as does the nonsensical but patently scatological and bawdy rhyme about a naughty parish priest and what he does in the sacristy to his so-called sisters. Maina Mendes loves to repeat the absurd sounds she knows are forbiddingly coarse because Hortelinda, though relishing them, strives to keep them from her mistress's hearing. It is in this context — two worlds so close together and so absurdly sundered apart — that Maina Mendes learns how to respect the absurd: 'Por toda a vida Maina Mendes sagraria assim, dessa crua distância, o direito ao absurdo dos demais e seu' [During her entire life Maina Mendes would thus consecrate, from that crude distance, her and others' right to the absurd] (pp. 24–26). Early on in her career, we observe, Maria Velho da Costa is already showing how congenial to her Lewis Carroll's nonsense would be.

The concept of the absurd crops up again later in *Maina Mendes* in the voice of Maina's son, Fernando (p. 177). Unlike his mother, Fernando surrenders to the absurd and ends up committing suicide (p. 278). In contrast, and not unlike her first major character, Maria Velho da Costa thrives on the absurd, often playing on the affinities of the absurd with nonsense and paradox. The writer's handling of the absurd has striking affinities with Lewis Carroll's serious nonsense. A critic once spoke of Carroll's *Alice* books as 'the most enchanting nonsense in the English language'.[3] I prefer to call it *serious* nonsense because I consider it a very serious enterprise to display the power of language to speak and unspeak at the same time, to speak us and speak for us while making us believe that we are the ones speaking, or, as such a self-conscious writer as Maria Velho da Costa puts it in great awe: 'Como se fôssemos nós que nos escrevêssemos' [As if we were the ones writing ourselves].[4]

I have pointed out elsewhere, without elaborating on the topic, the many allusions to the *Alice* books to be found in several of Maria Velho da Costa's novels.[5] In *Maina Mendes*, published in 1969, there seems to be no such explicit

---

[3] See Woollcott's introduction to Lewis Carroll, *The Complete Works*, intro. by Alexander Woollcott (New York: Vintage Books, 1976), p. 5.
[4] Maria Velho da Costa, *O mapa cor de rosa*, illustr. by Oscar Zarate (Lisbon: Dom Quixote, 1984), p. 141.
[5] See M. Irene Ramalho Santos, 'Gender, Species and Coloniality in Maria Velho da Costa', in *Gender, Empire, and Postcolony: Luso-Afro-Brazilian Intersections*, ed. by Hilary Owen and Anna M. Klobucka (New York: Palgrave Macmillan, 2014), pp. 191–201; also a slightly longer Portuguese version in Maria Irene Ramalho, 'A violência da cultura: sexo, espécie e colonialidade em Maria Velho da Costa', in *Representações da violência*, ed. by António Sousa Ribeiro (Coimbra: Almedina, 2013), pp. 51–63.

allusion. However, the novel does tell the story of a young girl surviving in a world of absurdities, some of them of her own making, and relinquishing speech 'para não ser incomodada' [to avoid being bothered], as a surrogate author metaleptically explains in a later novel.[6] In *Myra*, the author's latest novel (2008) and another story of a young girl surrounded by absurdities, some of which are also of her own making, there are not only explicit but also oblique allusions to the *Alice* books, such as significant language distortions with parodic effects, or animals satirically commenting on the seemingly absurd actions of their human masters. *Myra*'s eponymous heroine gains in being compared (and contrasted) with Maina Mendes: while Maina Mendes's major weapon of survival is self-imposed muteness, Myra's is fierce vocalism. As if, and I am paraphrasing the author elsewhere, all speech were compensatory of some silence.[7]

No wonder Maria Velho da Costa's handling of language should remind us of Lewis Carroll. Like him, she excels in pushing language inventively to its nonsensical and paradoxical limits. As I write this, I have in mind Gilles Deleuze's philosophical reflections on sense, nonsense, and paradox in *Logique du sens* (1969).[8] Deleuze's reflections are heavily inspired by Lewis Carroll's writings, both Carroll's fiction and Charles L. Dodgson's science, though fiction seems to arouse Deleuze's philosophical imagination in a far more productive way than science. Like so many other philosophers, Deleuze always finds in poets the most fertile soil for his philosophical reflections, particularly on the complex problem of language. *Et pour cause*. Are not poets the most sophisticated deconstructors and demythifiers of language? In *Logique du sens*, poets provide the philosopher with the finest sense for the nonsense and paradoxes of language, names, naming, renaming, and calling. Poets like Valéry, Mallarmé or Borges, alongside Lewis Carroll, provide sense to Deleuze. In *The Logic of Sense* he explores many forms of paradox in the Western philosophical tradition, including a paradox he calls 'the paradox of Lewis Carroll' (pp. 41–43; 28–30). This is when he comments on the paradox of regress, or of indefinite proliferation, performed by the White Knight in Chapter VIII of *Through the Looking Glass and what Alice Found There* (1871). The White Knight tells Alice the name of a song he is about to sing to her by going over an absurd, successive proliferation of names, revealing what each successive name is called, and explaining what *calling the thing names* does to the *sense of the thing*. In the case in point, *the thing* is the White Knight's farewell song to Alice. The many

---

[6] Maria Velho da Costa, *Missa in albis* (Lisbon: Dom Quixote, 1988), p. 377. Asked what she is writing, a writer-character in the novel replies: 'a história de uma menina que se faz muda para não ser incomodada' [the story of a little girl who pretends to be dumb to avoid being bothered].

[7] 'Toda, toda a escrita é compensatória de um silêncio' [All, all writing compensates for silence]; Maria Velho da Costa, *O mapa cor de rosa*, p. 16.

[8] Gilles Deleuze, *Logique du sens* (Paris: Minuit, 1969); *The Logic of Sense*, trans. by Mark Lester with Charles Stivale, ed. by Constantin V. Boundes (New York: Columbia University Press, 1990). Pages included in the text from now on, original followed by translation.

different names the eponymous heroine of *Myra* keeps calling herself and her dog in Maria Velho da Costa's latest novel come to mind. Only when her beloved Gabriel Orlando is dying does Myra reach the true sense of herself by telling him at last that her real name is Myra, and the dog's name is Rambo/Rimbaud. Ironically, in the self-intertextuality of Maria Velho da Costa's novels, the 'proliferation of names' had already been used by Orlando himself in *Irene ou o contrato social* (2000).[9]

The simplest example of paradox, and the most relevant for my purposes here, is the play on words, or pun: it is a paradox because it yields more than one sense at the same time and does not let you dismiss any one of them. Both, or all of them, make sense, which can be terribly confusing. As when a dumbfounded Alice unwittingly listens to the mouse's sad tale in Chapter III of *Alice's Adventures in Wonderland* (1865) as a long, meandering tail. The perplexing absurdity of the tale/tail episode results from the two homophone words (as also, in the same episode, Alice's confusion between 'not' [negative] and 'knot' [tie]), which reminds us that poetry is precisely, as eighteenth-century British poet, Christopher Smart, once put it, 'sound reasoning' — or sense-making sound.[10] Or, I would dare to say, sense-making *nonsense sound*. At some point during the maddening dialogue between Alice and the Duchess in Chapter IX, one of the Duchess's 'morals' turns out to be a parody of an English proverb — 'Take care of the sense, and the sounds will take care of themselves.'[11] Such a parody, as Deleuze remarks, ends up suggesting a close link between the logic of sense and 'ethics, morals or morality' (pp. 44; 31); but what the philosopher fails to make explicit is that the logical link is *poetry* itself as *sound reasoning*. Maria Velho da Costa's parodic rewritings or mistranslations of proverbs, famous names and titles or well-known lines of poetry, often in unexpected juxtapositions, appear galore throughout her fiction, with puns and absurd word-play mercilessly highlighting the many absurd aspects of culture at large. A particularly impudent example in *Casas pardas* is when the aspiring writer Elisa, as she listens to the tremulous, mellow sounds of The Platters' 'Only You', and as if striving for the right phrase, 'translates' Shakespeare into 'a shaking pear' — or 'pera tremente' (p. 65).[12] The impudent 'translation' will be later repeated in *Irene ou o contrato social* (p. 164), a perfect homage to the prince of the English language and master of puns. It is the sounds of language that construct the sense of reality in the sounds of the poem-as-a-heterocosm, as M. H. Abrams taught us many years ago.[13] By playing with the abyss between word

---

[9] Maria Velho da Costa, *Irene ou o contrato social* (Lisbon: Dom Quixote, 2000), pp. 111–21. Page numbers included in text from now on.
[10] 'Sound reasoning' is Christopher Smart's brilliant definition of poetry. See *Jubilate Agno*, ed. by W. H. Bond (Westport, CT: Greenwood Press, 1966), pp. 106–08.
[11] The parodied English proverb is 'Take care of the pennies, and the pounds will take care of themselves'. The other 'morals' are all well-known proverbs.
[12] '[...] as coisas que Eu já vi e não sei dizer, tios Guilhermes, shakes pear, pera tremente e tel quel, do platter [...]'.
[13] For the poem as a second nature or a heterocosm, see Meyer Howard Abrams, *The Mirror and the*

and thing, poetry problematizes what we usually call linguistic communication, and calls reference into question, often to such extreme performances as Carroll's nonreferential nonsense in 'Jabberwocky.'

Like Carroll, or perhaps I should add, like any other strong poet, Maria Velho da Costa, who has often fiercely denied being a writer of poetry [meaning verse],[14] consciously depends on the polysemy and opaqueness of language for her most striking creative and subversive moments. Consider her musings on the word 'cravo' [carnation], the red flower-symbol of the bloodless Portuguese Revolution of April 1974. In a brief introduction to the collection of this title, she explains that she doesn't even like the flower, which seems too aggressively phallic to her, at the same time that she shows great fascination with all the meanings and sensations evoked by the Portuguese word 'cravo' itself: the beautiful red flower, of course, but also the aggressive spike, the uglifying wart, the musical harpsichord, and the spicy clove.[15] *Cravo* was published in 1976: how many contradictory and potentially absurd meanings does Maria Velho da Costa invite us to hear in the iconic phrase 'A Revolução dos Cravos' only two years after the April revolution? The linguistic perplexities of Carroll's Alice cannot but come to mind: think, for example, of the various confusing meanings of 'draw' and 'well' in the dormouse's 'treacle' story in Chapter VII of *Alice's Adventures in Wonderland*.

I am not suggesting 'influence', a concept of which anyone writing about poetry (in the broadest and deepest sense of the term) should be wary. I prefer to speak of constellations of poets. Moreover, literature, or poetry (again, as always in all my criticism, in the broadest and deepest sense of the word), is always written in literature, or in poetry. The work of Maria Velho da Costa, whom I do not hesitate to call, after Harold Bloom, a *strong poet*, is peppered with citations or allusions to literature in many different languages and from many different cultures. She often italicizes her usually unidentified allusions. In *Myra*, on page 173, for example, *'um tigre a arder'* clearly evokes the 'tyger burning bright' of William Blake's famous poem. More interestingly, in the context of this article, in *Irene ou o contrato social*, Orlando takes leave of his sister one day by invoking the haste of Alice's White Rabbit in the italicized phrase *I'm late, I'm late, for a very important date* (p. 49), which actually comes from the 1951 Disney film, *Alice in Wonderland*.

In her epigraphs, her allusions are very explicit and straightforward. Epigraphs are links in the great chain of an author's pact with their readers. Maria Velho da Costa's first book of creative writing, *O lugar comum* (1966),

---

Lamp: Romantic Theory and the Critical Tradition (New York: Oxford University Press, 1971), pp. 35, 327.

[14] See 'Entrevista a Maria Velho da Costa: uma flor no deserto' by Tiago Bartolomeu Costa in the newspaper *Público*, 13 January 2013. In this interview, Maria Velho da Costa confesses she never wrote poetry and that she has abandoned all her youthful experiments with the genre. But I believe that what she actually means is that she never wrote or writes in *verse*.

[15] Maria Velho da Costa, *Cravo* (Lisbon: Moraes, 1976), pp. 11–13.

opens with a French epigraph taken from the Senegalese writer, Cheikh Hamidou Kane. It is one of two epigraphs in this collection of five short stories. The title of the first story, to which the Kane epigraph is attached, 'Exílio Menor', summons obliquely the major, painful exile narrated in Cheikh Kane's postcolonial novel, *L'Aventure ambiguë* (1961), to which Maria Velho da Costa alludes again in *Casas pardas* and *Myra*.[16] The import of the second epigraph to the story to which it presides is more mysterious, even verging on the paradoxical. It purports to be the Egyptian Pharaoh Akhenaten's 'Hymn to the Sun' (the sun being the god Aten, source of all life). However, the story calls itself 'A velada' [The Wake] and the poem, indeed identified as 'Amenophis IV, Hino Solar' [Hymn to the Sun], speaks rather of the dark shadows of death. And appropriately so, given the narrative that follows, the story of a little boy learning how to grow up and live on as he mournfully holds in his arms the dead body of a cat his father has just accidently run over.

Maina Mendes, on the other hand, resorts very generously to epigraphs, at least one per chapter. They come in Portuguese, Spanish, French, English and German. Maria Velho da Costa's epigraphs are no doubt her way of paying homage to her favourite authors and works, both canonical and noncanonical; but they are no less her way of composing her own constellation-of-poets. For the purposes of my argument in this article, I focus on the English epigraphs of *Maina Mendes* in counter-chronological order, which is also opposite to the author's inclusion of them. Thus, the most recent English quote, used last, is from 'Fixing a Hole' by John Lennon and Paul McCartney in the Beatles album *Sgt. Pepper's Lonely Hearts Club Band*, released in 1967 (p. 205). A few pages earlier (p. 191), Maria Velho da Costa resorted to a brief passage from Virginia Woolf's *The Waves* (1931). On page 149, the epigraph comes from Shakespeare's *King Lear*, an exchange bordering on the meaningful nonsensical between Lear and the Fool. Finally, the author offers, as her second epigraph, a passage from 'Carthon', one of *The Poems of Ossian*, concocted by James MacPherson in the eighteenth century from ancient sources.[17] Years later, in *O livro do meio*, co-authored with Armando Silva Carvalho, Maria Velho da Costa reminisces about a certain D. Maina Mendes de Sousa who was one of the pillars of her childhood.[18] Nonetheless, I can only imagine how delighted she must have

[16] Maria Velho da Costa, *O lugar comum* (Lisbon: Moraes, 1966). Cf. Cheikh Hamidou Kane, *L'Aventure ambiguë* (Paris: Julliard, 1961), p. 104. The relevance for Maria Velho da Costa, as a writer and as an engaged citizen, of this novel about colonialism and the power relations between African and European cultures is reaffirmed at least twice in her novels: in a passage of *Casas pardas* (Lisbon: Moraes, [1977] 1986), p. 308; and in an even more striking passage of *Myra* (2008): 'Como pudemos perder para quem não tem razão? Pensou Myra, que tinha lido isto num dos livros de Rolando [...] *L'Aventure ambigüe*, de um Sheik preto, Amidou Kane' [How could we lose out to those in the wrong? Myra thought. She had read it in one of Rolando's books [...], *L'Aventure ambigüe*, by a black Sheik, Amidou Kane].
[17] See James MacPherson, *The Poems of Ossian and Related Works*, ed. by Howard Gaskill, with an Introduction by Fiona Stafford (Edinburgh: Edinburgh University Press, 1996), pp. 127–37 (p. 128).
[18] Armando Silva Carvalho/Maria Velho da Costa, *O livro do meio* (Lisbon: Caminho, 2006), pp. 118, 135, 158, 175, 271, 316, 383, 403.

been to encounter, in *Ossian*'s 'Carthon', Moina, the beautiful wife of a Gaelic warrior and the mother of his son, three tragic members of a tragically doomed family.[19] Today as yesterday, us as them — the author seems to intimate — life has never been easy to live, families not always helpful, as 'The Family' by Paula Rego (1988) also shows.[20] The complexities of polyglot and multicultural families may also underline the name Maria Velho da Costa, always keen on interlingual punning, has biracial Orlando give to his female dog, a present from his Jewish-German stepfather: Meine, from the German possessive *meine* [mine] (pp. 45; 90; 92; 114). Later, the spelling of Meine will slightly change and Orlando acknowledges that the homophonous Maina is the name of a book with misfortune (pp. 139; 149; 168; 174; 179; 180; 185; 186; 187; 189; 192; 196; 197; 211; 217).

Maria Velho da Costa is unquestionably a cosmopolitan writer. All her novels, occasionally resorting to other languages beside Portuguese, are intertextually rich with references to works of literary imagination. Portuguese literature and culture, including her own fiction (as we have just seen), but by no means exclusively, are her main sources. More attention must be paid to her affinities with English.[21] The author taught Portuguese at King's College London in the 1980s, writing some *crónicas* for the Portuguese periodical *A Capital* during her first years in London.[22] One of them, featuring Nuno Bragança's novel *Square Tolstoi* (1981), begins with a sample of Alice's voice in the already mentioned Chapter VIII of *Through the Looking Glass*. Let us first reflect on the title of the chronicle: 'Square Tolstoi, Gordon Square, Eighth Square.' Square Tolstoi is a plaza and garden honouring Leo Tolstoy in Paris, the city where Nuno Bragança lived, loved, worked, wrote novels, and plotted against the Portuguese dictatorship in the 1970s. The plaza figures prominently at the closure of Bragança's novel, as a very drunk Bragança-like protagonist reenacts his many aspirations, desires and frustrations by invoking and apostrophizing such subversive writers as Henry Miller, Albert Camus, André Breton, José Bergamin, and Tolstoy himself, only to end up wondering despondently: 'Mas escrever porquê?' [But why write ?].[23] Gordon Square, also

[19] To the best of my knowledge, Estela Couto Berger is the only reader of *Maina Mendes* so far to give due relevance to the *Ossian* epigraph, no doubt precisely because of Berger's emphasis on patriarchy and family relations in Maria Velho da Costa's fiction. See Estela Couto Berger, *A audácia da diferença: percursos femininos na ficção de Maria Velho da Costa* (Faro: Universidade do Algarve, 1998), p. 96.
[20] For an interesting analysis of 'an intersemiotic dialogue' between Maria Velho da Costa's *Myra* and Paula Rego's 'visual poetics', see Ana Gabriela Macedo, 'Material Culture, New Corpographies of the Feminine and Narratives of Dissent: *Myra*, by Maria Velho da Costa and Paula Rego — an Intersemiotic Dialogue', in *The Edge of One of Many Circles: Homenagem a Irene Ramalho Santos*, ed. by Isabel Caldeira, Jacinta Matos and Graça Capinha, 2 vols (Coimbra: Imprensa Nacional da Universidade de Coimbra, 2017), II, 54–71.
[21] MVC holds a degree in English and German from the University of Lisbon and taught English in secondary school in the 1960s.
[22] The texts published in *A Capital* were then collected in *O mapa cor de rosa* (Lisbon: Dom Quixote, 1984). See the essay in this volume by Maria Luísa Coelho.
[23] Nuno Bragança, *Square Tolstoi*, in *Obra Completa* (Lisbon: Dom Quixote, 2009), pp. 409–583 (pp. 579–81).

a garden in Bloomsbury, London, resonates with the literary references of the Bloomsbury Group. In her chronicle Maria Velho da Costa even imagines Virginia Woolf strolling there, smoking, talking to herself, creating. Finally, Eighth Square is, we might say, Maria Velho da Costa's own invention: it refers to Chapter VIII of *Through the Looking Glass*, entitled 'It's My Own Invention', and is thus an imaginative place of poetic and magical reverberations as well.

Chapter VIII of *Through the Looking Glass* narrates how Alice was attacked by the Red Knight and saved by the White Knight. The hilarious parody of the chivalric code when a preposterous good knight gallantly comes to the rescue of a damsel in distress from an equally preposterous bad knight is comical enough. As soon as the Red Knight goes away, however, the ludicrous narration becomes mixed with shades of kindness and tenderness. The White Knight guides Alice to the end of the woods while the two of them engage in pleasant conversation, no matter how laughable and absurd. The ridiculous White Knight keeps falling off his no less ridiculous horse and paraphernalia, but Alice is always there to help him up again. And he insists on telling her all about his nonsensical inventions, to which she responds sweetly enough. Gradually, the scene becomes gentler and gentler, and even moving, as the moment arrives to say farewell. It is not difficult to imagine Lewis Carroll (who is also the scientist and inventor Charles L. Dodgson) taking leave of his beloved Alice Pleasance Liddell.[24] The passage Maria Velho da Costa chose to open her chronicle (presumably in her own translation) is taken from Alice's thoughts as she watches the White Knight going away into the forest and falling on his head one more time:

> Alice disse para si própria, a vê-lo ir. Lá vai ele! Mesmo de cabeça, como de costume. De qualquer das maneiras lá vai andando bastante bem — é de ter tanta tralha pendurada à volta do cavalo.] (p. 137)[25]

'Square Tolstoi, Gordon Square, Eighth Square' is ostensibly about *Square Tolstoi*. Bragança's novel is mentioned in the title, of course, and in the last line of the first paragraph, right after Maria Velho da Costa wrote that she was as happy as Alice at the end of Seventh House. She means Chapter VII of *Alice's Adventures in Wonderland*, when a tiny Alice finally manages to grow enough to reach the beautiful garden. Maria Velho da Costa, in turn, is happy because she enjoyed reading her friend Nuno Bragança's new novel. But what is truly fascinating to me is how Maria Velho da Costa weaves the *Alice* books into her rather cryptic response not just to Nuno Bragança's novel but also to the author as a captivating man of many adventures and many more misadventures

---

[24] See Donald Rackin's eloquent essay on this scene: '"And here I must leave you": Death, Love, and the White Knight's Farewell', in Rackin, *Alice's Adventures in Wonderland and Through the Looking Glass: Nonsense, Sense, and Meaning* (New York: Twayne Publishers, 1991), pp. 127–52.

[25] The original reads: ['It won't take long to see him *off*, I expect,'] Alice said to herself, as she stood watching him. 'There he goes! Right on his head as usual! However, he gets on again pretty easily — and that comes from having so many things hung round the horse — '; Lewis Carroll, *Complete Works*, p. 248.

('Everything, everything is autobiographical', she remarks).²⁶ First, there is the reference to the garden (or the gardens). Alice was happy because she finally managed to find herself in the garden. Maria Velho da Costa, on the other hand, failed to go to Gordon Square, as she intimates she usually does on that particular day of the week, so she has to reconcile herself with just talking about the garden. And so she does — for the next page and a half of this four-and-a-half page chronicle. The memory of Virginia Woolf's tragic end puts her back on track, but not without associating the English novelist with the Eighth House and a Queen that is gone (at the end of Chapter VIII of *Alice's Adventures in Wonderland*, the Queen of Hearts is indeed gone). It is then that Maria Velho da Costa feels she has to remind her readers (or perhaps herself) that her current piece of writing is very much about *Square Tolstoi* and her fellow novelist and dear friend, Nuno Bragança. In the two pages that follow, Maria Velho da Costa does indeed write about *Square Tolstoi*, inside out, as it were, and about Nuno Bragança. She skilfully borrows from his novel words, sensations and feelings; she invokes figures, scenes and dialogues; she reimagines contexts and consequences. All this in order to trace a solid portrait of a writer struggling (like herself) with exile, language-in-exile, and himself as a man burdened, like Alice's White Knight, with 'too much material' (p. 140, in English in the original).

How not to go back to the incipit of the chronicle in which Alice watches the White Knight, encumbered with all his gadgets, fall down and get up again one last time? I would be even tempted to surmise that the White Knight comes to Maria Velho da Costa as a fitting figure for the novelist who also wrote a novel entitled *Directa* (1977), which is the Portuguese word for an all-nighter — or white night.²⁷ As she writes feelingly about Nuno Bragança, Maria Velho da Costa can't help but think of herself as well. I quoted at the beginning of my article a sentence from this chronicle: 'As if we were the ones writing ourselves'. We are not, she continues, we but write each other. Is she suddenly reminded that some paragraphs of *Maina Mendes* fill with bliss the writer/protagonist of *Square Tolstoi*?²⁸ We are, she concludes, all of us, mere stuff hanging from the horse. The author of fiction is no more than a performer of the paradox of writing as inter- and intra-textual promiscuity.²⁹ To the question — 'Why

---

²⁶ 'Tudo, tudo é autobiográfico' (p. 141). How autobiographical everything really is, we learn in the gossipy 'milieu book' (*O livro do meio*) Maria Velho da Costa co-wrote with Armando Silva Carvalho twenty-three years later. Already quoted above (see note 18).
²⁷ Nuno Bragança, *Directa* (Lisbon: Moraes, 1977).
²⁸ '... fui relaxar o corpo num banho de tina e saboreando alguns parágrafos de Maina Mendes. Experimentava uma felicidade imensa por ter encontrado e haver escrita, e lugar nesta para mim' [I took a bath and relaxed my body while savouring a few paragraphs of *Maina Mendes*. I was feeling an immense happiness because there was writing and I had found it and a place in it for me.]. *Square Tolstoi*, p. 550.
²⁹ The writer as actor in Maria Velho da Costa is discussed in Maria José Carneiro Dias, *Maria Velho da Costa: uma poética de au(c)toria* (Lisbon: Imprensa Nacional – Casa da Moeda, 2018), esp. Chapter 3 ('A ficção é um palco: "comme au Théatre"'). Dias also calls attention to the intricacies of intratextuality in Maria Velho da Costa's fiction (esp. pp. 207–10).

write?' — Maria Velho da Costa will later reply in *O livro do meio* (p. 161), drawing on Bragança's writing and her own: it is an absurd question, like asking why breathe.

In 1983, while in London, teaching at King's College and writing the chronicles of *O mapa cor de rosa*, Maria Velho da Costa published a new novel, entitled *Lucialima*, with an exquisite cover by Paula Rego.[30] There is no explicit reference to the *Alice* books in this novel, which is made up of several relatively independent stories implicitly intertwined at the end by the novelist's narrative. But the little girl who is the protagonist of one of them, Lucinha, is clearly an Alice figure.[31] Both little girls suffer an experience that sets them on the way to wondering about who they really are: Alice accidentally falls down the rabbit hole, Lucinha becomes blind, apparently as the result of a car accident. In this sense, we could say that Maina Mendes is also an Alice figure, not to mention that Alice, Maina and Lucinha are all mother-deficient, in one way or another. But in *Lucialima*, a book peopled all over by birds and many other kinds of animals, there is a fantasy scene that cannot but immediately send us back to *Alice's Adventures in Wonderland*. Lucinha experiences a strange hallucination that reflects her anxiety about the misencounters of her parents whose constant bickering she frequently overhears (pp. 153–66). She has an absurd conversation with a weird creature sitting on a mushroom, a conversation that is rather like a scene of instruction touching upon one's sense of being and identity. When asked by Lucinha who she is, the creature identifies itself as 'eu sou eu' [I am I], which leads Lucinha to call the creature, in a kind of logic of nonsense, 'Eukié' [I that is]. This conversation of who is who cannot but bring to mind again *Alice's Adventures in Wonderland*. At the end of Chapter IV, a very tiny Alice is looking for something to eat or drink, with the hope of regaining her proper size, when she comes across a caterpillar sitting on a mushroom. In Chapter V, when asked by the caterpillar, 'Who are *you*?', Alice is embarrassed because, after so many changes of size (i.e. of identity), she no longer knows who she really is. When the caterpillar asks her to explain *herself*, Alice's reply — 'I can't explain *myself* […] because I'm not myself' — sounds like a metaleptic commentary on Lucinha's anguished perplexities about herself and her parents. Alice gets from the mushroom the munching magic that will help control her size (i.e. her identity) and ultimately go on to live a normal life in the real world. Lucinha, whose blindness, like Maina's muteness, is not physiological, is left in the realm of fantasy that alone appeases her anxiety.

In *O livro do meio*, the twofold autobiographical and very indiscreet epistolary exchange with Armando Silva Carvalho, which is a scathing critique of the Portuguese cultural milieu at the beginning of the twenty-first century,

---

[30] Maria Velho da Costa, *Lucialima* (Lisbon: O Jornal, 1983).
[31] For a clever reading of the novel's title as bringing together the names of the two nobler characters — Lúcia, the Child, and Lima, the Man-Maker of the Revolution — see Berger, *A audácia da diferença*, p. 122.

we learn that Maria Velho da Costa also sees herself sometimes as an Alice figure. In the letter of 1 March 2006 she writes that 'the Old Girl' is happy in her little house, even if occasionally she amuses herself by saying something that is actually not true: that she 'feels like Carroll's Alice, when the latter takes the potion that makes her huge and pushes her body through the house's openings, head through the chimney, arms and legs through the door and windows'.[32] But for the most meaningful engagement of Maria Velho da Costa with Lewis Carroll's meaningful nonsense perhaps we have to go back to *Casas pardas*, where the caterpillar episode is also evoked and 'Alice' is said to have become very fashionable (p. 229). At the beginning of the chapter entitled 'IV/ Casa de Elisa/Angelus', the aspiring writer Elisa, as she reflects on the situation in Portugal during the so-called Primavera Marcelista, introduces a curious fable: 'Fábula De Rerum Novarum ou A Raposa Europeia' [*The Fable of Rerum Novarum or the European Fox*] (p. 292). The title deliberately brings into a context of fable (in all senses of the word 'fable') Pope Leo XIII's encyclical of 15 May 1891, *De rerum novarum*, addressing the wretched conditions of the working class in Europe at the end of the nineteenth century. The fox points to the fable proper: the author's narrative of the voracious fox that ate so much it became the she-wolf of the myth of the foundation of Rome (or Europe) introduces the topic, so frequent in Maria Velho da Costa, of the violence of culture. Published three years after the Carnation Revolution, when finally the wretched conditions of the Portuguese working classes did begin to benefit from European social democracy, the novel, focusing on the period right before the end of Salazar's dictatorship, is somewhat sceptical about the goodness of European institutions. Alice-like, the protagonist, Elisa, feels tempted to see all the rulers as a mere pack of cards (pp. 293–94). In the last chapter of *Alice's Adventures in Wonderland*, titled 'Alice's Evidence', the evidence is the following: 'Who cares for *you*? [...] You're nothing but a pack of cards'.

Missa in albis is arguably the most complex of Maria Velho da Costa's novels. Resorting to a maddening variety of parodic allusions and misquotation of people's names, titles and events, *Missa in albis* is the perfect evidence that great literature is written in literature, great poetry, in poetry. Narrated by multiple voices often difficult to distinguish, and thus perplexing the reader as to the 'author's' true voice, *Missa in albis* is Maria Velho da Costa's richest work in wordplay and seemingly absurd and paradoxical situations and relationships. The text woven by the novelist, however, coincides accurately with the fabric of the Portuguese nation in the 1960s and the 1970s, up to and shortly after the Carnation Revolution. 'Everything is autobiographical', Maria Velho da Costa admits in her chronicle on Nuno Bragança's *Square Tolstoi*. My re-quoting this is not an invitation to search for the author's self in her fiction, a futile task from

---

[32] '[A Rapariga Velha] diz, o que não é bem verdade, que se sente como a Alice de Carroll, quando toma a poção que a faz enorme e sair-lhe o corpo pelas aberturas da casa, a cabeça pela chaminé, braços e pernas por janelas e porta' (p. 41).

the point of view of literature and poetry: once included in fictional narrative, real life immediately becomes fiction. Rather, it is to draw attention to an 'Alice' that suddenly pops up in *Missa in albis* (pp. 357, 358, 361, 412), bringing along Carroll's Cheshire cat and an unmistakable allusion to the relative madness or sanity of dogs and cats in Chapter VI of *Alice's Adventures in Wonderland* ('Pig and Pepper'). Finally: what to make of Maria Velho da Costa's Elisa in *Casa pardas*? Elisa, whose name, by the way, is almost an anagram of Alice, and whose evocation of *Alice*'s 'A Mad Tea Party' encouraged her to enter a succession of 'casas' [homes], not 'pardas' [dun], but 'parvas' [dumb] (*Casas pardas*, p. 294). This is Carrollian nonsense at its best as embraced by Maria Velho da Costa throughout all her work. Or, as the unidentified (?) author of the passage in question in *Novas cartas portuguesas* says, Alice keeps growing in volume 'de volume em volume' [from volume to volume].[33]

To conclude: there is no doubt that Carroll's *Alice* books have played a very important role in shaping Maria Velho da Costa's imagination and poetics. As we have definitively learned from Robert Douglas-Fairhurst's *The Story of Alice*, Lewis Carroll used nonsense and the absurd obliquely, often perhaps even unwittingly, to depict the social contradictions of Victorian society, as in a fable.[34] Maria Velho da Costa, on the other hand, uses nonsense and the absurd deliberately, to denounce the glaringly unfair inequalities of Portuguese society, while caricaturing the resilient pretensions and potential for corruption of its pre- and post-April Revolution ruling classes.

---

[33] Maria Isabel Barreno, Maria Teresa Horta, Maria Velho da Costa, *Novas cartas portuguesas*, edição anotada, ed. by Ana Luísa Amaral (Lisbon: Dom Quixote, 2010), p. 98.
[34] For an illuminating study of the *Alice* books in the context of a Victorian society shaken by Darwin's *On the Origin of Species* (1859), see Robert Douglas-Fairhurst, *The Story of Alice: Lewis Carroll and the Secret History of Wonderland* (London: Harvill Secker, 2015), especially Chapter 12.

The Polyhedral Victim and the Patchwork Abuser: A Comparative Study of Names and Naming in Vladimir Nabokov's *Lolita* (1955) and Maria Velho da Costa's *Myra* (2008)

Tom Stennett

University of Oxford

As Myra, the eponymous heroine of Maria Velho da Costa's 2008 novel, dresses for her master/lover Orlando Gabriel on the night of her sixteenth birthday, she likens herself to 'uma Lolita velha' [an old Lolita] and 'uma ninfa de mariposa desabrochada da pupa. Ridícula, com uma previsão de sobrevida de um dia, ou dois' [a nymphic butterfly newly emerged from its cocoon. Ridiculous-looking, with a life expectancy of a day, or perhaps two] (*Myra*, p. 150).[1] It is no coincidence that Myra is Russian, and that she is compared to the preferred creature of the lepidopterist Vladimir Nabokov, the Russian author of the English-language novel *Lolita* (1955).

Myra is described as an 'old' and 'nymphic' Lolita because she has just turned sixteen — two years older than the fourteen put forward by Humbert Humbert, *Lolita*'s narrator and the titular child's kidnapper and abuser, as the upper age-limit for a nymphet; a hebephilic[2] fantasy that Humbert sketches in an early part of the novel:

> Between the age limits of nine and fourteen there occur maidens who, to certain bewitched travellers, twice or many times older than they, reveal their true nature which is not human, but nymphic (that is demoniac): and these chosen creatures I propose to designate as 'nymphets'. (*Lolita*, p. 16)[3]

Nymphets are sexualized fantasies that exist only in the eyes of the paedophilic beholder; they are demonic doubles of human referents. In the abuser's mind, the nymphic form is 'truer' than her human equivalent.

As Myra looks at her image in the mirror, she refuses to define herself, or let another define her, in terms of anyone else:

---

[1] Maria Velho da Costa, *Myra* (Lisbon: Assírio e Alvim, 2008). All translation of quotations from *Myra* are my own, and follow the Portuguese in brackets, along with a page number.
[2] Hebephilia is the persistent sexual preference by adults for early adolescent children.
[3] Nabokov, *The Annotated Lolita*, ed. by Alfred Appel (Harmondsworth: Penguin, 2000).

Portuguese Studies vol. 35 no. 2 (2019), 228–43
© Modern Humanities Research Association 2019

> Agora talvez ganhasse, no horror da beleza, no horror da beleza do duplo, de ser dupla de outrem, *substidupla*, riu-se. [...]
> E não é assim que se ama, se adora, com a carga de ressuscitar a memória de alguém, outrem?
> Não, disse Myra nobremente, diante do espelho, Se não sou preferida, não sou ninguém [...]. (*Myra*, p. 149)
>
> [Now perhaps she gained, in the horror of beauty, in the horror of a doppel-beauty, of being someone else's double, a substi-duo. She laughed to herself. [...]
> Is it not thus that we love, we adore — with the charge of resuscitating the memory of someone, of someone else?
> 'No,' said Myra nobly, in front of the mirror. 'If I am not the chosen lover, I am no one [...]'.]

Myra, who has no meaningful contact with any girls of her own age throughout the novel, refuses to identify with the 'outras raparigas' — those young girls, like Lolita, that she reads about in novels or watches on film: 'É estranho, disse Myra, eu não me apaixono como as outras raparigas. Não perco a cabeça' ['It's odd,' said Myra, 'I don't fall in love like other girls. I don't lose my head'], p. 150. Through the voice of her protagonist, Velho da Costa establishes a relationship with *Lolita* at the same time that she distinguishes her heroine from Nabokov's: when away from the gaze of the predatory adults that stalk the novel's pages, Myra is no double or substitute, nor is she unreal like those girls that she has read about or watched.

The episode in front of the mirror underlines Myra's ability, honed throughout the novel, to take on new identities. These personae serve to protect her chosen identity, associated with the name 'Myra', that she only shares with her faithful hound, Rambo.

In this article, I examine the significance(s) of names and the act of naming in *Myra* and *Lolita*. First, I consider the implications of the 'extratextuality' of these novels' eponymous protagonists, given that the method of intertextual decoding, encouraged elsewhere in both novels, is thwarted if the reader attempts to look for literary/cultural predecessors for Lolita or Myra. Second, I argue that identities serve as sham (*Lolita*) and fragile (*Myra*) protection respectively in the novels. Myra's adoption of personae entails a deflection of the unblinking look that is cast upon her by the dangerous adults that she meets on her tour of Portugal. In *Lolita*, the novel's fictional editor uses false identities (putatively) to conceal the identity of the abused child from his readership. The crucial difference is that Myra names herself as a part of a survival strategy; Lolita is named by her abusers, who commandeer her story and her literary representation. Myra has an agency that is denied Lolita. Last, I situate Nabokov's decision to write a narrative from the perspective of a male abuser, and Velho da Costa's determination to centre her novel around a female victim, in the specific contexts in which these texts were conceived.

Lolita and Myra: Extratextual Protagonists

Whereas the novels *Myra* and *Lolita* are replete with intertextual references (Myra and Humbert both being very well-read), the names 'Myra' and 'Lolita' do not point to clear predecessors. Lolita's intertextuality is controlled by her abuser, Humbert Humbert, and by the author, Nabokov. Myra, an outsider in Portugal, negotiates the dangerous world of Velho da Costa's novel through the invention of false identities. In *Myra*, make-believe is a survival strategy; in *Lolita*, control of the narration of the eponymous protagonist's story is ensured by Humbert Humbert through the construction and control of her identity. Whereas Myra adeptly inserts herself in a transcultural textuality, Lolita is inserted in an intertextual genealogy of her writers' creation.

Lolita's main body is a text written by Humbert Humbert while in prison. His account is framed by a foreword written by John Ray Jr., the fictional editor. As is the case with 'Lolita', Humbert Humbert is not the fictional author's real name; the moniker is an identity chosen to safeguard the writer's identity from the reading public.

Humbert's text is the account of his 'love' for Lolita, whom he meets when he accepts a teaching position at a school in the fictional New England town of Ramsdale. In the novel, Lolita is also referred to as 'Dolores Haze' — an approximation of her real name chosen by John Ray. Humbert soon becomes sexually obsessed with the then twelve-year-old Dolores, whose mother Humbert marries. Humbert murders the mother and kidnaps Dolores, whom he sexually abuses for several years while they travel across North America, stopping for a time in the fictional town of Beardsley. During a second road trip, Humbert is followed by the playwright Clare Quilty, whom Humbert had met in the hotel where he first raped Dolores. While in Texas, Dolores, having fallen ill, disappears from the hospital where she was being treated. Several years later, when Dolores has reached the age of seventeen, Humbert receives a letter from her telling him that she is now living in Coalmont, Tennessee; that she is married to a Richard Schiller, pregnant and in dire financial difficulty. Humbert tracks down Dolores, who tells him that she was not abducted: she left of her own volition with Quilty, from whom she later escaped. Humbert tracks down Quilty and murders him. The novel ends with Humbert's arrest. Lolita's fate is absent from the final chapters. A rereading of Ray's foreword reveals that a 'Mrs. "Richard F. Schiller"' had died in childbirth, prompting the publication of Humbert's text (*Lolita*, p. 4), for the fictional author had stipulated that his novel should only be published after Lolita's death (pp. 308–09).

The intertextual genealogy of Lolita (novel and protagonist) is constructed and controlled by Humbert and by Nabokov. Humbert states that Lolita's only precursor is another inhabitant of the novel's literary universe: 'Did she have a precursor? She did, indeed she did' (p. 9) — Annabel, a childhood love of

Humbert's.⁴ In a 1964 interview with *Playboy*, Nabokov explains his choices for the various names given to Lolita, and her abuser's unusual moniker. The author places an emphasis on the importance of the 'lyrical lilt' of the nymphet's name:

> One of the most limpid and luminous letters is 'L.' The suffix '-ita' has a lot of Latin tenderness, and this I required too. Hence: Lolita. However, it should not be pronounced as you and most Americans pronounce it: Low-lee-ta, with a heavy, clammy 'L' and a long 'o.' No, the first syllable should be as in 'lollipop,' the 'L' liquid and delicate, the 'lee' not too sharp.⁵

In contrast, Humbert Humbert's name was chosen for its sinister suggestiveness:

> The double rumble is, I think, very nasty, very suggestive. It is a hateful name for a hateful person. It is also a kingly name, and I did need a royal vibration for Humbert the Fierce and Humbert the Humble.⁶

If 'Lolita', pronounced correctly, afforded Nabokov's ears pleasure, his narrator, at the beginning of the novel, describes the sensuous enjoyment that he experiences when pronouncing the three syllables that constitute the name that he has given to his nymphet: 'Lo-lee-ta: the tip of the tongue taking a trip of three steps down the palate to tap, at three, on the teeth. Lo. Lee. Ta' (p. 9). The function of Lolita's name is lyrical — in the sense of poetic phonetics, and of lyric poetry: 'Another consideration was the welcome murmur of its source name, the fountain name: those roses and tears in "Dolores." My little girl's heart-rending fate had to be taken into account together with the cuteness and limpidity.'⁷

The novel *Lolita* has its own precursor, a novella written in 1939, but discarded by Nabokov, called Волшебник (translated by his son Dimitri as *The Enchanter*) and signed by 'V. Sirin', a pseudonym in Nabokov's Russian works. The anonymous pubescent girl in the novella is a spectral presence, spending most of the narrative away from the (also unnamed) male abuser. Unlike Lolita, who, according to Humbert, invites her abusers' advances, the girl in *The Enchanter* screams in fear and tries to escape when her step-father attempts to rape her in a hotel room as she sleeps. Dimitri Nabokov writes in his postface, 'On a Book Entitled *The Enchanter*', regarding the relationship between Волшебник and *Lolita*: 'Dolores Haze may, as [Vladimir] Nabokov says, be "very much the same lass" as the Enchanter's victim, but only in an inspirational, conceptual sense'.⁸ Lolita's place in Nabokov's textual universe is strictly controlled by the author, his son and the fictional narrator.

---

⁴ One possible literary precursor for *Lolita* has been identified by James T. Bratcher — a character from Mayne Reid's *The War Trail* (1857) — but neither Humbert nor Nabokov directs the reader towards Reid's novel. James T. Bratcher, 'Lolita: A Probable Source of Nabokov's Name for his Temptress', *Notes and Queries*, 56.3 (2009), 427.
⁵ Alvin Toffler, 'Interview: Vladimir Nabokov', *Playboy*, January 1964, <http://reprints.longform.org/playboy-interview-vladimir-nabokov> [accessed 14 October 2016].
⁶ Ibid.
⁷ Ibid.
⁸ Dimitri Nabokov, 'On a Book Entitled *The Enchanter*', in *Novellas: The Eye, The Enchanter, The Original of Laura* (London: Penguin Classics, 2012), pp. 183–213 (p. 213).

Myra is a Russian child immigrant who begins the novel as a stranger to and within Portuguese culture. As she reads books and watches films, Myra inserts herself in a transcultural textuality, constructing her identities in and through cultures, inventing 'contos' [short stories] to fool potential predators, whilst preserving her chosen identity, Myra.

Myra tours Portugal with a former fighting dog, Rambo/Rimbaud, having escaped from her family, who live with other Eastern European immigrants in a warehouse in the coastal town of Caparica, south of Lisbon. Thereafter, Myra traverses a world filled with predatory adults, including the lecherous German Kleber and his lover, the austere artist Mafalda, who hosts Myra in her 'Casa Grande'.[9] Having escaped Mafalda's house, Myra is eventually taken into the household of the Cape Verdean *mestiço* Gabriel Rolando/Orlando. Gabriel persuades Myra to move with him to Lisbon, but they are stopped on their way by three men, who shoot Gabriel and kidnap Myra, taking her to a brothel in Porto. The novel ends with Myra's inevitable ('Tem de ser' [It has to be]; *Myra*, p. 221) suicide, as she jumps out of her new bedroom window clutching her only friend, the dog Rambo/Rimbaud.

Myra's name immediately signals her foreignness, for 'y', like 'k' and 'w', was only re-introduced to the Portuguese alphabet in 2009, under the Portuguese Language Orthographic Agreement of 1990, having been initially abolished in the Orthographic Agreement of 1945.[10] Once re-introduced into the Portuguese alphabet, the usage of these letters was restricted to acronyms, foreign words not rendered into Portuguese, or nouns and adjectives derived from these terms.[11]

On the novel's first page, the narrator frames Myra as an outsider, like the *blinis* about which the protagonist reminisces. Her initial identity lies outside the cultural-linguistic system that she has entered, having abandoned her remaining family in Caparica, and before that her native Russia: 'Myra lembrou-se da neve em cima dos telhados de ouro e loiça. E os *blinis* que não tinham nome nesta terra. Ao princípio nada tinha nome' [Myra remembered the snow that covered the gold and china rooftops. And the *blinis* that had no name in this land. In the beginning, nothing had a name] (*Myra*, p. 9). The narrator recognizes that the foreign object, as an intruder in the receiving culture's linguistic framework, is at first anonymous. Myra will have to accept a label if she wants to participate in this dangerous world, as opposed to remaining mute like Maina Mendes, the eponymous protagonist of another Velho da Costa novel. Variously Sonia/Sophia to Mafalda and Kleber; Maria Flor to a Friar and a Nun who feature in Chapter 9; Elena, to a blind man whom the protagonist meets in Chapter 10; and finally, Ekaterina/Kate to Gabriel Orlando — Myra's

---

[9] 'Casa Grande' in Portuguese has clear colonial overtones, as the term traditionally refers to the large rural properties ('Big Houses') of slaveowners in the northeast of Brazil.
[10] The Portuguese Language Orthographic agreements were international treaties designed to standardize spelling in the Portuguese language across continents.
[11] 'Acordo Ortográfico da Língua Portuguesa. Assinado em Lisboa a 16 de Dezembro de 1990', <http://www.priberam.pt/docs/AcOrtog90.pdf>, p. 6 [accessed 2 December 2016].

identity is never fixed, shifting according to circumstance. For Ana Filipa Prata, the name Myra points to the protagonist's myriad identities.[12]

Names as Shields: Identity as Fragile/Sham Protection

Unlike in *Myra*, the reader of *Lolita* never learns the eponym's surname. Lolita is a sexualized, fantastical identity foisted by Humbert upon the young adolescent girl that he kidnaps and abuses. Lolita is not the girl's only mask. The moniker Dolores Haze, which approximates her real name, should serve to protect the child's identity from prying readers, but the fictitious editor John Ray sees no 'practical necessity' to alter the original name radically. The fictional surname Haze rhymes with the girl's real family name and her forename, Dolores, has not been changed because 'her first name is too closely interwound with the inmost fiber of the book' (*Lolita*, p. 4). Ray glibly provides, 'for the benefit of old-fashioned readers', several details that would allow anyone interested 'to follow the destinies of the "real" people beyond the "true" story' (p. 4). Nabokov's fictional editor thus directs the reader, presumed to be a man ('as the reader will perceive for himself', p. 4), towards the information relating to the events of the novel, and thereby tacitly encourages the 'inquisitive' reader to discover more about the case, exposing the people imbricated in the story. In this respect, Ray resembles Humbert, who, at several points in the narrative, attempts to expose the real names of people to whom he has taken a dislike. Ray acknowledges the existence of such moments:

> Save for the correction of obvious solecisms and a careful suppression of a few tenacious details that despite 'H.H.'s [Humbert Humbert's] own efforts still subsisted in his text as signposts and tombstones (indicative of places or persons that taste would conceal and compassion spare), this remarkable memoir is presented intact. (p. 3)

The editor's carefree attitude towards the privacy of the *people* involved in the drama leaves us wondering whether Ray was entirely scrupulous in his rectification of these moments of aberration; where the factual erupts into the fiction. Of course, the novel *is* a fiction, and as such Lolita, Mona Dahl (another 'nymphet'), and the rest are not in any danger of being exposed — because they do not exist, except as literary constructs. Nevertheless, the similarities between Ray and Humbert underline the fact that the dangers of this fictional world extend beyond the monstrous Humbert. In the novel, the abuse of the vulnerable, embodied by Lolita, is rampant, goes unnoticed, often escapes punishment until it is much too late, and, because of characters like Ray, continues even after the victim has extricated herself from the clutches of a tormentor.

---

[12] Ana Filipa Prata, 'Transgression, Transdifference and Abjection in Maria Velho da Costa's *Myra* and Teresa Villaverde's *Transe*', *Portuguese Studies*, 33.2 (2017), 202–18 (p. 206).

Ray's supposition that a substantial proportion of *Lolita*'s readership will be interested in the 'real' Lolita seems particularly pertinent nowadays, given contemporary questions over the role of the media and the public gaze in causing undue, added distress to victims of sexual or physical abuse, and the issue of whether victims' names ought to be published by the media.[13] Although the purpose of Ray's words is not to highlight that particular issue, the fact that both Ray and Humbert feel that they can use Lolita's name(s) as they wish demonstrates the power that these characters have over her. Humbert Humbert's double name reflects his doubled power over Lolita: on the one hand, the protagonist Humbert enjoys, for most of the novel, almost absolute control over her — a defenceless girl whose stasis should not be misinterpreted as assent; on the other, the second and later Humbert, the narrator, takes charge of the evocation and the ordering of the story's events, but also of the representation of the novel's heroine, who is denied the agency of telling her version of events.

Myra *is* a storyteller, but her narratives and identities are mendacious fictions. Myra deflects the various objectifying looks that are cast upon her by the male predators that inhabit the novel's fictional universe through her hasty invention of alter egos to protect her chosen identity: 'Myra'.[14] However, Myra is not merely an image, nor is she solely subject to the male predatory gaze that Laura Mulvey suggests is present in the Freudian scopophilic look that traditional film induces the male spectator to cast on the female form, which is 'displayed for his enjoyment (connoting male phantasy)'.[15] For Mulvey, through a second look, 'that of the spectator fascinated with the image of his like set in an illusion of natural space', the objectification of the female form inherent in the first look is extended to 'the control and possession of the woman within the diegesis', as the male spectator identifies with the more complete image of himself: the central male protagonist.[16] Whereas the 'control and possession' of the *girl* by a male spectator/reader, encouraged obliquely by the author through the devices of the fictional editor and the narrator, applies more readily to *Lolita* and its framing texts, the interplay of looks in *Myra* is complex: Myra is both (self-reflexive) spectator and spectated.

The danger of being looked at is encoded in the name 'Myra'. In the novel's penultimate chapter, Maribel, the girl Myra meets having been kidnapped and

[13] See, for example, Lisa M. Jones, David Finkelhor and Jessica Beckwith, 'Protecting Victims' Identities in Press Coverage of Child Victimization', *Journalism: Theory, Practice and Criticism*, 11.3 (2010), 347–67 (p. 348).
[14] For a reading of *Myra*'s 'poetics of a resourceful survival strategy structured by a strong intertextual network, discursive and narrative artificial, and cultural subversion' (p. 204), see Ana Filipa Prata, 'Transgression, Transdifference and Abjection in Maria Velho da Costa's *Myra* and Teresa Villaverde's *Transe*', esp. pp. 205–14.
[15] Laura Mulvey, 'Visual Pleasure and Narrative Cinema', in *Film Theory and Criticism: Introductory Readings*, ed. by Leo Braudy and Marshall Cohen (New York and Oxford: Oxford University Press, 2009), pp. 711–22 (p. 717).
[16] Ibid.

taken to D. Adalgisa's brothel, performs a song:

> Mira-me Miguel
> Como estoy de bonitinha
> Xaia de burel
> Camijinha de estopinha.
>
> [Look at me, Miguel
> How pretty I am
> A woollen skirt
> A little linen shirt.]
> (*Myra*, p. 216)

'Mira(r)', a verb that exists in Portuguese, but which is more commonly used in Mirandese, seems to refer to the unblinking (male) gaze to which Myra is subject throughout the novel, and which the song's constructed female voice invites.

The chapters that recount Myra's sixteenth birthday, which takes place in Gabriel's 'Casa Branca', alternate between Mulvey's first scopophilic look, and its rejection in favour of a three-dimensional and sympathetic, but not idealized, portrayal of Myra. Similarly, the text hesitates between the representation of Gabriel's relationship with Myra as a heterosexual, male domination of the female body on the one hand, and a harmonious love-bond on the other.[17] Both representations are subverted.

Chapter 17 is tinged with a distinctive filmic quality, beginning with a general reference to cinema that suggests that what follows will take place behind the lens of a camera: 'Nonóia [t]razia um sorriso maior que a boca dela e uma bandeja de hotel de cinco estrelas, como ela só vira em filmes, ou séries de luxo brasileiras' [Nonóia beamed a smile broader than her mouth should allow and carried a serving tray of the sort that only exists in five-star hotels, and which Nonóia had only ever seen in films, or classy Brazilian TV series] (*Myra*, p. 139). The chapter is punctuated with references to specific films, such as several of Pasolini's movies (p. 140), *Long Day's Journey into Night* (p. 144), and possibly the 1997 film version of *Lolita* (p. 150).[18]

The narration moves like a lens across Myra, focusing on her clothes and on her fragmented body, with each outfit that Myra dons, and the concomitant rituals of (un)dressing, loaded with symbolic, if ambiguous, meaning. The nuptial nightdress (one of the household staff, Nonóia, calls it a 'Vistide di noiva'; p. 140) that Myra receives as a present from Gabriel represents the handing over, in the novel's twisted patriarchal order, from the girl's absent father to her mutilated husband. Myra's first menstruation in the novel's opening chapter coincides with her flight from her family, and her entry into the dangerous underworld that she traverses. Orlando's dress commemorates

---

[17] Gabriel's age is never specified. When the fifteen-year-old Myra first encounters him, the anonymous narrator remarks that he could be in his twenties or thirties (*Myra*, p. 90).

[18] It is unclear whether Myra refers to the Lolita in Nabokov's novel, or that of the 1997 film version.

Myra's sixteenth birthday: the age when a girl becomes a woman in this world, for Myra's mother and grandmother both had their first children aged sixteen (pp. 140–41). The date marks Myra's sexual initiation; Gabriel waits for Myra to reach the age of consent for fear of being accused of being a paedophile (pp. 106–07).

Myra's second outfit, a swimming costume 'loaned' by her lover/master, is forcibly removed during a sexually explicit scene, after she has been rescued from an unidentified sea creature (p. 143). Following the undressing scene on the boat, Myra's reformulates her tragic mantra, 'Não vou chorar', to the ambiguous: 'Não vou chorar, nem de alegria, pensou Myra, a água do mar faz isso por mim ['I won't cry, not even for joy,' thought Myra. 'The seawater will do that for me'] (*Myra*, p. 143).

Myra's and Gabriel's love bond attempts to transcend the colonial dynamics of violence and coercion that structure the underworld portrayed in the novel. Their efforts are futile. Having shown Myra his mutilated genitals, Gabriel declares his love: 'O amor, o teu amor, fria donzela. Quero o que já tenho, mas consentido. Sem recalcitrância, sem jogos de poder, ó russinha. Desde que te vi, vi que me convinhas. Em ti *deponho toda a minha pena*' [Love, your love, frigid maid. I want what I already have, but with your consent. Without reluctance, without power games. Oh, my little Russian! When I first saw you, I knew that you and I were meant to be. In you *I lay down all my pain/pen*] (*Myra*, p. 168). The italicized text is a reference to the poem by Luís de Camões addressed to a black slave called Bárbara. The verse in question is a bawdy pun playing on the double meaning of 'pena' in Portuguese, which can refer to 'pain' or 'shame', as well as the poet's phallic 'pen'. In his declaration of preference for a loving relationship devoid of power games, Gabriel makes direct reference to a poem that operates on the very sexual (and imperial) power games that he disavows.[19] In the case of Gabriel's ironic rewriting, the 'pena' is a double signifier of an absence: it points to his mutilated penis and the psychic pain provoked by the memory of it, which is revealed to Myra at the end of her birthday. Like Myra's first 'master', Mafalda, Gabriel is 'Prospero and Caliban at the same time';[20] a master with a body violently marked by colonial violence.

Gabriel is framed as a predator at several moments: he is 'Beast' to Myra's 'Beauty' and a Bluebeard who rears the child Myra for her sexual initiation on her sixteenth birthday. The murkiness of Gabriel's and Myra's relationship is underlined in the description of the 'powerphiles' (*poderófilos*) that populate *Myra*'s underworld: 'Uma criança cede, cede sempre. Pode chorar, mas cede. Não tem outro remédio. E até pode gostar, o que não é menos horrendo' [Children give in, they always give in. Cry they might, but they always give in.

---

[19] Luís de Camões, *A Lírica de Luís de Camões: Textos Escolhidos*, ed. by Maria Vitalina Leal de Matos (Lisbon: Editorial Comunicação, 1981), pp. 81–82.
[20] Ana Filipa Prata, 'Transgression, Transdifference and Abjection in Maria Velho da Costa's *Myra* and Teresa Villaverde's *Transe*', p. 210.

They have no other choice. And, just as horrendous, they might even enjoy it] (p. 218). Although the novel's structure suggests that Gabriel's love is the best that Myra can hope for — the 'Casa Branca' is her last stop before the brothel and her premature death — a more sinister reading remains open: that Myra declares that she is in 'love' and that she is 'happy' is no guarantee that her bond with Gabriel is not that of a vulnerable teenager in the thrall of someone who loves power. Myra is wary enough of her master/lover that she only reveals her name to Gabriel as he lies dying on the roadside.

Humbert's Bizarre Mask, Myra's Canny Disguises

Like Myra, Lolita is a girl who 'might even enjoy' her captivity by a powerphile. As Dimitri Nabokov notes, in his comparison of Lolita and her prototype — the girl in *The Enchanter* — the latter is: 'perverse only in the madman's eyes; innocently incapable of anything like the Quilty intrigue'.[21] When Humbert catches up with Dolores, several years after she disappears from a hospital, she tells him that she was not abducted by Clare Quilty: she left willingly.

Lolita's escape from Humbert underlines the slipping control that the abuser has over his victim as Lolita grows up. However, the abuser's control over Lolita's identities is fragile at best *throughout* the text on the level of representation. The reader is made aware, from the text's second paragraph, that Lolita and her many, splintered forms are highly artificial creations:

> She was Lo, plain Lo, in the morning, standing four feet ten in one sock. She was Lola in slacks. She was Dolly at school. She was Dolores on the dotted line. But in my arms she was always Lolita. (*Lolita*, p. 9)

These sentences are particularly revealing about what happens to Lolita's identity in the text: she is hewn by Humbert into a series of sexualized images, behind which may lie the 'real' Lolita, the 'true' version that John Ray encourages us to seek, but which Nabokov, a patent detester of mimesis and 'realism', seems to reject both in his afterword to the novel,[22] and through the device of Ray. There is no 'real' Lolita to find other than that imagined by her abuser.

Nabokov was highly conscious of the dangers inherent in writing a book like *Lolita*: Ray's foreword and Nabokov's afterword underline three major concerns. First, that the book will be dismissed, 'not based on my treatment of

---

[21] Dimitri Nabokov, 'On a Book Entitled *The Enchanter*', p. 213.
[22] In 'On a Book Entitled *Lolita*', Nabokov evinces his suspicion of the term 'reality', and questions whether the term, in the realm of literature, has any meaning: '[...] I was faced by the task of inventing America. The obtaining of such local ingredients as would allow me to inject a modicum of average "reality" (one of the few words which mean nothing without quotes) into the brew of individual fancy [...]', *Lolita*, p. 312. Nabokov parodies 'realistic' writing: 'Some of the reactions [from publishers to the manuscript of *Lolita*] were very amusing: one reader suggested that his firm might consider publication if I turned my Lolita into a twelve-year-old lad and had him seduced by Humbert, a farmer, in a barn, amidst gaunt and arid surroundings, all this set forth in short, strong "realistic" sentences ("He acts crazy. We all act crazy, I guess. I guess God acts crazy." Etc.)', p. 314.

the theme but on the theme itself' (p. 314) — a subject to which I will return later. Secondly, Nabokov is wary of the reader who will disparage *Lolita* for its lack of realism, a critique that Nabokov rejects by asserting his preference for 'aesthetic bliss', or 'a sense of being somehow, somewhere connected with other states of being where art (curiosity, tenderness, kindness, ecstasy) is the norm' (pp. 314–15). Thirdly, Nabokov is alert to that brand of reader who looks for biography in the fiction, who sees Ray and Humbert as manifestations of the author. Nabokov's novel, as well as the metatexts that frame it, are attempts to deny the existence of a (more) 'truthful' reality hiding behind the masks worn by the characters that populate *Lolita*: Humbert Humbert and the artificial vizard(s) that the girl he abuses is forced to wear.

The image of the mask is introduced by Ray in relation to the strange name of *Lolita*'s narrator, whose 'bizarre cognomen is his own invention; this mask — through which two hypnotic eyes seem to glow — had to remain unlifted in accordance with its wearer's wish' (p. 3). Nabokov tempts the reader to make the leap from fictional narrator to author, whilst also denying that very possibility. He does a similar thing in his afterword, where he adopts the language of *Lolita*'s narrator in a text that mocks readers who have interpreted the novel as a semi-biographical work: 'The first little *throb* of *Lolita* went through me late in 1939'; 'I find [*Lolita*] to be a delightful presence now that it quietly hangs about the house like a summer day which one knows to be bright behind the *haze*' (p. 311; 316, my emphasis). Nabokov teases his readers, daring them to make the (il-)logical leaps from protagonist, narrator or fictional editor, to author.

Here, one of the crucial differences between *Myra* and *Lolita* emerges. Like Nabokov, Velho da Costa is aware of the performative, theatrical aspect of identity. However, in *Myra*, there is no such play when it comes to the possible existence of a lingering identity behind the various disguises that Myra dons. Along with her guard dog and companion Rambo, Myra's names and slap-dash identities are her only defence against the potential predators she encounters.

Myra only willingly reveals her given name to one other human being in the novel — to Gabriel Orlando:

— *Kiss me, Kate.*
— Myra, chamo-me Myra, chamo-me Myra, meu amor.

['*Kiss me, Kate.*'
'Myra. My name is Myra. My name is Myra, my love.'] (*Myra*, p. 192)

At the zenith of vulnerability and despair, Myra's masks fall as she rejects Kate — simultaneously an abbreviated form of Ekaterina, the identity that Myra creates for Gabriel, and Gabriel's *Kiss me* 'Kate' — a Humbertian artifice. Myra spends the remainder of the novel exposed, as her kidnappers sneeringly address her by the name that she reveals to Gabriel: 'Que ela gosta mesmo é de cães, não é *Miss* Myra?' [She really *does* like dogs, don't you Miss Myra?] (p. 194). Neither Myra nor Rimbaud, who is recognized as a successful fighting dog, will last out the night. The coincidental timing of Myra's unmasking and her premature death is not innocent: Myra's suicide/murder[23] occurs at the point when she exposes her *chosen* identity. Myra is forced out of hiding with the death of Gabriel. This Myra — one denied the possibility of telling her own story through her mendacious *contos* — cannot be reconciled with the novel's dangerous underworld. Exposed to her kidnappers, Myra does not invent a new identity before her suicide on the novel's last page.

Myra's ability to adopt different roles and outwit the predators that threaten her is testament to her talents as a performer who is able to thwart, at least for a time, an overbearing, kyriarchal power structure.[24] Maria Irene Ramalho Santos has written that, in contrast to the nonverbal Maina Mendes, 'the polyglot Myra refuses to be pinned down by a name. She calls herself [...] different names, in freedom-fighting gestures of hidden sense'.[25] Unlike 'Lolita', a sexualized identity foisted upon the 'real' girl that Humbert kidnaps and abuses, 'Myra' is a chosen identity, constituted of and protected by the alter egos that are hastily invented by the protagonist. These multiple identities are constitutive of a tessellated, supra-identity, 'Myra': a name that gathers meaning as the child grows, even if that meaning is not allowed to burgeon to its full potential. This supra-identity, constituted of myriad, fleeting personae, serves to protect a different Myra: the Russian adolescent who only reveals herself to her dog and to her lover as he gives out his dying breath. This hidden Myra embodies the childhood that is denied her.

In an article on the importance of place names in *Lolita*, Monica Manolescu-Oancea argues that in Nabokov's stated project to 'invent' America, the author creates a continental patchwork described over the course of the novel: 'Nabokov's America is best rendered, visually and kaleidoscopically, by the image of the patchwork, "the crazy quilt of forty-eight states" that features in *Lolita*'.[26] Nabokov's spatial quilt is constituted of a 'rainbow of "realities"',[27] a combination of real and fictional place names that create a 'motley'[28] textual space, which is navigated by 'a spatial discourse of seduction', oriented along the 'geometrical shapes of voluptuous digression'.[29] Manolescu-Oancea remarks that Nabokov's invented North America reflects Humbert Humbert's

---

[23] '[Myra] Lembrou-se de Ernst Kleber, o bom alemão, *os suicidas são sempre assassinados*', [[Myra] Remembered the words of Ernst Kleber, the good German: *suicide is always murder*], p. 220. The notion that suicide is always murder had appeared in Costa's 1983 novel *Lucialima*.
[24] Elisabeth Schüssler Fiorenza, 'Introduction: Political Construction of Feminist Biblical Interpretation', in *But She Said: Feminist Practices of Biblical Interpretation* (Boston, MA: Beacon Press, 1992), pp. 1–18.
[25] M. Irene Ramalho Santos, 'Gender, Species and Coloniality in Maria Velho da Costa', in *Gender, Empire and Postcolony: Luso-Afro-Brazilian Connections*, ed. by Hilary Owen and Anna M. Klobucka (New York: Palgrave Macmillan, 2014), pp. 191–202 (p. 197).
[26] Monica Manolescu-Oancea, 'Inventing and Naming America: Place and Place Names in Vladimir Nabokov's *Lolita*', *European Journal of American Studies*, 4.1 (2009), para. 1 of 47.
[27] Manolescu-Oancea, para. 12 of 47.
[28] Manolescu-Oancea, para. 13 of 47.
[29] Manolescu-Oancea, para. 24 of 47.

patchwork configuration: 'Genetically and metaphorically, Humbert is a quilt himself'.[30] She notes that the intrusions of fictional place names 'allow Nabokov to invent and at least appropriate America by (partially) naming it all over again'.[31] This reflection might be applied equally to Humbert's renaming and subsequent appropriation, on the levels of diegesis and literary representation, of the child that he abducts. To name and rename is the prerogative of the powerful; of people (typically men) like Humbert, the white male abuser.[32] In 'On a Book Entitled *Lolita*', Nabokov rejects moral charges against his work. However, it is telling that Nabokov is more interested in creating a multi-faceted America and a complex figure out of the predatory Humbert than he is in creating a rounded character out of Lolita. This is not to say that Nabokov sides with his 'creature', Humbert; he clearly does not: 'there are many things, besides nymphets, in which I disagree with him' (*Lolita*, p. 315). Nabokov privileges the voice of the presumed interesting male predator, even if he does so to disparage him. Meanwhile, the victim is silenced by Humbert and Ray, who take control of her narrative and her literary representation.

Writing against Moral Policing, Writing at the Heart of a Scandal

How might this difference in approach to the sensitive topic of paedophilia be explained? The contexts in which *Myra* and *Lolita* were produced, and published, are fundamental to understanding the authors' respective treatments of similar subject matter.

In the book *Girls Lean Back Everywhere: The Law of Obscenity and the Assault on Genius*, Edward de Grazia dedicates a chapter to the difficulties that Nabokov encountered in trying to publish *Lolita* in France, the USA and the United Kingdom, including the 'lolitigation' levelled against the Olympia Press, the French publishing house infamous for its catalogue of 'd.b.'s (dirty books) run by Maurice Girodias.[33]

In the United States, the legal framework regarding obscenity in literature was unclear at the time that Nabokov first sent manuscripts of *Lolita* to North American publishers in 1954. In 1948, the Supreme Court had been called upon to rule on a case brought against Edmund Wilson's *Memoirs of Hecate County*, which had been suppressed on obscenity charges by the Court of Special Sessions of New York. A tied vote of 4–4 resulted in the lower court's decision being upheld. Grazia writes that 'the split and silent decision left

---

[30] Manolescu-Oancea, para. 18 of 47.
[31] Manolescu-Oancea, para. 30 of 47.
[32] John Ray Jr. on the novel's title: '*Lolita, or the Confession of a White Widowed Male*, such were the two titles under which the writer of the present note received the strange pages it perambulates' (*Lolita*, p. 3).
[33] For an account of the trials and tribulations of *Lolita*'s publication in France, see Edward de Grazia, *Girls Lean Back Everywhere: The Law of Obscenity and the Assault on Genius* (London: Constable, 1992), pp. 255–72.

authors and publishers hopelessly adrift in a sea of conflicting lower court judicial decisions and opinions'.[34] Changes in the law developed gradually: in the 1957 Roth case the Supreme Court 'held enigmatically that "obscenity" was not constitutionally protected expression, but also that literary and artistic "discussions" of sex having even the slightest social importance ought to be constitutionally protected'.[35] Grazia states that: 'Not until June 1959 [...] did the Supreme Court make it clear that a book could not be banned for its sexual immorality'.[36]

In the foreword to *Lolita*, Ray makes reference to the case brought against James Joyce's *Ulysses* in 1933 on the grounds of obscenity (*Lolita*, p. 4). After a Shakespeare and Company edition of *Ulysses* had been seized by customs in New York, the publisher, Random House, went to the federal court in an attempt to clear the obscenity charges brought against the Shakespeare and Company edition, and thereby make the novel available for publication in the USA. Sitting judge John H. Woolsey's ruling marked 'a new and, for its time, liberal approach to the definition of the obscene', for he 'held that the work as a whole had literary merit but no aphrodisiacal impact on the average person'.[37]

Through the device of Ray and in 'On a Book Called *Lolita*', Nabokov demonstrates that he was highly conscious of the dangers of trying to publish a book like *Lolita* in the USA, fearing the prospect of criminal charges and dismissal from his teaching position at Cornell University. Nevertheless, in the context in which the novel was composed and then published, *Lolita* stands as a challenge to North American obscenity laws, as the author, in various guises, goads the sort of reader that he disparages in 'On a Book Entitled *Lolita*' to label his novel and its writer(s) and editor obscene. At the same time that Nabokov mocks the reader who looks for autobiographical details in fictional works, he dares his readership to identify Nabokov-the-artist with Humbert and Ray.

Whereas Nabokov interrogates the question of decency in literature in a climate of McCarthyism through the first-person narrative of a child abuser, Velho da Costa's novel is a work produced at a time when a decades-old child abuse scandal, involving a state-run institution and powerful men positioned in several circles of the Portuguese elite, was putting enormous pressure on the country's legal system, the State, and the media.

Velho da Costa had previously experienced legal (and political) difficulties with the publication of her collaborative project *Novas Cartas Portuguesas* in 1972.[38] In 2008, she published *Myra* against the backdrop of the Casa Pia

---

[34] Grazia, p. 250.
[35] Grazia, note on p. 250. Grazia states that 'Not until June 1959 [...] did the Supreme Court make it clear that a book could not be banned for its sexual immorality'.
[36] Grazia, note on p. 250.
[37] Grazia, p. 30. For an account of the various controversies that *Ulysses* provoked in the United States, including the 1933 judgement to which John Ray Jr. refers, see Grazia, pp. 7–39.
[38] For a study of the book's reception in Portugal, see Ana Luísa Amaral, Ana Paula Ferreira and Marinela Freitas (eds), *New Portuguese Letters to the World: International Reception* (Oxford: Peter Lang, 2015), pp. 11–48.

scandal — a case of child sexual abuses dating from the mid-1970s involving children and employees at the Casa Pia, a state-run institution for the care of under-privileged children and orphans in Lisbon. The story broke in November 2002,[39] provoking a media circus involving newspapers, television and radio, with all arms of the Portuguese media bearing the brunt of stern criticism and 'humiliation'.[40] After a drawn-out legal process, six men were formally charged on 3 September 2010 — a group that included a doctor, a lawyer, a TV presenter, a retired ambassador, and a former Casa Pia governor. It is no accident that the kidnapper who wants exclusive access to Myra is a 'doutor' — in Portugal, a term normally used as a marker of social status, designating a man holding a university degree.

In *Myra*, the author's focus is not on the scandal that paedophilia provokes. *Myra* is the story of an exceptional girl who is denied her childhood in a world where no one, not even the victim, can be innocent. Myra *is* complicit in this guilty world: in Chapter 7 she attempts to kill Mafalda, a course of action that places the reader in a moral dilemma: 'Yes, it is self-defence in the interest of survival, but the question remains: Where is the line to be drawn?'[41] One of the most vulnerable members of this dangerous society, Myra is left desperate: 'Myra is a loser in all senses of the word: a foreigner (a Russian girl in Portuguese lands), a woman, a child'.[42] Myra is not Beauty (to Gabriel's Beast), Kate or the rest by choice: these identities are necessary to deflect the predators that threaten to discover her inner identity. In Mafalda's house, Myra remarks: 'A minha vida não é igual às outras [...]. Fui proibida de existir. Fui roubada de poder ser' [My life is not like others' [...]. I was prevented from existing. I was robbed of being] (*Myra*, p. 55). Unlike Lolita, whose death is a footnote to Nabokov's story, Myra's fate takes centre stage. With *Myra*, a testament to the worth and importance of untold narratives like that of her protagonist, Velho da Costa reminds her readers that human stories are too often forgotten amidst the scandal.

In *Lolita*, the control of names and the process of naming are key to the power that the novel's various abusers have over the young girls (Lolita, Mona Dahl) that feature in the novel. Even where the false identity 'Dolores Haze' should protect its bearer, this semi-constructed identity is in fact a deliberately fragile defence that only half-conceals the abused girl who lies behind the vizard wrought by the fictional editor. In Velho da Costa's novel, the contingent

---

[39] An article published twenty-one years earlier by the Portuguese tabloid *Tal e Qual* in July 1981 called 'Prostituição masculina tinha Mercado na Casa Pia' [Male Prostitution had a Market in the Casa Pia] had been ignored by the Portuguese press and the public. Madalena Oliveira, 'A Casa Pia e a imprensa: jornalistas em acto de contrição: a impiedade das críticas ou auto-regulação?', in *Casos em que o jornalista foi notícia*, ed. by Manuel Pinto and Helena Sousa (Porto: Campo das Letras, 2007), pp. 125–48 (p. 126).
[40] Oliveira, p. 136.
[41] Santos, p. 194.
[42] Translated from the Portuguese. Maria de Fátima Marinho, 'Myra ou o contrato de identidade(s)', *Convergência Lusíada*, 36 (2016), 94–100 (p. 95).

identities that Myra invents at moments of great peril are fundamental to her survival strategy in the dangerous underworld that she traverses. The multiplication of names and their attendant identities results in a polyhedral identity. The difference in narrative perspective between *Myra* and *Lolita* results in Velho da Costa's protagonist being a nuanced — imperfect — protagonist, whilst Nabokov's and Humbert's Lolita is relegated to a problematic silence.

Reviews

Feminine Singular: Women Growing Up through Life-Writing in the Luso-Hispanic World, ed. by MARIA-JOSÉ BLANCO AND CLAIRE WILLIAMS (Oxford and New York: Peter Lang, 2017). xiv+ 369 pages. Print and ebook.

Reviewed by DEBORAH MADDEN (University of Manchester)

Feminine Singular: Women Growing Up through Life-Writing in the Luso-Hispanic World is an edited collection of fifteen chapters that identify 'women who have written or expressed their sense of identity' (p. 3) through a diverse range of genre and media. It skilfully and effectively eschews two fundamental critical concerns of gynocentric scholarship: the potential to imply a homogenous female experience and the resulting inference that women's output follows similar generic traits; and forming *sub*categories that, not unexpectedly, are not afforded the same critical currency as those associated with men. Including chapters on poetry, diaries, autobiographies, biographies, travel writing, memoirs and visual art, the volume offers thought-provoking critical analyses that critique, unpack and contest — both implicitly and explicitly — androcentric cultural and critical practices. With a focus on artists and texts from Portuguese- and Spanish-speaking countries, geographical regions justifiably deemed by the editors 'proudly, gloriously patriarchal' (p. 1), this volume manifests its political agenda to confront the social, cultural and political legacy of societies that assumed women had 'no individual intellectual purpose' (p. 1) by only including female critics.

The editorial decision to include such a diverse range of material not only makes for an intriguing, intellectually engaging piece of scholarship, but also exemplifies the need to allow the selected texts and authors to *self*-represent; a critical approach that underpins all of the analyses. The reader is aided by an informative introduction that provides crucial cultural, critical and socio-political context, detailed textual analyses and concise historical summaries to inform the discussions. Though helpfully organized into six sections that broadly categorize the primary texts by genre — writings during religious incarceration, diaries, memoirs, poetry, fictional (auto)biographies and visual biographies — it is the intriguing points of comparison that arise throughout the collection that exhibit the strength of this work.

The innovative critical approach of *Feminine Singular* is exemplified by its opening chapter: an examination of trauma and desire in writings by Teresa de Ávila, Carmen Laforet and Rosa Chacel that offers a fresh perspective on three (of very few) canonical Spanish women writers by astutely juxtaposing their works. The critical benefit of crossing geographical, temporal and thematic boundaries becomes abundantly clear when comparing the 'cathartic and restructuring potential of autobiographical writing' (p. 61) explored in texts by Antónia Margarida de Castelo Branco and D. Leonor de Almeida Portugal, both Portuguese aristocrats confined to convents against their will, with an analysis of Olga Alonso's more overtly political *Testimonios*, deemed a 'cathartic response to the traumatic gap between her expectations of revolutionary participation and the reality of her time in rural Cuba' (p. 109).

The self-conscious critique of gender, genre and representation that underpins this collection informs many of the analyses, including chapters dedicated to Fernanda de Castro's *Ao fim da memória*, Margarida Tengarrinha's *Quadros de Memória* and Agustina Bessa-Luís's biography of her close friend, the painter Maria Helena Vieira da Silva; it is also explored in Laura Freixas's first-hand reflections on editing, translating and authorship — an unexpected but welcome addition to the volume that exemplifies its unorthodox selection criteria. Thought-provoking examinations of Liliana Lara's *Abecedario del estío* and poetry by Adília Lopes explore how the politics of authorship are indexed in literary conventions and generic traits, while examinations of scrapbooks produced by Carmen Martín Gaite and Julia Fons — the latter perhaps as unknown as Martín Gaite is famous — demonstrates the importance of examining a diverse range of creative forms if we are to augment our understanding of female creativity and (self-)representation. It is, therefore, only fitting that a chapter on Helena Almeida's self-portraits, produced under the claustrophobic environment of the *Estado Novo*, is the final analysis in the collection, as her photographs delineate how she uses her body as 'an active participant in a communicative process that involves the artist, the viewer and the artwork' (pp. 337–38).

Somewhat paradoxically, it is Silvia Roca Martínez's examination of Isabel Allende's apparent disidentification with Chilean women in *Mi país inventado* that characterizes a core premise that recurs throughout this feminist volume: the ethical responsibilities of self-representation when speaking from a position of collective otherness. Susan Bozkurt's conclusion that Ana Luísa Amaral's poem 'Carta a Minha Filha' recognizes how 'a freer and more nourishing environment for future generations of women writers [...is] only possible for the woman poet once the dominant cultural traditions are overcome' (p. 224) is, in one sense, realized in Maite Usoz de la Fuente's examination of Elvira Lindo's *Lo que me queda por vivir*, as she argues for a need to 'unpack the gender and value connotations attached to generic labels such as autobiographical and autofictional, and vindicate the literary worth of autobiographical fiction' (p. 240).

The immanently feminist character of this volume is multifaceted. In particular, credit is due for including a range of figures and/or texts unknown to most critics of Lusophone and Hispanic studies, while the concise overview of key female-authored texts in the Introduction and detailed footnotes in the chapters facilitates — and invites — further research. Complementing an increasingly transnational, multilingual approach within Hispanic and Lusophone Studies, *Feminine Singular* is essential reading for feminist critics of all extractions and for scholars of life-writing, who will be aided by excellent translations, and makes an important contribution to scholarship of Lusophone, Hispanic, Iberian and feminist studies.

Eleanor K. Jones, *Battleground Bodies: Gender and Sexuality in Mozambican Literature* (Oxford: Peter Lang, 2017). xxxv + 209 pages. Print and ebook.

Reviewed by Dorothée Boulanger (University of Oxford)

A decade after the seminal works of Phillip Rothwell and Hilary Owen on gender and sexuality in Lusophone African literature, a new wave of publications by young researchers (Ana Martins, 2012, Maria Tavares, 2018) pursues the intricate exploration of gender, power and identity in the former Portuguese Third Empire. Eleanor Jones's *Battleground Bodies*, based on the author's doctoral dissertation, provides a compelling illustration of how much feminist epistemologies can contribute to postcolonial studies. Focusing on poetry and fictional narratives of Mozambique and crossing them with historical sources and political discourse, Jones analyses how gender and the body have been systematically mobilized in the construction, critique and subversion of collective identities and power struggles, before and after independence in 1975. From the construction of the black body as inferior and deviant under slavery and colonialism, to the post-independence regime's obsession with women's bodies as carrying, birthing and feeding the new nation, corporeality has been a key site of power struggle in Mozambique. One of Jones's main arguments in *Battleground Bodies* is that, under the pen of Mozambican postcolonial writers, these highly patriarchal corporeal norms have been exposed and parodied, transforming the body into a weapon at the service of resistance literature.

The monograph opens with an introductory chapter which sets out the work's disciplinary framework (from psychoanalysis to queer and black feminist theory) and locates it within the broader field of Lusophone postcolonial studies. Though some of these introductory paragraphs dwell for too long on previous major publications on the subject (Owen and Rothwell's *Sexual/Textual Empire* in particular), they will prove a useful companion for students of Lusophone African studies and Lusophone gender studies. More importantly, the opening pages bridge pre- and post-independence periods to analyse how, despite a radical project of emancipation, Mozambique's nationalist ruling party, FRELIMO (Frente de Libertação de Moçambique), not only maintained patriarchal norms but made them a cornerstone of its policies and propaganda.

The first full chapter proposes a history of gender and sexuality in Mozambique, focusing on the twentieth century while offering some insights into the earlier period of Portuguese occupation. Highlighting the parallels between the lexicon of reproduction and cultivation, it lays bare the twofold (male) Portuguese anxiety to make the African land fertile and to perpetuate their own presence. After examining how Gilberto Freyre's Lusotropicalist fiction allowed the *Estado Novo* in the 1950s and 1960s to transform this narrative of failure into a success story of miscegenation and racial harmony, where black women's bodies became instrumental to the colonial project, Jones focuses on the post-independence implications of these gendered legacies. Judiciously using Sara Ahmed's concept of 'non-performativity', by which a speech act is produced to avoid its effective realization, Jones shows how FRELIMO denounced women's colonial and 'traditional' oppression while rejecting feminism and locating child-rearing and cultural transmission in the exclusive realm of women.

One of the most original and successful aspects of the monograph lies in its privileging of a comparative perspective, with each of the three ensuing chapters exploring specific themes in the works of two Mozambican authors, generally across generations and genders. Chapter 2 for instance, looks at masculinities in the poetry of José Craveirinha and the novels of Paulina Chiziane. Through perceptive close readings of Craveirinha, it reveals how the poet, in his attempts to counter colonial propaganda, adopted a masculinist stance replicating colonial gender binaries, equating agency with virility and constructing 'mother Africa' as a passive figure. Jones rightly notes that most critics have emphasized Craveirinha's anticolonial discourse and its connections to the negritude movement, but rather ignored the hyper-sexualized and heterosexist tones of his poems. She then moves on to build an inspired comparison with Paulina Chiziane's novels, which, in their satirical portrayal of masculinities in crisis, offer a parodic version of the hypersexualized African big man. Chiziane thus calls out the masculinism pervading anticolonial aesthetics and denounces FRELIMO's hypocritical defence of African women by exposing the violence women are subjected to in the postcolony.

Through the works of Noemia de Sousa and Ungulani Ba Kha Khosa, Chapter 3 looks at how Mozambican authors resisted dominant conceptions of femininity during the late colonial phase and after independence. Sousa deployed narrative strategies that playfully evaded rigid feminine identifications and gendered language, embracing a more ambiguous and evanescent narrative identity. In the works of Ba Kha Khosa, on the other hand, this transgressive fluidity is exaggeratedly corporeal, inscribed in Black women's bodies through an aesthetics of excess and abjection. Using Kristeva and Butler, Jones persuasively shows how Khosa's grotesque depictions of major symbols of femininity, such as menstruation or childbirth, knock down (Western) feminine ideals of purity and light to evoke instead experiences of pain, torture and degradation that pervade war-ridden post-independence Mozambique.

Chapter 4 pursues the uncovering of the impact of extreme and prolonged violence in Mozambique in its analysis of 'exceptional states' (suicide and hunger) in the works of Lília Momplé and Suleiman Cassamo. Recalling, with

Achille Mbembe's concept of 'necropolitics', how Africa has long symbolized death in Western consciousness, Jones highlights the parallel between colonial and patriarchal oppression in two narratives by Momplé and Cassamo ending in the suicide of their main protagonist. If Jones's examination of hunger and food as gendered symbols of oppression and deprivation illuminates how FRELIMO replicated the colonial connection between women and domesticity, it might have benefited from a more anthropological perspective on 'the politics of the belly' highlighting the intrinsic link between power and ingestion in Africa.[1]

Sharp and clear in its writing, ambitious and stimulating in its thematic and comparative layout and scope, *Battleground Bodies* is an important contribution to Lusophone African literary studies and to Lusophone postcolonial studies more generally. It is an engaging read that produces brilliant close-readings while conveying a subtle and complex understanding of Mozambique, convincingly showing the continued relevance of resistance literature in Portuguese-speaking Africa.

MARIA TERESA HORTA, *Point of Honour: Selected Poems of Maria Teresa Horta*, translated by LESLEY SAUNDERS and introduced by ANA RAQUEL FERNANDES (Reading: Two Rivers Press, 2019). 237 pages. Print.

Reviewed by ANA FILIPA PRATA (Universidad de los Andes)

Point of Honour is the first anthology of poetry by Maria Teresa Horta published in English. It presents a selection of more than eighty poems chosen by Horta herself and her husband, the late Luís Barros, and translated by Lesley Saunders, a contemporary British poet. This book constitutes a landmark in the reception of this major Portuguese poet who is mostly known internationally for being the author, together with Maria Velho da Costa and Maria Isabel Barreno, of the *Novas Cartas Portuguesas* [*New Portuguese Letters*], published in 1972.

The chosen title for this collection — taken from one of the poems — is a very enlightening editorial decision: this anthology is meant to be a real point of honour for Horta's literary work; it is both a poetic statement and a moment of consecration of a singular and revolutionary voice that has shivered patriarchal discourses and conservative mores in Portugal throughout the last decades.

Maria Teresa Horta has been consistently publishing since 1960, from the inaugural *Espelho incicial* [*First Mirror*] to *Estranhezas* [*Oddities*], her last book published, in 2018. Horta has thoroughly cultivated a poetic work that is nowadays unanimously considered groundbreaking in both rhetorical and thematic terms, elaborating sensual and erotic expression, defying a conventional representation of womanhood and its imagery, aiming at the creation of an independent feminine discursive location. This anthology gives an account of this historical evolution and poetic consolidation; each of Horta's

---

[1] Jean-François Bayart, *The State in Africa: The Politics of the Belly*, 1st English edn (London: Longman, 1993).

books published from the '60s up to the first decades of the twenty-first century is represented by two to five poems, which fosters a comprehensive approach to her profuse poetic creation.

This bilingual edition opens with an introduction by Ana Raquel Fernandes, whose recent research draws mainly on female Portuguese and English authors. Fernandes provides very valuable information on Horta's literary trajectory, but also on the political and social commitment of the author during the times of dictatorship, stressing her engagement in the defence of women's rights. Fernandes briefly comments on several poems and highlights the main themes in Horta's poetry such as women's bodies and sexuality, social and literary insubordination, the representation of mother and motherhood, and the intertextual and intermedial references often present in her poetry, especially in her recent publications. There follows a translator's note in which Lesley Saunders comments on her first approach to Maria Teresa Horta's poetry, how she came to meet her, and how these translations are the result of a fruitful dialogue between these two poets. Even if Saunders does not have a deep knowledge of Portuguese language — as she admits — she has managed through the dialogue with the author to immerse herself in the poetic essence of Horta's poetry and 'bring it across' to English-speaking territory. The thorough translations by Lesley Saunders are an example of what Haroldo de Campos called 'transcreation': Saunders goes beyond literal reformulations and reinvents through English syntax the particular rhythm and musicality of Horta's vibrant compositions.

Leslie Saunders presents a very interesting recreation of Horta's poetry that was already noticed and acclaimed in 2016, when she won the Stephen Spender Trust Award for the translation of 'Poem', also present in this anthology. Saunders goes far beyond literality and introduces strangeness into the English version of Teresa Horta's poetry, making visible the fingerprints always inherent to the task of the translator. Her translations differ deeply from Ana Hudson's much more literal versions, published on the web platform 'Poems from the Portuguese' in 2010. Saunders' decision will please some readers but disquiet others — especially those who can understand Portuguese and compare both versions displayed in the book. This translation has thus the interest and the value of expressing the poetic tension between two different languages and between each one's own particular musicality. It also focuses on the dialogue and negotiations between two different cultures, in order to bring together shared interests and common battles.

Point of Honour is indeed a great introduction to Horta's universe and to the dialogical features of her poetry. However, there are some editorial details that could have been considered more attentively, especially given the importance and the expected impact of a first edition of this Portuguese poet in English.

The book includes an epigraph with an unpublished poem by Maria Teresa Hora, 'Canto Eterno' [Forever Song], a poem that can be read as an *ars poetica* or an illustration of Horta's poetic labour, the song of Eurydice writing violently against obscurity. Regrettably, the first approach to this wonderful surprise is interrupted by an orthographic fault right in the very first verse in Portuguese ('Pudesse eu transformer-me no meu verso'), which strikes the attention of the reader. Nevertheless, and despite this small disturbance, the most important fault that importunes the reading experience of Horta's book is perhaps that it does not include an index, but only a sort of table of contents with information on the selected poems. That is certainly useful to locate the author's work in time and specific publications, but it is noticeably insufficient for an easy handling of the anthology. Clear indications on the pages are lacking and would have been suitable to locate specific poems and approach both original and translation effortlessly. At the end of the book (pp. 234–37), there is a section dedicated to 'translator's notes on the translations' that provides useful information for understanding the specificities of some of the Portuguese 'untranslatables' (as Emily Apter would say), such as *saudade*, for instance. There is valuable and important historical and cultural data. Nevertheless, and again, there is no indications on the poem's specific pages that some notes will be provided at the end, which have been useful to the reader in order to avoid a somewhat peripatetic reading experience.

Despite some editorial aspects that can surely be corrected in future editions, *Point of Honour* stands out as a celebration of Horta's poetry. Through the inspired voice of Leslie Saunders, it establishes Maria Teresa Horta as one of the must-read poets of our times, not only within the Portuguese-speaking world, but also in dialogue with other authors and texts, important at this particular moment of growing intolerance and indifference, both in Europe and in Great Britain. As Ana Raquel Fernandes states, it is an invitation to 'think about ways of resisting oppression and silencing'. *Point of Honour* ranges over more than half a century and it testifies to the engagement of its author who was also an important protagonist in the political and social struggles that took place in the last decades of the twentieth century in Portugal. To be sure, this publication will contribute to the recognition of a unique poetic voice that advocates a revolutionary poetry and militates against patriarchal and conservative traditions, while liberating the expression of the singularities of women's bodies and discourse.

Take Six: Six Portuguese Women Writers, ed. by MARGARET JULL COSTA (Sawtry, Cambs.: Dedalus, 2018). 251 pages. Print and ebook.

Reviewed by SUZAN BOZKURT

With *Take Six*, edited by Margaret Jull Costa and published by Dedalus Europe, English-speaking readers are given a glimpse of the extraordinarily rich and varied production in short-story writing by Portuguese women writers in the twentieth and twenty-first century. Undoing canonical perceptions, where the 'proper model for fiction [...] was the nineteenth-century novel',[2] their short fictions open up a window onto the seemingly ordinary minutiae of daily life, the small things that end up questioning the way the world operates: a woman's screams in front of a prison wall in 'The Silence', by Sophia de Mello Breyner Andresen, denounce the injustices and brutality of dictatorship; the significant role a bicycle plays in 'The Instrumentalina', by Lídia Jorge, gives its owner a sense of freedom that leads to his insubordination of family rule. But, don't be mistaken. Smallness, of course, is not the aim of these stories; they don't shy away from asking the big questions of life. 'Who's going to waste five or ten minutes thinking about hope?', asks Maria Judite de Carvalho's Mariana in 'So Many People Mariana'. 'God [...] is bored and in a bad mood', muses the blind man in Hélia Correia's 'Twenty Steps', and 'every now and then he'll [...] stick out his cane so someone trips and falls down the steps', adds a disillusioned Rosa. Nor can their authors be called 'small' or insignificant. Sophia de Mello Breyner Andresen (1999), Agustina Bessa-Luís (2004) and Hélia Correia (2015) have all received the highest honour available to writers in the Portuguese language, the Prémio Camões. Maria Judite de Carvalho (1995), Teolinda Gersão (2002) and Hélia Correia (2014) have also been singled out for their shorter fictions in the awarding of the Grande Prémio de Conto Camilo Castelo Branco, Portugal's most prestigious prize for short-story writing.

It is, therefore, hardly surprising that Margaret Jull Costa, who has won numerous awards and prizes for her work as a translator, describes the writers united here in this volume as 'some of Portugal's finest writers [...] [and] six of my favourite authors'. She certainly brings to these translations a passion that can only be found in a true eagerness to convey the shining radiance of these authors and stories, celebrating the production of women writers in Portugal in the twentieth and twenty-first century. *Take Six* takes a well-earned place in Dedalus's series 'Celebrating Women's Literature, 2018–2028', appealing to readers who are interested in European fictions as well as women's writing. Another remarkable feature of this anthology is its collaborative nature, where, under the overarching editorship of Jull Costa, a younger generation of translators tries their hand. Some translations render visible and readable stories that would, otherwise, have been condemned to a life in a dusty library, available only to the connoisseur and expert. Victor Meadowcroft's and Jull Costa's translations skilfully bring to life such gems as Agustina Bessa-Luís's short stories, written in the 1950s and currently awaiting a reprint in their original language, where, in 'On the Road to Emmaus', a shiny blue motorbike speeds down dusty country lanes in a long forgotten rural Portugal of cosy *tavernas* and travelling salesmen.

The availability of *Take Six* as an ebook opens up this publication to a younger and more mobile readership — and which genre could be better than the short

[2] Robert Shapard and James Thomas, *New Sudden Fiction: Short-Short Stories from America and Beyond* (New York: W. W. Norton, 2007), p. 14.

story to appeal to a generation constantly on the move? 'If you don't have time to read a novel, you can read a short story. On the underground, in a bus, in a dentist's waiting room',[3] remarks Teolinda Gersão in an interview. Her short-short stories[4] such as 'The Red Fox Fur Coat', where a woman turns into a fox in breath-taking brevity, are example of an international wave in experimental fiction that crosses transnational (language) boundaries and have been included in English-speaking anthologies, such as Shapard and Thomas's *New Sudden Fiction* (2007) and online literary magazines, such as the *Threepenny Review*, for many years. But this undoubtedly strong anchorage of the authors and stories of the *Take Six* volume in national and international canons is, in my opinion, also one of its weaknesses. Some, like 'So Many People Mariana' and 'Twenty Steps' are re-translations of material already available in English; others, such as most of Teolinda Gersão's stories have here, for the first time, come to rest in print, but have been around online for a while. With authors like Hélia Correia, Lídia Jorge and Teolinda Gersão being present in several other recent translation anthologies of Portuguese short fiction — *Storytelling: Memory, Love and Loss in Portuguese Short Fiction* (2016); *Tempo da História Esplendor do Conto / Beyond History: The Radiance of Short Stories* (2018) and *Lisbon Tales* (2019) — one has to ask whether these six authors are not rapidly becoming 'mulheres extraordinárias',[5] exemplary and exemplified women writers that stand for a whole generation of female authors, overshadowing other promising writers of their own and younger generations.

---

[3] Rodrigues da Silva, 'Teolinda Gersão: Quem conta um conto...', *Jornal de Letras, Artes e Ideias*, #835, 2–15 October 2002, p. 10.
[4] Shapard and Thomas, p. 15.
[5] Hilary Owen and Cláudia Pazos Alonso, *Antigone's Daughters? Gender, Genealogy and the Politics of Authorship in 20th-century Portuguese Women's Writing* (Lewisburg, PA: Bucknell University Press, 2012).

Abstracts

Teresa Margarida da Silva Orta (1711–1793): A Minor Transnational of the Brown Atlantic
ANA MARGARIDA MARTINS

ABSTRACT. This study offers a reinterpretation of Teresa Margarida da Silva Orta's standing in Afro-Brazilian literature, by presenting an analysis of her 1752 novel, *Máximas de virtude e de formosura com que Diófanes, Clymenea e Hemirena, príncipes de Tebas, venceram os mais apertados lances da desgraça*, in light of the author's chosen themes and under-researched maternal Afro-descendancy. Grounding Orta's historical and literary agency in the framework of 'minor transnationalism' (Lionnet and Shih 2005), it is argued that the field requires a new understanding of Afro-Brazilian contributions to literature in Portuguese that links the struggles and writings of pioneering Afro-descended women writers in a lateral and non-hierarchical way.
KEYWORDS. Minor transnationalism, Afro-descended women writers, Brown Atlantic, geographical mobility, gender performance.

RESUMO. Este estudo apresenta uma reinterpretação da reputação de Teresa Margarida da Silva Orta no seio dos estudos literários Afro-brasileiros, através de uma análise do seu romance de 1752, *Máximas de Virtude e de Formosura com que Diófanes, Clymenea e Hemirena, príncipes de Tebas, venceram os mais apertados lances da desgraça*, à luz dos temas escolhidos pela autora e da sua pouco-investigada afro-descendência materna. Fundamentando a agência literária e histórica de Orta no conceito de 'transnacionalismo menor' (Lionnet e Shih 2005), defende-se que a área dos estudos literários Afro-brasileiros necessita de uma nova visão do que se entende por literatura negra de mulheres em português, visão esta capaz de ligar as escritas de artistas Afro-brasileiras de forma lateral e não-hierárquica.
PALAVRAS-CHAVE. Transnacionalismo menor, escrita de mulheres afrodescendentes, Atlântico Pardo, mobilidade geográfica, performance de género.

The Empires Write Back: Tracing Transnational Indias in the Work of Maria Ermelinda dos Stuarts Gomes
HILARY OWEN

ABSTRACT. This paper analyses the work of the Indo-Portuguese woman writer and thinker Maria Ermelinda dos Stuarts Gomes. In it, I read her early twentieth-century publications as representative of how the non-canonical, 'peripheral', raced and colonized voices of women's rights entered into dialogue with hegemonic Republican feminist voices of the metropolis such as Ana de Castro Osório, who knew and mentored Gomes. I contend that Gomes provides a telling example of the shifting and at times contradictory political subjectivities that are created for women, as well as the discursive possibilities that are opened up, when we review 'empire' and 'nation' as plural transnational phenomena. I show how Gomes's evolving position on Goan independence, and on the status of British India, make her a rare dissident voice among first-wave feminists in the context of Portugal's stridently nationalist reaffirmations of empire in the 1920s and '30s.

KEYWORDS. Republican feminism, Goan independence, Maria Ermelinda dos Stuarts Gomes, Ana de Castro Osório.

RESUMO. Este artigo analisa as obras da escritora e pensadora indo-portuguesa Maria Ermelinda dos Stuarts Gomes. As suas publicações, datadas do início do século XX, são representativas das vozes não-canónicas, 'periféricas', e colonizadas que tentaram promulgar os direitos das mulheres em diálogo com as vozes feministas republicanas e hegemónicas da metrópole, como Ana de Castro Osório que conhecia, e pretendia orientar, Gomes. Argumento que Gomes fornece um exemplo revelador das subjetividades políticas e às vezes contraditórias e instáveis que emergiram para as feministas coloniais daquela altura, bem como das possibilidades discursivas que se abrem quando analisamos 'império' e 'nação' como fenómenos transnacionais e plurais. Eu mostro como o posicionamento de Gomes em defesa da independência de Goa e da Índia Britânica evoluiu e desenvolveu, fazendo dela uma rara voz dissidente entre as feministas da primeira onda, no contexto das reafirmações nacionalistas do imperialismo no Estado Novo, nos anos trinta em Portugal.

PALAVRAS-CHAVE. Feminismo republicano, independência goesa, Maria Ermelinda dos Stuarts Gomes, Ana de Castro Osório.

Early Twentieth-Century Portuguese Feminist Writers as Transnational Cultural Mediators: Virgínia de Castro e Almeida and Ana de Castro Osório
CHATARINA EDFELDT

ABSTRACT. This article considers the role of Portuguese feminist writers and intellectuals of the early twentieth century as important transnational cultural mediators, who functioned both as promoters of Portuguese culture and literature across national borders and as importers of ideas that were in circulation at that time. The article traces how the correspondence between the prominent intellectual Ana de Castro Osório (1872–1935) and the translator Göran Björkman (1860–1923), together with Virgínia de Castro e Almeida's (1874–1946) reception and dissemination of the feminist thinker Ellen Key (1849–1926), illustrate the cross-cultural exchange between Portugal and Sweden, thus highlighting how these Portuguese intellectuals functioned as transnational beacons for the circulation of ideas. The article's overarching aim is to highlight the role played by these Portuguese women writers as mediators

in the transnational processes of cultural exchange, which underpinned and shaped the modernization of Portuguese early twentieth-century culture.
KEYWORDS. Portuguese first-wave feminism, cultural mediators, Ana de Castro Osório, Virgínia de Castro e Almeida, Göran Björkman.

RESUMO. Este artigo considera o importante papel das escritoras e intelectuais feministas portuguesas do início do século XX enquanto mediadoras culturais e transnacionais, que funcionavam, tanto como disseminadoras da cultura e literatura portuguesas além fronteiras, como importadoras de ideias que estavam em circulação na época. O artigo explora a correspondência entre a proeminente intelectual Ana de Castro Osório (1872–1935) e o lusófilo e tradutor Göran Björkman (1860–1923), juntamente com a recepção e disseminação das ideias feministas da pensadora Ellen Key (1849–1926) por parte de Virgínia de Castro e Almeida (1874–1946), a fim de ilustrar o intercâmbio transnacional e cultural entre Portugal e Suécia, destacando assim essas intelectuais portuguesas como mediadoras transnacionais na circulação de ideias. O objetivo principal do artigo é destacar o papel desempenhado por essas escritoras portuguesas enquanto mediadoras nos processos transnacionais de intercâmbio cultural, que sustentaram e moldaram a modernização da cultura portuguesa do início do século XX.
PALAVRAS-CHAVE. Feminismo português da primeira vaga, mediadoras culturais, Ana de Castro Osório, Virgínia de Castro e Almeida, Göran Björkman.

'Nem uma coisa nem outra': Nomadic Subjectivity in the 'Crónicas' of Ilse Losa
ROSA CHURCHER CLARKE

ABSTRACT. A rare example of successful non-native writing in Portuguese literature, Ilse Losa uses her cultural duality to present a multiplicity of perspectives and transgression of borders in keeping with feminist philosopher Rosi Braidotti's 1994 characterization of Nomadic Subjectivity. In the *crónicas* of *À Flor do Tempo* (1997), Losa frequently shifts between distant geographical landscapes and linguistic contexts, bringing figures from (principally) German and Portuguese cultural history into contact with one another, consistently blending and bending boundaries between their separate spheres. Combining a collection-wide analysis with close readings, this article examines how Losa's transnational identity has influenced her *crónica* writing and how this might link to Braidotti's theory of Nomadic Subjectivity.
KEYWORDS. Ilse Losa, *crónica*, nomadic subjectivity, transnational.

RESUMO. Ilse Losa, um raro exemplo de uma escritora estrangeira a escrever em português, usa a sua dualidade cultural para apresentar uma multiplicidade de perspectivas e uma transgressão de fronteiras que faz eco da 'subjetividade nómada' definida pela filósofa feminista Rosi Braidotti (1994). Nas crónicas de *À Flor do Tempo* (1997), Losa frequentemente alterna entre paisagens e

contextos linguísticos distantes, misturando (particularmente) figuras da história cultural alemã e da portuguesa, fundindo e ultrapassando as fronteiras dessas esferas tradicionalmente separadas. Através de uma análise da coleção de crónicas como um todo, bem como de *close readings*, este artigo analisa como a identidade transnacional de Losa influenciou as suas crónicas, e como esse aspeto pode ser relacionado com a teoria da 'subjetividade nómada' de Braidotti.
PALAVRAS-CHAVE. Ilse Losa, crónica, subjetividade nómada, transnacional.

'O mapa cor de rosa' by Maria Velho da Costa: Migration, Dis-location and the Production of Unstable Cartographies
MARIA LUÍSA COELHO

ABSTRACT. This article considers the texts written by Maria Velho da Costa when she was living in London, in the early 1980s. Taking a closer look at the *crónicas* initially published in the Portuguese newspaper *A Capital*, at a time when the relationship between Portugal and its European others was under intense scrutiny, and subsequently compiled in *O mapa cor de rosa: cartas de Londres* (1984), I argue that the process of dislocation experienced by the writer encouraged her to develop a literary cartography with unstable geographic and cultural boundaries and through which personal, national and linguistic identities and locations are seen as hybrid and always in transit.
KEYWORDS. Maria Velho da Costa, migration, *crónicas*, hybridity, Luso-British relationships.

RESUMO. O presente artigo analisa os textos escritos por Maria Velho da Costa enquanto esta viveu em Londres, nos inícios da década de 80 do século XX. Centrando a discussão nas crónicas inicialmente publicadas no jornal português *A Capital*, num período em que a relação entre Portugal e a alteridade europeia era intensamente escrutinada, e subsequentemente compiladas em *O mapa cor de rosa: cartas de Londres* (1984), defende-se que o processo de deslocação experienciado pela escritora encorajou-a a desenvolver uma cartografia literária de contornos geográficos e culturais instáveis e através da qual identidades e posicionamentos subjetivos, nacionais e linguísticos são entendidos como híbridos e permanentemente em trânsito.
PALAVRAS-CHAVE. Maria Velho da Costa, emigração, crónicas, hibridismo, relações luso-britânicas.

Éukié: Maria Velho da Costa's Alice and the Absurd
MARIA IRENE RAMALHO

ABSTRACT. This article is a first approach to Maria Velho da Costa's art of fiction in the light of Lewis Carroll's nonsense and is mainly concerned with poetic language as social and cultural criticism.

KEYWORDS. Maria Velho da Costa, Lewis Carroll, poetic language, social criticism.

RESUMO. Este artigo é uma primeira reflexão sobre a arte narrativa de Maria Velho da Costa à luz do *nonsense* de Lewis Carroll e debruça-se, em particular, sobre a linguagem poética enquanto crítica social e cultural.

PALAVRAS-CHAVE. Maria Velho da Costa, Lewis Carroll, linguagem poética, crítica social.

The Polyhedral Victim and the Patchwork Abuser: A Comparative Study of Names and Naming in Vladimir Nabokov's 'Lolita' (1955) and Maria Velho da Costa's 'Myra' (2008)
TOM STENNETT

ABSTRACT. In this article, I compare the function of names and the act of naming in Vladimir Nabokov's *Lolita* (1955) and Maria Velho da Costa's *Myra* (2008). I situate Nabokov's decision to write a narrative from the perspective of a male abuser and Velho da Costa's centring her novel on a female victim in the specific contexts in which these works were published. Whereas *Lolita* stands as a challenge to North American obscenity laws in the 1950s, *Myra* was written against the backdrop of a child abuse scandal, involving a state orphanage and powerful men from the Portuguese elite.

KEYWORDS. Identity, obscenity, intertextuality.

RESUMO. No presente artigo, comparo a função de nomes e do ato de nomear em dois romances: *Lolita* (1955), de Vladimir Nabokov, e *Myra* (2008), de Maria Velho da Costa. Situo a decisão de Nabokov de escrever uma narrativa a partir da perspectiva de um agressor masculino e a de Velho da Costa de ter como foco narrativo uma vítima feminina nos contextos específicos em que essas obras foram publicadas. Enquanto *Lolita* desafia as leis norte-americanas contra a obscenidade nos anos 50 do século XX, *Myra* foi publicado no contexto de um escândalo de abusos sexuais de menores, que envolveu um orfanato estatal e homens poderosos da elite portuguesa.

PALAVRAS-CHAVE. Identidade, obscenidade, intertextualidade.

www.ingramcontent.com/pod-product-compliance
Lightning Source LLC
Chambersburg PA
CBHW071405290426
44108CB00014B/1695